PRAISE FOR
Getting Rich Outside
the Dollar

"MUST READING FOR ALL SERIOUS INVESTORS. In an interesting, lively style, Weber and Reiss tell what factors drive currencies, economies, and stock markets—and what this all means for Americans. . . . I would advise investors to pay close attention to what Weber and Reiss have to say—it could prove financially rewarding."
—Albert J. Fredman, coauthor of *Investing in Closed End Funds* and *How Mutual Funds Work*

"EXCELLENT. . . . Opens the minds of American investors to endless opportunities for making money outside the U.S. and outside the U.S. dollar. Citing explicit ways to invest, the book shows how to multiply profits by investing in fast-growing economies and at the same time make extra profits when the currencies of those markets become more valuable against the dollar. To my knowledge, no other book has ever done this before."
—Edgar Gunther, Ph.D., International Financial Adviser

"Weber can write like a dream, and here he lets the readers in on his secrets in highly readable and sparkling prose. For anyone interested in conserving or expanding his capital in today's increasingly complex and tangled world, THIS BOOK IS A MUST!"
—Murray N. Rothbard, author of *America's Great Depression* and *What Has Government Done to Our Money?*

more . . .

"Weber and Reiss' book is the best primer available on the way the currency markets work. It's full of good, practical suggestions on how average people can make sure they're not only not hurt by fluctuations in currencies, but can profit from them."
—Doug Casey, author of *Crisis Investing* and *Crisis Investing for the Rest of the '90s*

"Opens up phenomenal new opportunities waiting overseas for armchair investors. . . . Unlike so much of the trash that's published today, the advice in this book really works. If you ignore it, you'll have less security, less income, and yes, even less fun."
—Daniel Rosenthal, President, The Institute for the Preservation of Wealth, Inc.

"I truly enjoyed reading this new book—one of the most thorough and certainly most up-to-date primers on foreign exchange and overseas investing for individuals. The authors correctly point out the long-term forces that will tend to make the dollar less valuable over time. And before laying out specific investment advice, they give one a rare chance to see each of the major world currencies from its historic perspective and to appreciate just how differently each country values its currency."
—F. Mark Turner, Chief Investment Officer and Managing Director/Global Bonds Putnam Investments

"The authors have done a superb job of making the complex world of currencies and currency trading readily comprehensible to the ordinary investor. The book is full of insights and practical information."
Adrian Day, author of *International Investment Opportunities* and editor of *Adrian Day's Investment Analyst* newsletter

CHRISTOPHER WEBER is an investment consultant and the author of eight books on economics as well as newsletters on investing both in the U.S. and abroad.

LEONARD REISS was president of Schwab and Beatty, Inc., and served on the board of Precious Metals Reports, Inc., and Littleton Rare Coins.

Getting Rich Outside the Dollar

Christopher Weber and Leonard Reiss

WARNER BOOKS

A Time Warner Company

This book is sold with the understanding that the publisher is not engaged in rendering legal or investment services, and professional advice may be advisable before undertaking specific investments. The information contained in this book is as timely as possible. However, the publisher disclaims responsibility for accuracy of the text.

Chart on p. 30 courtesy of Aden Research, P. O. Box 754-1007 Centro Colon, San José, Costa Rica; charts on pp. 45, 52, 60, 63, 69, 76, 84, 101, 110, 282, 304, and 350–351 courtesy of BCA Publications Ltd.; charts on pp. 304 and 305 courtesy of *Harry Browne's Special Reports*; chart on p. 344 from *The Hyperinflation Survival Guide: Strategies for American Businesses*, sponsored by Figgie International Inc.

Warner Books, Inc., 1271 Avenue of the Americas, New York, NY 10020

 A Time Warner Company

Printed in the United States of America
First Printing: August 1993
10 9 8 7 6 5 4 3 2

Library of Congress Cataloging-in-Publication Data

Weber, Chris.
        Getting rich outside the dollar/Christopher Weber and Leonard
Reiss.
            p.   cm.
        ISBN 0–446–39396–7
        1. Foreign exchange.   2. Dollar, American.   3. Money.
4. Investments.   5. Finance, Personal.   I. Reiss, Leonard.
II. Title.
HG3851.W39   1993
332.45—dc20   92-43090
                                                              CIP

Cover design by Mike Stromberg
Book design by H. Roberts

ACKNOWLEDGMENTS OF THE AUTHORS

▼

Chris Weber wants to acknowledge the people who helped develop his interest in foreign currencies: "When I was a boy, my father always brought back coins from numerous trips abroad. This gave me an early appreciation for the different monies of the world. Later, Jerome Smith, Hans Weber and Erich Stoeger made it possible for me to travel the world and learn about foreign currencies and banking practice. Franz Pick and Nicholas Deak spent a combined 130 years as currency experts and each before he died gave me all the time and insights I could have hoped for.

As for the book itself goes, I want to thank Len Reiss who first broached the idea that it should be done and was an inspiration all the way through. Gloria Crocker did a fine job of typing the manuscript. Jack Williams and numerous European bankers reviewed the manuscript and made very valuable comments.

Leonard Reiss wants to express his appreciation to Nicholas Bratt and E. Mark Turner of Scudder, Stevens and Clark, and to M. David Testa of Rowe Price-Fleming International. They were more than ordinarily generous of their hospitality and time and even altered their travel schedules to give him valuable insights into international investing. He is also indebted to Norman Tepper of Value Line Reports for showing him little-known ratings on mutual funds without which some of the chapters he wrote would not have been as comprehensive. Jim Conover and Tom Collins reviewed the manuscript and made detailed suggestions. Tom was also a wonderful screen for title ideas (as was my wife, Lynn).

Both authors owe a debt to literary agent Oscar Collier and Warner Books senior editor Tracy Bernstein, both of whom believed in the book from the outset and thereby made it possible, and to senior editor Susan Suffes who carried it through to publication.

Because of the esoteric nature of foreign currencies and securities markets, the job of copyeditor on this book was extremely challenging. Both authors acknowledge the superb job done by Mel Minter.

This book is dedicated to
"my Carolines"
and to
Lynn Sherman

TABLE OF CONTENTS

INTRODUCTION

▼

You're Already Investing in Currencies

Put your hand in your pocketbook or wallet. What do you find?

Dollars, of course.

What's in your savings account, your money market fund? What is your mortgage valued in? How do you express the value of your stocks and bonds?

Unless you're one of those rare Americans who have opened a foreign bank account or bought even a modest amount of foreign currencies or securities—everything you own is in dollars.

But even if you've *never* owned any currency but dollars, you have been and you still are a currency investor. Because— whether you realize it or not—by holding dollars you have, in effect, chosen *not* to hold yen, marks, pounds, or Swiss francs.

Every time you put money into your savings account or buy a CD at your bank or buy stocks or bonds at your broker, your investment immediately becomes dependent upon the

integrity and value of the currency it is denominated in—the
U.S. dollar.

And if for the past twenty years everything you own has
been in dollars, that may not have been the best thing for
your financial health.

If your savings are in dollars, and the dollar's value falls
against other currencies—something it has done fairly often in
our time—then your standard of living has fallen along with it.

Most Americans think of foreign currencies as risky. But
when they hold dollars instead, they are also taking a currency
risk. Because if the dollar falls, their ability to spend their
money as they wish shrinks. And sometimes it shrinks dramatically.

You Are Not Trapped in the Dollar Forever

There is no law—nor has there ever been one—that prevents
you from owning British pounds, German marks, or Swiss
Francs. No doubt some American presidents have done it.

There is no law against your opening a secret Swiss bank
account and filling it with the currencies of other strong and
dependable countries.

There is no reason why you shouldn't buy the government bonds of other sovereign nations—and considering how
well those bonds pay, there is plenty of reason why you
should.

After all, we like foreigners to buy U.S. bonds. Why
shouldn't we buy theirs?

And if you find some Dutch or Japanese or Italian company with an excellent chance for growth and profit, it might
make a lot of sense, at the right time, to invest a modest
amount of your money there, if for no other reason than to
diversify what you now own on Wall Street.

Why You Should Consider Your Escape Routes Now

Perhaps you've considered yourself—and shown your kids—how to get out of your house in case of a fire. It makes sense to do that, even if you're almost sure it will never happen.

During the last twenty years and more, your dollars have lost a lot of their value compared to the value of stronger currencies. Against the Swiss franc, the Japanese yen, the Austrian schilling and the German mark, your dollars have lost up to 75 percent of the value they once had.

Regardless of what the dollar is doing when you read this, it has the potential to fall again and fall to a sickening degree. You don't want everything you own—all of your net worth—to go down when that happens.

Our book will show you the escape routes.

We will show you where to keep your money in another currency while it earns a very good rate of interest and is as safe or much safer than in your own hometown bank.

We will show you which currencies have done the best over time and which still show the best promise for the future.

We'll show you how to squeeze a higher rate of return out of your bank deposits or CDs that are denominated in another currency. We'll show you how to leverage your bank deposits—if you don't mind a little extra risk in order to achieve a higher rate of return.

And if you want to put some of your money in the strongest foreign bonds or the fastest-growing economies and stock markets, we'll show you how to do that with an 800-number call to highly rated mutual funds. We'll even tell you what numbers to call.

We'll tell you how to judge when your money would be best off in dollars and how to profit by a dollar rally, even if it is temporary. And we'll tell you when your money will be safer and earn more in another currency.

Face it. Now and for the rest of your life, you are destined to be an investor in some currency or other. Why not learn how this opportunity, this choice that is your legal right, can make you richer?

That's what this book can help you do.

▼

PART I

How to
Free Yourself
from an
Endangered Dollar

▲

CHAPTER 1

▼

The Future Belongs to Those Who Think Internationally

Less than fifty years ago, our country sat on top of the world.

We grew more food than we could eat. We made more and better cars than anyone else. Our assembly lines, our skyscrapers, our movies, our telephone system, our advertising, our superhighways, our plumbing were all the envy of people around the globe. Our scientists won the lion's share of Nobel Prizes. Even our athletes dominated the world of sports, bringing home trunkfuls of medals from the Olympics.

And—oh, yes—our dollars were good as gold.

We could travel to Europe and buy antiques, art masterpieces, Paris fashions, Italian sportscars, villas on the Riviera, and Swiss timepieces at what seemed like giveaway prices, because our dollars at that time were worth two, three, and four times the number of francs, marks, pounds, and lire that they now fetch.

When any of us went abroad, we could travel like royalty and never feel the pinch of high prices. We could stay and eat at top-rated establishments for a month and pay roughly the same number of dollars that we'd have to pay today for only two or three days of similar luxury.

Earlier in the century we had felt that our way of life was protected by two enormous oceans. We really didn't need the rest of the world. They accused us of being isolationist in our thinking, and we were.

We had refused to enter the League of Nations. We kept strict quotas on those whom we would allow to become American citizens; we virtually excluded all Asians. We paid lip service to teaching foreign languages in our schools: we didn't teach them very well, almost no one mastered a tongue other than English, and nobody much cared. Our schools taught history but only American history. We hardly showed foreign films. Foreign cars were an oddity. Few went to Europe. Almost nobody went to the Far East.

World War II changed all this.

Thanks, in part, to our economic aid, nation after nation—formerly humbled and impoverished—raised itself and took aim on "the good life." All the world wanted a standard of living that, before, only America had enjoyed.

As those nations grew in strength, so did their economies, so did their stock markets, and so did the value of their francs, pounds, marks, and yen.

As they rose, we—by comparison—fell.

The U.S. Begins to Lose Dominance

By 1970 the system of fixed exchange rates that had been put in place twenty years earlier to help the world recover from the war in an orderly fashion was no longer working. So the free world decided to end fixed rates of exchange and let their currencies "float" to find their own market-determined value.

Ending fixed rates of exchange coincided with the end of American dominance. In 1970 we accounted for half the world economy. By 1990 our share had shrunk to a third or less. In 1970 the capitalization of our stock markets represented two-thirds of all stock markets in the world. Today it is closer to one-third.

But the most dramatic change that followed the end of fixed exchange rates was, of course, what happened to the dollar. It went into a twenty-year decline.

From 1972 to 1978, for example, the dollar lost 60% of its value against the Swiss franc. In 1972 a good Swiss watch might have sold for SFr400 and cost Americans who traveled there only $100; you could then get SFr4.0 to the dollar. In 1978 the same watch would cost $250, because our dollars no longer bought SFr4.0. We could only get SFr1.6 for each of them.

Businesses Adjust to the Change

American businesses in the sixties looked at changes in the world economies and the changes in the value of the dollar versus other currencies, and what they saw was a chance to make more money. The rising economies in Europe offered them not only new markets for American goods and services but the likelihood of bringing home profits in strengthening francs, marks, and pounds that would boost their profits when translated into dollars.

In the seventies we began to hear the phrase "multinational corporations." We also began to hear that Ford, Colgate, and IBM were making more profits abroad than they were making in the United States. To serve these companies, American advertising agencies, PR firms, auditors, and law firms agreed to set up offices in Europe and Asia. At first they dragged their feet; later they were gleeful about profits earned in francs, marks, pounds, and yen.

Businesses did well in those years. But not the average American.

The average American still had all his investable funds— savings accounts, stocks, bonds, mutual funds, IRA accounts, etc.—in dollars. As other currencies bought more and more, our dollars bought less and less. And we Americans began to feel the pinch.

Even some of the luxuries that middle-class Americans had always taken for granted—putting our children through a good college, retiring to a large sunbelt home, taking cruises to the Mediterranean—had to be replaced by retirement plans that were painfully more modest and by student loans that would take half a lifetime to repay.

The bad news of the last twenty years may not just end there.

For the foreseeable future you are likely to see our economy represent a smaller and smaller part of the gross world output. You're likely to see the stock markets of Japan and Germany extend the rises they have begun. You are also likely to see stocks of emerging countries such as Turkey, Malaysia, Mexico, Brazil, Chile, and Indonesia as much as double and triple in less than a year, while ours are content to rise 10% to 15%. And there's no telling when (or by how much) the dollar will continue to decline.

But don't let this make you feel trapped.

If American businesses can learn to stay on the right side of a declining dollar and to profit from changes around the world rather than lose out to them, well, so can you.

This book will help you do that:

• We'll show you how—without ever leaving your armchair—you can send your money around the world in search of profits that are simply hard to find here.

• We'll show you how to earn rates of interest on your savings that are sometimes 10 to 30 percent higher than what you now earn. Not in dollars but in a currency that is getting stronger.

• We'll show you the advantages of keeping your money at a triple A–rated bank where your financial dealings can be nobody's business but your own.

• We'll show you how to invest in top-rated government

bonds that pay substantially higher interest than ours and are just as safe.

• We'll help you explore overseas stock markets, where yearly gains that are double and triple that of the S&P 500 Index often seem almost commonplace.

• We'll show you how easy it is to deploy at least part of your assets into some currency other than the dollar, so that you never again have to worry about a dollar crisis trashing the value of everything you own.

Don't Count on U.S. Dominance

As you read this book, the dollar may be enjoying a brief rally. Or even a year or so of firmness. When that happens, it is very natural for us to hope that the worst is over and to assume there is no need to protect ourselves against another fall in the dollar.

That would be a dangerous assumption to make. The dollar has rallied a number of times during the past twenty years. Markets always fluctuate. Yet any investor who took heart during those rallies and continued to hold all his assets in dollars ended up with dollars that were worth less and less.

As you are reading this, our stock markets may be registering new all-time highs. And if you look only at our stock markets, you may feel you are invested in the best of all places. But right now, it is almost certain that elsewhere in the world—where local labor is skilled, amazingly hardworking, and incredibly cheap—foreign capital is flowing in like a flood. And local stock markets are making ours look tame. Elsewhere in the world, regional agreements are creating booming development. And for the first time those countries are depending only on each other and not counting the United States in.

As you read this, our bank regulators may be announcing that the worst is over and that you can now be sure your money is safe in any American bank. But elsewhere in the world, you will find banks that are more highly rated than the one where you probably keep all your cash. At these triple A–rated European banks you have the chance to earn substantially more interest, and as currencies change in value, these banks let you move from weaker currencies to stronger ones. (Would your bank let you do that?)

What You Should Be Thinking and Doing Now

There is no need, unless that is already on your mind, to switch all of your money out of the dollar today. It is enough for now to read this book and decide what it would be best for you to do and when to start doing it.

You can start with as modest a step as opening a small Swiss franc account at one of the American banks we describe in chapter 13. Or you can put some money in a mutual fund made up of international stocks or bonds. Or you can look into the advantages of banking overseas. In chapter 12 you'll learn how easy it is to open such an account and what advantages you can gain by keeping some money there, and in chapter 13 you'll find a directory of great European banks that love to work with Americans.

In the chapters that follow, you'll learn all the techniques that top professionals use to squeeze more profit out of money kept abroad. It doesn't matter if you are a timid investor or an aggressive one, there are ways you can take advantage of higher interest rates abroad and faster-growing stock markets and better-performing currencies. And all the while, you'll be protecting yourself against a dollar plunge.

Let's Plan a Trip to Europe

Assuming that the whole idea of having some of your money deployed in another currency appeals to you, let's see how trying out another currency can get you some of the good things in life.

Let's imagine that you went to Europe recently and were stung by how much things cost there. Still you love traveling and you'd like to be able to afford a trip abroad every two years for the foreseeable future.

Here's how you might be able to do it—just by opening a foreign currency account.

Imagine for starters that you put a portion of your money (say, $10,000) into a regular savings account in one of the great European banks. It's not hard; you can do it all by mail. Let's say your account is in England, Germany, Switzerland, Holland, Denmark or Austria. And let's say you ask the bank to hold your deposit in an Austrian schilling CD.

As you will see in chapter 5 and again in chapter 11, few currencies have paid Americans as rich a return on their money as the schilling. In fact, during a twenty-year period in the seventies and eighties, you would have earned over 35 percent a year total return in an Austrian schilling CD.

So if you choose the schilling, two years from now you should at the very least have the satisfaction of having put your money into a strong currency that keeps earning a high rate of interest. And, if the dollar starts down again, the dollars you converted into schillings could be worth 25 percent more counting both the interest earned and any rise in the value of the schilling.

If it works out that way, your $10,000 bank deposit will have brought you a two-year gain of possibly $5,000, which would surely make your next trip to Europe a lot less expensive than the last one.

While you are in Europe, you could pay a visit to the bank that holds your schilling CD. There you are likely to find a banker who has time to chat. And if you ask him for the best way he could suggest to invest your money over the next two years, you may be surprised to find how helpful he can be.

Keep notes about your visit to the bank. Then when tax

time rolls around, show those notes to your accountant. He might think it's perfectly OK to write off some of the expenses of your trip.

Becoming a Citizen of the World

By reading this book and becoming more international in your thinking, you may start something that can change your life.

American is still a great country, still the single greatest country in the world. But our position in that world *is* changing.

Once we dominated. Now Europe is creating a single economy that will probably be larger than ours. With the addition of Eastern Europe, that economy could become a colossus. Japan's growth never seems to stop for very long. It dominates another part of the world. Our area of domination, on the other hand, keeps shrinking. We seek special trade arrangements with Canada, Mexico, and South America because we are so much less important than we once were in the rest of the world.

Japan's currency has a good future. Switzerland, Austria, Germany, and all the currencies that are tied to the European Economic Community also have a promising future. The only major world currency that has traders worried is the dollar.

So once you decide to take a more international point of view—once you decide not to keep all your assets in dollars—you can start to share in the good things that are happening around the world, rather than be a victim of them. When the newly elected prime minister of a major country announces moves to strengthen his economy, you'll know how that is likely to affect his currency, and you can change your investments accordingly. When you meet citizens of other countries and observe whether they are more or less educated or hardworking than the average American, you can then square those observations with what you already know about their currencies and the growth of their stock markets.

Through your investments you will become more a citizen of the world. That is what we all must be in order to survive financially today and thrive tomorrow.

▼

CHAPTER 2

It's Time to Stop
Losing Money
on the Dollar

If today you're feeling less confident financially—that is, if you don't feel you can afford luxuries you once bought without thinking twice—there could be a very simple explanation.

Your dollars are simply not worth what they once were.

Since our government cut the dollar's last link to gold back in 1971, the dollar (your dollar) has lost three-quarters of its value—that's right, three-quarters of its value—against the Swiss franc.

You don't even have to go back that far or use the world's most revered currency as an example. More recently, in just a little over a year (May 1989 to October 1990) the dollar lost 27% against a minor currency, the Spanish peseta, and 35% against the Austrian schilling.

That's what you lost. But let's see what, in that same brief time, you could have gained.

What You Might Have Gained in the Right Currency

If in May 1989 you had deposited $3,000 of your money in Austrian schillings, by May 1990 your money would have been worth over $5,000. You would, in other words, have made over 67% on your money just by letting it sit in a bank for little more than a year.

It wasn't the interest that would have made you richer. (Some currencies pay incredible interest rates, but Austrian interest rates were roughly the same as ours then.) You would have been made richer by the changes that took place in the value of the dollar and the schilling.

In May 1989 an Austrian schilling was worth just over 7¢. By October 1990 the same schilling had soared in value to almost 11¢. While this jump took place in little more than a year, it was no flash-in-the-pan rise. The schilling has been climbing against the dollar for a generation.

Go back to the year 1970, and you'll soon see what being in the right currency (instead of the dollar) would have done to your net worth.

Three thousand dollars of your money put into an Austrian schilling bank account and simply kept there, safe and sound, drawing regular interest, averaging about 5%, would by 1990 have grown to $24,712.

In other words, your money would have grown eightfold! Just salted away in a bank. With no need for you to lose a single night's sleep about what was happening on Wall Street.

Dollar Is No Match for Strong Foreign Currency

Ever wonder why foreigners have been buying up so much of America? Once again, it comes back to the sad, steady decline of the dollar.

Let's imagine that you and a Japanese businessman are both standing in front of an office building in Austin, Texas.

The building is for sale. The price is $30 million. You both saw the same building in 1970. Then the price was only $10 million. So today—at triple its former price—you are not all that interested in buying the building. To you it's no bargain.

To the Japanese businessman, however, it's a whole 'nother thing!

In 1970, when the price was only $10 million, the Japanese businessman would have had to pony up ¥3.57 billion to buy it. That is what $10 million translated into in 1970.

Now let's jump to 1990. The price of the building has tripled from $10 million to $30 million. But not in yen. At the 1990 rate of exchange, $30 million translates into ¥3.9 billion. For the Japanese businessman the price hasn't tripled. It's hardly gone up at all! So he says, "I'll buy it." And you, with weaker dollars, turn it down.

We used a Japanese businessman as our example. But roughly the same opportunity to get a bargain was within the reach of a German businessman or anyone who holds German marks. Ditto for Swiss franc holders.

While the price tripled in dollars during those twenty years, it went up much, much less in German marks. In 1990 a German could have bought the building for only 22% more than what he would have had to pay in 1970.

And listen to this: a Swiss would actually have paid less for the building in 1990 than he would have in 1970. At a price of $10 million dollars in 1970, he would have had to hand over SFr43.1 million. But in 1990, when the price went up to $30 million, he would only have had to pay SFr37.5 million to buy it. That's what it means to keep your money in a really strong currency.

It is very painful for us Americans to see how cheaply a foreigner (using his strong currency) can buy our properties and to realize that we no longer can afford them, simply because our currency is so weak. But the picture actually gets worse when you consider how the incomes of the Japanese, German, and Swiss have been rising in this period. They have been working harder. They have been making things that the world wants at prices that the world adores. So their economies have risen and so have the incomes of the Japanese, Swiss, and German people.

The Japanese businessman who could have bought the Texas office building in 1990 for only a few more yen than he'd have paid twenty years before no doubt had more money to spend on a real estate investment than he had in 1970. After all, as his currency got stronger and stronger, his cost of living got cheaper and cheaper. Chances are he saved a lot in those twenty years and had more money to spend on buildings than the comparable American businessman.

The American businessman had the opposite experience. As the dollar kept going down, he could see his cost of living going up and his bank account having a hard time rising as fast as the cost of things he wanted to buy. So he put off buying; he had to.

For the American, with less to spend and with little enthusiasm for buying, the price was now triple. And for the Japanese businessman, who had become more prosperous—and could easily have spent more—the price had hardly changed at all.

When you realize that since 1970 the incomes of most Germans, Swiss, Japanese, and others holding strong currencies have risen tremendously just in terms of their own marks, francs, and yen, the reason they have been buying up America gets even more clear.

Since the Japanese businessman was earning more in 1990, you could say he had to work less (maybe half as much) to earn ¥3.9 billion needed to buy the building. So instead of the price going up 9% for him in twenty years, it actually went down in terms of hours spent to earn it. You might indeed say that, for him, the building became 41% cheaper, not 9% more expensive. For the American the price seemed to triple, but in terms of work needed to earn those dollars, the price he would have to pay was even more punishing than that. (In fact, let's not dwell on it, it's too painful.)

Seen from that perspective, it is no surprise that foreigners have been able to buy so much of America. The real wonder is that they haven't bought more.

Good News or Bad—The Dollar Fell

Chances are the forces that caused the dollar to decline in value against other currencies have not exhausted themselves. Once a major trend is in place, it tends to continue; temporary changes in that trend should not be allowed to draw you into complacency. With time, new reasons for shunning the dollar—reasons few could have anticipated—keep springing up.

Take the Japanese businessman who bought the office building in Austin, Texas, in mid-1990. Suddenly late that year, the Japanese stock market (which was dangerously over-priced) plummeted by 40%. The Japanese businessman is forced to sell the building. To stay liquid, he may also be forced to sell some U.S. Treasury bonds that he bought because they paid more interest than bonds in his home country. Now interest is less important to him; he needs cash and he needs it in yen.

Such dumping of dollars might have little to do with the intrinsic worth of the dollar at the time (except that dollars are less likely to be dumped if their future value is held in high regard.) The combined effect of the fall in the Japanese stock market in 1990 and the low regard for the dollar at that time, however, meant that dollars were dumped—making the value of your dollars less.

It didn't much matter what was going on in the world in the late eighties. The dollar kept falling for all kinds of perceived reasons and, seemingly, for no reasons at all.

• The Japanese stock market soared, the dollar fell. The Japanese stock market plunged, the dollar fell.
• Wall Street soared from 1985 to 1987, the dollar fell. Wall Street collapsed in October 1987, the dollar fell. Wall

Street recovered, the dollar fell. Wall Street fell again, so did the dollar.

• Our country's trade deficit rose, the dollar fell. The trade deficit fell, so did the dollar.

• When the economy looked strong, the dollar fell. And when the economy looked weak, the dollar fell.

• On the announcement of the unification of Germany—which should cause a heavy drain on marks from West to East Germany—you'd have expected the mark to fall against the dollar. But, no, it didn't happen that way. The mark rose to a record and the dollar fell.

• And most worrisome of all, as war broke out in the Middle East, instead of being viewed as a safe haven for money around the world (as it always had been before), the dollar was shunned and it fell. The Swiss franc and the Japanese yen soared instead.

Just imagine! The currencies of two countries that produce no oil at all rise at a moment that the oil reserves of the world are threatened. And the currency of our country—with our comparatively rich oil reserves—falls.

The situation was puzzling even to currency experts at the time. Just when they thought the dollar had fallen too much and was due for a bounce, the dollar fell once again. The bounce didn't come until about eight months later. And when it did, it seemed like the proverbial "dead cat bounce."

Why the Dollar Keeps on Falling

In order to understand why the dollar keeps falling, it's useful for us Americans to take a good hard look at ourselves—even if we don't like what we see.

A nation is generally made up of diverse groups of people. But when a country is viewed from outside, it takes on the personality of a single individual. The world thinks of Japan as one kind of person (you fill in what kind of person you think Japan resembles), of Germany as another kind of person—and so on.

What kind of person do you suppose the world thinks of when they think of our country?

They probably picture a rich, spoiled brat living off a rapidly diminishing trust fund and refusing to do what is necessary to provide for a secure future. Why? Because to take needed action might mean some unpleasant sacrifices. When you recall the latest congressional fight over taxes or the S&L scandal or the way we have drifted from work to leisure, ask yourself whether the image of America as a spoiled brat isn't largely justified.

You yourself may not fit that picture. Chances are you don't. The fact that you are reading this book suggests that you have worked hard and you have earned assets that you want to protect. Perhaps you have traits more in common with American values of old, or European or Asian values of today.

But if all your hard work has done for you is earn you assets that are denominated in dollars, you may largely have labored in vain.

Your wealth, be it in real estate, securities, or CDs, is reckoned in dollars, the currency of a nation that is eating its seed capital. Your precious savings are in the currency of a country that refuses to save. Your very future is wrapped up in a currency where the leaders view the future simply a place to push off unpaid debts.

That's the way the world sees us. And if your assets are tied up in dollars, the world will be reluctant to give you much for them.

You don't have to take this punishment anymore.

What happened to the dollar in the late eighties was awful, and it can happen again. But you don't have to stand by idly and let it make you poorer. You can move some of your money into a stronger currency now and more of it later as the threat to the dollar becomes more obvious to you. It has never been easier to do this.

In the last few years, perhaps in response to the awful slide in the dollar, half a dozen or more new ways to get out of the dollar have become available. The easiest, perhaps because it is so close to home, is to put some money in an American bank that offers Swiss franc, mark, yen, or pound accounts. Until 1990, it was virtually impossible to do this. But now you can. In chapter 10, we'll tell you which banks do this and how to contact them.

You can also put some money in a mutual fund specializing in international stocks, international bonds, or international currencies. That's also very easy. It might take nothing more than calling an 800 number.

And it's surprisingly simple now to open a currency account overseas without ever leaving home.

Some of the greatest (safest) banks in the world are in countries where the local currency has, over time, risen against the dollar. These banks have for years been offering easy-to-open deposit accounts not only in their own currency (Swiss franc, mark, pound, yen, schilling, etc.) but in any of the major currencies of the world.

In a few days you can open an account in any of these banks by mail or fax. They offer old-world service regardless of the size of your account; good personal service still lives at the great banks of Europe. They pay interest rates that will probably gladden your heart. They generally charge far less to exchange your dollars into a foreign currency than a bank in this country. And according to international rating services, these banks are probably far safer than the one you now have money in.

At any of these banks, you can own an account holding any of the top fifteen currencies or a combination of currencies of your own choice. Also these banks offer a lot of foreign currency savvy; they have been dealing in them for centuries and helping some of the richest people in the world conserve their wealth this way. They can help you move your money around whenever you think it will grow faster in another currency.

Like the economies in which they operate, these banks
have stayed extremely competitive. They want your business.
So they are, by comparison with American banks, very flexible, very efficient, inexpensive for their customers, and more
anxious to serve.

There is an another strong reason for having some of
your money in an overseas bank. What money you have there
and what it earns is nobody's business but yours. The banks
in Europe have a high regard for bank account secrecy. They
don't rush to report your financial dealings to anyone but
you—not to the government or your spouse or your business
partner. Your overseas bank account cannot normally be sub-
poenaed.

We'll introduce you to eight of these great banks, tell
you whom to contact there and what to tell them. You'll learn
this in chapters 12 and 13.

It's Time for You to Stop the Bleeding

All Americans have taken a terrible beating because of the
decline in the dollar. But our guess is that less than one person
in a thousand has done anything to protect himself against
another dollar fall.

The premise of this book is that the dollar—whether it
stabilizes briefly or just keeps on going down—will end up
losing money for you over the next ten years unless you decide
to do something about it. It might be very wise for you to
move a little or a lot of your money out of the dollar on a
time schedule that is comfortable for you. You don't have to
stay out of the dollar forever. You can move back into dollars
whenever you need to or whenever you think the dollar is
due for a bounce. There are even plenty of ways to make
money outside the dollar during those periods in which the
dollar rallies.

But right now, realize that as a holder of dollars, you are

in danger. No insurance company would insure you against another big fall in the dollar. But you can provide that insurance yourself.

Use what you learn in the upcoming chapters to devise a plan that fits your assets and your needs.

CHAPTER 3

▼

How to Turn
a Wobbly Dollar
to Your Advantage

Chances are, when you think about your net worth, you think of it in dollars. You may say to yourself: "I'm now worth a hundred thousand" or "half a million." But the dollar sign is there, even if unsaid.

So it must be at least a little unnerving to you when you read in the newspaper: "The dollar fell yesterday against all major currencies."

What *is* happening to your dollars?

The price or value of the dollar in terms of other currencies varies almost every day. Like anything else that is publicly traded, its value responds to supply and demand, in this case the supply and demand for dollars in the global currency markets.

If your paper says that the dollar fell yesterday against the German mark, fetching only DM1.74 (or three pfennigs less than the day before), it implies that someone holding German marks (and hoping to buy U.S. dollars) made the last bid of the day and he offered to pay DM1.74 for each of the dollars he wanted to buy. The same German buyer might have paid DM1.77 the day before. So on the second day, the dollar was reported to have fallen against the German mark.

To oversimplify, that's all there is to it.

The same day, your paper probably said that the dollar also went down against the Swiss franc and the Austrian schilling, because these currencies often move in concert with the mark. The dollar went down against the franc and schilling because holders of those two currencies had bid less for dollars that day than they had the day before.

Or perhaps the price of dollars (in terms of those currencies) changed that day because of demand that started in this country; perhaps Americans hoping to buy francs and schillings had to bid more dollars in order to get the francs and schillings they needed. As Americans bid up the dollar price of francs and schillings, like a teeterboard, the franc and schilling price for dollars came tumbling down. And your newspaper reported that the dollar had fallen.

Needless to say, when we Americans import a lot of foreign goods and services—and have to pay for them in foreign currencies—we automatically put upward pressure on the price of those currencies and downward pressure on the price of our dollars. When we buy a lot of francs, marks, pounds, and yen, we not only make our dollars seem less valuable, we also encourage those who hold francs, marks, shilling, pounds, and yen to think they don't have to pay as much for the dollars they want to buy.

The dollar, however, doesn't always move the same way against all currencies. The same newspaper report might also have reported that the dollar on that day went up against the Japanese yen, indicating that holders of yen had to bid more than the day before in order to get dollars they needed to buy American farm products or to settle accounts that had to be settled in dollars (like oil purchases) or simply to speculate on the future price of dollars or yen.

Why Does the Dollar Go Down?

The value of the dollar goes down for the same reason that a share of AT&T goes down or the price of a house that someone has to sell in a hurry. It goes down because potential buyers are simply unwilling to pay any more than the lowered price.

If investors hear that AT&T has been slapped with a big lawsuit, they may want to dump the stock. So the stock goes down. If the house that is being sold is in a problem neighborhood, it may take a lot longer to sell it. And the owner might have to drop his price more drastically to get a buyer before he moves.

And so it is with the dollar.

Whenever more people who own British pounds have an urgent need for dollars for business purposes or to pay for traveling in the United States, they are more likely to bid up the price of the dollar. And it will be reported in the paper that the price of the dollar (in pounds) went up.

And it isn't just a matter of *need* that sends the price (the value) of dollars up or down. Sometimes investors, speculators, central banks around the world sense that the dollar has risen beyond its true value (that it is, so to speak, "overbought"). So they don't want to get "caught" holding a lot of dollars. Their trading instincts tell them they'd better get out of dollars and into marks or some other rising currency. This could spur an exodus from the dollar and bring about a quick and sharp change in its exchange rate, i.e., the rate at which it can be exchanged into other currencies.

Take an example that really happened during the years 1985 to 1988. The dollar went down steadily for those years against all major currencies, but its fall was especially steep against the Swiss franc. Late in 1988, when currency investors or speculators got a hint that the dollar had "bottomed" against the franc and was ripe for a rise, perhaps only a temporary one, they piled into the market and bid more and more in francs to get the dollars they were sure would soon be worth a higher price in francs. The franc fell and the dollar rose in very short order.

How a Falling Dollar Crimps Your Standard of Living

If the dollar were always firm or rising (as was once the case, when our economy dwarfed all others), Americans would have less need to look abroad for investment opportunities. For one thing, under an always rising dollar, our security markets are more likely to outpace those in other countries. For another, your strong dollars could buy a lot more in imported luxuries, and you could far more afford luxurious hotels and restaurants when you traveled abroad.

As chart 1 on page 30 clearly shows, however, the value of the dollar over the last twenty years has been far from firm and rising. In fact, it has traced what is called a down-channel, reaching lower highs before turning down and lower lows before turning up. It has drifted, it seems, inexorably lower, sending out ominous signals about its future.

The effect of a falling dollar on your standard of living has been painful. If in 1970 your net worth (the value of your house, car, savings accounts, your stocks and bonds, retirement fund, etc.) came to $180,000, you could have turned that net worth into assets worth SFr775,860, because in 1970, $180,000 was worth that many Swiss francs.

Twenty years later, an American whose net worth was $180,000 could turn it into fewer than SFr230,000. In twenty years a net worth of $180,000 had lost three-quarters of its value in terms of the Swiss currency. To be sure, the franc was the strongest world currency in that time, but your own experience probably tells you that in recent years your dollars have lost value against most of major currencies.

If you traveled abroad seven years ago and then again recently, you probably wince when you think how much less you can get overseas for your dollars—that is, how much

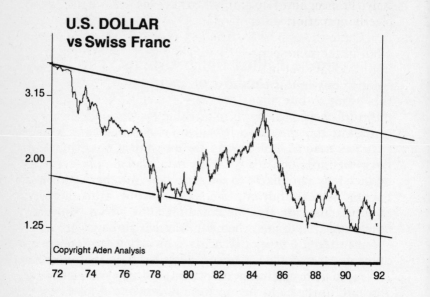

U.S. DOLLAR vs Swiss Franc

Copyright Aden Analysis

Stuck in a deadly down-channel: The dollar (when strong) struggles to ever-lower highs and (when exhausted) ever-lower lows. An ominous sign for the future.

more it now costs for a first-class hotel or for a meal in a good restaurant.

If you bought an imported car seven years ago and then again recently, you know how many more dollars you had to pay for it.

If you loved to buy good French wines seven years ago, you might feel less enthusiastic about them today. You might even find yourself shifting to California or Chilean wines, where your dollars have some of their old buying power.

The prices you pay for goods made in this country may have gone up over the past decade, but nowhere near as much as the prices for goods from Japan, German, Switzerland,

Italy, France, and England, where the local currencies have clearly outperformed the dollar.

Quite the opposite is true for people in other countries who, in the same period, have held most of what they own not in dollars but in Swiss francs, marks, or yen. What they want to buy in this country is cheap for them. In fact, what they want to buy almost anywhere is cheap for them after they turn their greatly appreciated currency into the currency of the country they are visiting.

You may have seen foreign tourists scooping up everything they see in our shops. Once they turn their money into dollars, they can't believe how cheap things are here. Japanese tourists will even buy Japanese cameras here because the yen they brought with them (when turned into dollars) brought the price of the cameras down to less than the price at home. What foreigners have to pay (in their money) for hotels, restaurants, and rental cars when they visit this country feels a lot less to them than what we have to pay in dollars when we travel to Europe.

The same goes for foreign investors. They find it easier to buy our farmland, our office buildings, even some of our large corporations, advertising agencies, publishing firms, record companies, etc. On the other hand, what was once corporate America's growing appetite for companies in Europe has slackened because of how much less our dollars can buy there.

Don't Curse a Falling Dollar—Turn It to Your Advantage

Increasingly each year, Americans have found that one way to protect themselves against the erosive power of a falling dollar is to diversify their investments—to put some of their money into other currencies and into other stock and bond markets.

Chances are this will also happen to you, if it hasn't

already. Chances are that in the years ahead more and more
of your money will end up invested overseas. And its value
will be expressed in currencies other than the dollar.

• If you put money into a CD in a Swiss bank, for example, the value of your account will normally be reported to
you in Swiss francs, unless you specify you want it in another
currency.
• If you buy British gilts (bonds), they will pay you interest (recently quite a good rate of interest) in British pounds.
• If you buy shares in the Japan Fund, a no-load mutual
fund made up almost entirely of Japanese stocks and bonds,
you will be able to buy fund shares from the distributor in
New York and pay for them in dollars, at the fund's net asset
value that day. But the value of the individual stocks and
bonds in the fund's portfolio (the value that determines what
you pay for fund shares) will be set each day in Tokyo and
will, of course, be expressed not in dollars but in yen.

So as more of your money moves overseas, it will matter
a great deal to you what happens to the *dollar* value of the
Swiss franc, the German mark, the British pound, and the
Japanese yen—because those are some of the local currencies
your investments will be denominated in. And as they get
stronger against the dollar, you will be able to turn the marks,
francs, pounds, and yen that you have, in effect, invested
overseas back into more and more dollars that you can spend
at home.

For example, on any particular day your newspaper
might tell you that the dollar *fell* against the mark—and that
each dollar bought DM1.74 in the open market. The day
before, your paper might add, the dollar had brought as much
as DM1.77. Since each dollar bought about 2% fewer marks
that day, the dollar lost almost 2% of its value in relation to
the German mark.

If all your money had been held in *dollar* investments
that day, you would have reason to be unhappy. The dollar

had gone down. But every *mark* you had invested in German securities or German bank deposits went up in value by the same 2%, because when converted back into dollars, their mark value would have brought you more dollars. So your investments overseas tend to keep your portfolio level, to take the shock out of investing.

A 2% gain in the mark (the 1% drop in the dollar) mentioned above may not seem like much. But that was only one day. And when the dollar keeps falling like it did in the second half of the eighties, those little gains can add up to a surprising amount.

An Italian CD That Yielded 29.8% and a British CD That Yielded 45.9%

Imagine, for example, that you had put $10,000 into a Swiss bank account in 1985, asking that it be held for you in Italian lire (lire deposits were yielding 17.7% at the time and U.S. deposits were paying less than 10%). Under stable currency conditions, you could have looked forward to drawing out lire worth $11,770 at the end of that year—your $10,000 deposit plus the 17.7% interest earned. But that year, the dollar/lira market was not stable. The lira rose 12.1% against the dollar. So instead of growing to $11,770, your $10,000 investment actually ended the year being worth $12,980— a gain of 17.7% in interest and of 12.1% in the currency translation, for a total gain of 29.8%. That's a very good return even for growth stocks, but a remarkable gain for money kept snug in a bank.

If you had asked to have your money kept in British pounds, you would have had to settle for a lower rate of interest than in lire. In 1985 pound deposits were earning little more than dollar deposits—only 11.67%. All the same, you would have made out much better keeping your money in pounds than in lire because that year the value of the pound leaped against the dollar by 29.2%.

In the instance we've just described, your $10,000 deposit translated into pounds would have given you £8,929. Under stable currency conditions you would have expected your deposit to end up at year end as £9,972 (a 11.67% gain from interest earned) or about $11,167. But because of the sharp rise in the pound against the dollar that year (or to put it another way, the 29.2% fall in the dollar against the pound), you could have traded your year-end balance of £9,972 into $14,459.26—an almost 50% gain for the year.

Better-Paying CDs, Higher-Yielding Bonds, Faster-Growing Stocks, Stronger Currencies

What is true of foreign-currency bank deposits is also true of all investments that have their value based in another currency. Any change in the value of the dollar affects the net value to Americans of all foreign stocks, foreign bonds, and all mutual funds whose holdings are valued at the close of day on some foreign stock exchange and in some currency other than the dollar.

If you own shares in international stock or bond funds, you can expect the net asset value of those funds to rise faster during a period of dollar decline, because as the dollar declines, those funds enjoy the tail-wind effect of the rising value of the local currencies against the dollar. So when one adds the higher value of those currencies to the increased value of the stocks themselves, the result for American shareholders is a far better than average gain—sometimes a staggering gain.

A good example of this occurred in 1985 and 1986. While our stock markets (and domestic mutual funds) were doing very well—*booming,* in fact—mutual funds invested overseas did substantially better. A representative sampling of international stock funds posted gains of 41.17% in 1985 and 44.02% in 1986—far better gains than the booming Dow Jones Average.

In part that was because overseas markets were doing well—but only in part: International mutual fund managers get an extra lift from any rise of their local currencies against the dollar. They benefit from each drop in the dollar (rise in the value of the local currencies), because when the portfolio's local value is translated back into dollars, it's worth more dollars. Also, by concentrating their cash reserves in those currencies that are growing especially rapidly against the dollar, even the fund's cash reserves earn more money. In rare instances these managers may even short the dollar, i.e., sell dollars for future delivery hoping to buy them back at a much lower price. So there are many reasons for the managers of international stock and bond funds to pray for a drop in the dollar.

In those periods when the dollar is rising, fund managers have the privilege of hedging against that rise by selling short any currencies that are falling especially fast against the dollar, even if the currencies they sell have nothing to do with the fund's holdings.

Put the Dollar Damage Behind You

What has happened to the dollar (and to the standard of living that we once enjoyed) is painful, and when you look to the future, it is worrisome as well. But there are things you can do to protect yourself in that worrisome future.

When you understand what makes the dollar and other major currencies rise and fall, you'll know how to deploy your assets to better effect. You'll be able to deposit your savings at interest rates that beat U.S. rates by a mile and in currencies that are rising against the dollar. You will be able to seek out stocks and bonds and mutual funds that are rising faster than the Dow Jones Average and which give you extra profits instead of the losses you would have suffered from a falling dollar.

In short, you'll be able to keep the changing value of all major currencies always on your side, helping your net worth to grow instead of shrink.

▼

PART II

Sixteen Currencies You May Find More Profitable Than the Dollar

▲

▼

CHAPTER 4

Finding the Right Currencies to Invest In

There were, at last count, 175 different currencies in the world. This seems like you have too much choice—especially if you've been accustomed to investing in only one currency—but we can fairly easily whittle those 175 down.

The Dollar Didn't Fall Against All Currencies—Just the Leading Ones

You may have gotten the impression that the U.S. dollar has fallen against all the world's currencies over the past twenty years. This is not true, however. Here are some facts that may surprise you. Surprise number one: since 1970 the dollar has risen against most of the world's currencies. Surprise number two: from 1970 to 1990 only thirty-six currencies have risen against the dollar. All the rest either shadowed it or fell against it. And of those thirty-six, only sixteen rose in value by more than 25% over those two decades. Surprise number three (and perhaps the most striking fact of all): only five currencies—the "Fabulous Five"—doubled (or more) in value against the dollar during the past generation, a disastrous period for the greenback. And only one, the Swiss franc, more than tripled against it.

Keep in mind that we are talking about the pure currency. It does not take into account the interest rates, especially compounded interest rates, that boosted the gains from the exchange rate move alone. We'll see in chapter 10 how just staying in Swiss francs earning compound annual interest would have brought a 513% return from 1970 through 1991. And doing the same thing in Austrian schillings would have gained even more.

But when we speak of how much the dollar has fallen, we really mean how far it has fallen over a relative handful of currencies. Stay within the group, and you'll do well. Stay too far outside it, and you take your chances.

In 1990 the famous investment writer Harry Browne calculated how each one of the world's currencies performed against the dollar, first from 1970 and then from 1980 to 1990. Table 1 on pages 41–42 gives the 25 best-performing alongside the 25 worst-performing. (Only 135 of today's 175 currencies were tracked from the end of 1989 to the present.)

The Dollar's Seeming Strength in Parts of the World Leads Many Investors Astray

We have established that the U.S. dollar has lost 75% of its value against the Swiss franc in the past generation. It may shock you to know how many other currencies have done even worse, losing upward of 99.9% of their values against the *dollar*.

Ninety-five of the world's currencies have lost value against the dollar in the past twenty-odd years. Fully one-third of those lost over 90% of their dollar values, and two-thirds lost more than 50%. This happened at the same time the dollar was being kicked around by other leading currencies.

TABLE 1

**Appreciation/Depreciation (Percentage vs. U.S. Dollar)
from January 1, 1970, to January 1, 1991**

Best Record

1.	Swiss franc	+ 246.5
2.	Japanese yen	+ 181.7
3.	West German mark	+ 150.1
4.	Austrian schilling	+ 149.9
5.	Dutch guilder	+ 118.6
6.	Singapore dollar	+ 74.6
7.	Belgian franc	+ 57.4
8.	Luxembourg franc	+ 57.4
9.	Taiwanese dollar	+ 51.3
10.	Maltese lira	+ 38.9
11.*	Rwandan franc	+ 32.8
12.	Qatar riyal	+ 30.8
13.	United Arab Emirate dirharn	+ 29.8
14.	Libyan dinar	+ 26.9
15.	Bahrain dinar	+ 26.3
16.	Cuban peso	+ 25.5
17.	Kuwaiti dinar	+ 24.2
18.	South Korean won	+ 23.7
19.	Danish krone	+ 23.3
20.	Ethiopian birr	+ 20.8
21.	Djbouti franc	+ 20.6
22.	Saudi Arabian riyal	+ 20.0
23.	Mongolian tugrik	+ 19.2
24.	Malaysian ringgit	+ 13.8
25.	Iranian rial	+ 12.9

Worst Record

135.	Argentinian austral	− 99.9 +
134.	Bolivian boliviano	− 99.9 +
133.	Brazilian cruzeiro	− 99.9 +

Worst Record, cont.

132.	Chilean peso	− 99.9 +
131.	Israeli New shekel	− 99.9 +
130.	Nicaraguan cordoba	− 99.9 +
129.	Peruvian inti	− 99.9 +
128.	Ugandan shilling	− 99.9 +
127.	Uruguayan peso	− 99.9 +
126.	Yugoslavian dinar	− 99.9 +
125.	Laotian kip	− 99,9 +
124.	Vietnamese dong	− 99.9
123.	Zairian zaire	− 99.9
122.	Polish zloty	− 99.7
121.	Ghanaian cedi	− 99.7
120.	Turkish lira	− 99.7
119.	Mexican peso	− 99.6
118.	Lebanese pound	− 99.5
117.	Sierra Leonean leone	− 99.5
116.	Icelandic krona	− 98.5
115.	Somalian shilling	− 98.3
114.	Zambian kwacha	− 98.2
113.	Ecuadorian sucre	− 98.0
112.	Mozambican metical	− 96.9
111.	Colombian peso	− 96.5

*Currencies 11 through 25 valued as of August 4, 1990.

One unfortunate aspect of this is that in country after country where currencies have collapsed—Argentina, Brazil, Chile, Israel, etc.—the smartest people there, while abandoning hope in their own currencies, have usually chosen the dollar as the currency to tie their wealth to. We in the United States—victims ourselves of a falling currency—can only shake our heads sadly as we admit to them that they didn't make the best choice.

Those who denominated their savings in dollars are certainly better off than those who stayed with their own failing currencies, but anyone who put his or her savings in Swiss francs instead of dollars would have watched his or her wealth increase from the level of a serf to that of a king.

What We Americans Can Learn from Those Who Held On to Their Failing Currencies

The millions of citizens whose currencies have collapsed in the past few years could teach some lessons to us Americans. If you are worried about the value of your money, they'd now be quick to tell us, look outside your own borders.

But don't just look anywhere, and don't assume that a politically or militarily powerful country is the best place. It needn't be the currency of a strong country as much as that of a nation which has run its economic and financial system well. In particular, look at nations that have a proven track record of good management of their currencies. You needn't actually keep the currency of those countries in those same countries; you can keep them in a strong bank anywhere in the world. But wherever you keep them, you should own those currencies.

In the next four chapters we'll look at some of the currencies that have a proven record of outperforming the dollar. There is a lore about each currency, strong or weak, whose history and fortunes usually reflect those of the host country. By examining their life stories, so to speak, we not only gain an understanding of the particular currency—for instance, whether its recent strength is but a flash in the pan—but we also better understand the other country itself. In doing so, we become closer to that ideal of citizens of the world—at home everywhere and able to appreciate the best that each country has to offer.

CHAPTER 5

The "Fabulous Five"

1. The Swiss Franc: Star of the "Fabulous Five"

No currency has held its value better, not only over this past generation, but over the past 150 years, than the Swiss franc.

The modern Swiss franc was born in 1850, two years after the Swiss constitution put an end to cantons using their own currencies. The Swiss franc was declared equal to the French franc, each being defined as 4.5 grams of fine silver.

It is very interesting to see how those three values have done since then. Today it takes about four French francs to equal one Swiss franc. But most extraordinary of all is how the Swiss franc has held its value in terms of silver. After all, you'd expect the Swiss money to have gained against the French. But most currencies have lost value against silver over the past century or so, and most have lost big. Italy's lira has lost 99.9% of its silver value since 1862, when its value was also fixed at 4.5 grams of silver.

At recent ($4 per ounce) silver prices, 4.5 grams of silver

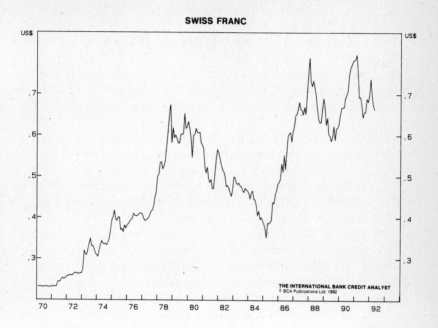

SWISS FRANC

The 20th-century's king of currencies: The Swiss franc is the currency that has dominated our time. None other has kept its value so well against the dollar (drubbing the greenback by almost sevenfold). The Swiss know how critical the franc is to their future and they have the national will to protect its value.

would be worth 58¢. And yet the Swiss franc has been recently worth closer to 70¢—20% more than the 4.5 grams are worth in American money. In short, while other currencies have faded against silver, the Swiss franc has shone more brightly.

This is worth noting because over time, paper currencies have always tended to lose value against commodities like silver. All currencies were once freely convertible into specific weights, or amounts, of gold or silver. But no other currency has held its value so well against the metal in whose weight it was first defined.

Let's take the U.S. dollar as a comparison. In 1850 the U.S. dollar was equal to 24.06 grams of silver (about three-quarters of an ounce). Today at $4.00 per ounce, 24.06 grams of silver are worth $3.10. That is to say, it would take $3.10 to buy the same amount of silver that only 58¢ bought in 1850.

Seen this way, the dollar has lost over two-thirds of its value, while the Swiss franc has increased its value by 15% over the same period as measured against the same unchanging commodity, silver, by which both were first defined.

In 1850 Switzerland's franc was also defined in terms of gold: 290.323 milligrams. This value held well for a long time. During World War I, Switzerland, like all the other European nations, went off the gold standard, but the damage done to the franc was minor compared to the value lost by every other European currency. By 1920 the Swiss franc had declined 22% against its previous value (to 226.5 milligrams of gold). But by 1929 it was back up to prewar value.

Then in the thirties Switzerland, like all nations, inflated to get out of the Great Depression. By 1940 the franc had fallen 29.25% against gold, to 205.35 milligrams. This meant a dollar rate of SFr4.32 per dollar (or 23.1¢ per Swiss franc), a price that would stay fairly stable until the early seventies.

Switzerland was so monetarily responsible during World War II that the franc rose dramatically against the dollar during the war. It reached a high of SFr2.27 per dollar (44.1¢) in December 1943.

In the seventies and eighties the Swiss franc soared against the dollar, increasing more than any other currency: from 22¢ to 81¢ (268%). But even so, the value of gold in Swiss francs went up even faster. In mid-1991 the franc was only worth about 44 milligrams of gold. Even the world's strongest currency has thus lost 85% of its value against gold in the past sixty years.

Gold doesn't pay interest, and it has been notoriously

volatile in recent years. But over the long term, it is a good measure by which to judge the value of all paper money. It is a sobering thought to realize that an ounce of gold could buy a good man's suit sixty years ago, just as it could today. And for even the strongest national paper currency to have lost so much of its gold value during that same time means that even the Swiss franc has not held its value against the things people need to buy. But if faced with the choice of where to put your interest-bearing savings over the past twenty years, no currency—except one (the Austrian schilling)—has done better than the Swiss franc. The reasons this has been true will be apparent as you read further in this book. But right now we can assert that when comparing currencies, the Swiss franc is the currency against which others must be judged.

What Makes Switzerland So Special?

Swiss political stability is without parallel in the world. For instance, Swiss voters have held the four main political parties in very nearly perfect equilibrium for over seventy years.

Yet what is so stable now was not always so. In the 1830s and 1840s Switzerland was one of the most turbulent countries in Europe. As an Austrian diplomat observed during that period, it was "the most perfect image of a state in the process of social disintegration. . . . [It] staggers from evil into upheaval and represents . . . an inexhaustible spring of unrest and disturbance." Battles between liberal Protestant and conservative Catholic cantons threatened to tear the country apart. In fact, some Catholic cantons contemplated joining Austria and held secret talks with Austria's Metternich.

When these talks became known, in 1847, civil war broke out. Federal troops prevailed in the brief war, which ended twenty years of guerrilla warfare and revolution throughout Switzerland.

Victor and vanquished worked together to write the Constitution of 1848, which has governed Switzerland ever since.

(It is now by far the oldest continually used constitution in Europe.) One cannot but be impressed that the stable Swiss constitution grew out of the trauma of a civil war. The stable American constitution was born of a united overthrowing of a foreign tyrant and is much easier to understand. But civil wars usually leave a legacy of bitterness for generations afterward.

A Mania for Independence

Why was this not the case with Switzerland? Fundamentally, it was because the constitution enshrined a central tradition of Swiss life: ultimate sovereignty rests not with a central government, but rather with the people. Specifically, power resides in the local neighborhoods, where free citizens are most able to control their lives. It stands to reason that the more power individuals have over their own lives, the more incentive they have to keep their country free, stable, and prosperous.

Accordingly, the most basic unit of Swiss political life, that unit from which everything else flows, is the local community government called the *Gemeindeversammlung*. There is no English word for this. *Municipality* comes close to *Gemeinde* but does not convey the same sense of community. Perhaps the best approximation to *Gemeindeversammlung* is the old-fashioned New England town meeting. There, the assembled citizens of the neighborhood decide the pressing questions facing their towns.

The *Gemeindeversammlung*, however, is far more potent and universal a force. One becomes a Swiss citizen only by first becoming a citizen of a *Gemeinde*. On all Swiss passports and official personal papers the name of the *Gemeinde* is prominent.

The singular thing is that this town could well be one that neither the citizen nor the past few generations of his family have ever seen. Citizenship in a *Gemeinde* stays with a family and its descendants even if they are no longer living there. The pull, however, remains strong. When the Swiss are asked "Where are you from?" most will answer instinctively with their *Gemeinde*, even though they may never have been there.

There were at last count 3,072 Swiss *Gemeinden* for roughly 6.4 million Swiss. This averages some 2,000 Swiss per *Gemeinde*. But they vary greatly in size: one might have as few as 12 people; at the other extreme Zurich has 370,000.

The existence of so many self-governing communities continually gives vent to frustrations that in other countries may be pent up until the boiling point. Some communities may be rabidly liberal, others very conservative: yet each can exist in its own area, where its own prejudices can be aired, and without fear that the prejudices of other communities will disrupt its way of life.

It is not too much to say that this strict decentralization and compartmentalization keeps Switzerland stable. Paradoxically, it also keeps the country unified in a way that other more centralized countries (for example, the former Soviet Union) are not. However else each *Gemeinde* or canton may differ from others, they all retain their essential "Swissness," that policy of respect for others that results in strength through diversity.

2. The Austrian Schilling

We are giving this currency a second place to the Swiss franc even though it is rarely mentioned in the same hushed tones as the franc, the mark, and the yen.

Why?

The schilling appears to have lagged behind the Swiss franc, the yen, and the mark in performance over the past generation. But not if you add accumulated, compounded interest to the excellent currency appreciation it has achieved against the dollar. After all, earning interest on bank deposits is the way virtually everyone keeps currency. Holding Swiss francs at the average deposit interest would have gotten you over 500% from 1970 through 1990—not bad at all. But by holding Austrian shillings and compounding their average interest rates, you would have made over 750% during that same period. The Austrian schilling has been little-known but extremely profitable for those few investors who have discovered it. A combination of currency appreciation and nice high yields have made the currency the unsung star of our time.

Most Americans don't know much about Austria. Some confuse it with Australia. But because it is so little-known and so profitable for some, Austria and its schilling deserve more in-depth background information. It could be a real find for you.

A Currency Star Is Born, Then Dies, Then Is Born Again

In December 1923 ten thousand of the inflated paper krone were exchanged for one new schilling. The krone (crown) had been Austria's money for centuries, but with the collapse of both the Hapsburg monarchy and the krone itself, it was decided that a clean break was needed. (*Schilling* comes from the German *Schild*, or shield. As we'll see, this was the same origin for the ecu.)

One schilling was defined as and was convertible into 211.72 milligrams of gold. Just how unsuccessfully currencies (yes, even this superb currency) have held their original gold value can be made clear in this fact: from 1923 to 1992 you'd have been far better off staying with the gold than with the schilling. At today's gold prices the 211.72 milligrams of gold by which the schilling was defined is worth over $3.10. Today one schilling is worth 87¢.

The thirties were bad years for the schilling. Its value fell by over 20%, but this wasn't the worst of it. Austrians first lost their freedom to take their money out of the country (exchange controls), and finally, in 1938, Nazi Germany abolished the schilling altogether.

The postwar monetary chaos ended in 1953. Austria joined the International Monetary Fund and fixed the schilling this way:

$$S1 = 34.18 \text{ milligrams of gold}$$
$$\$1 = S26$$

The turning point for Austria was 1952 to 1953. After that its stability and prosperity grew steadily. The schilling's value held steady at S26 per dollar from 1953 to 1970. Then, when the major currencies were allowed to seek their own level, the schilling began to climb. There are about S11 per dollar now. Put another way, at S26 per dollar, the 1970 starting point, each schilling was worth 3.85¢. Now, at S11 per dollar, the schilling is worth over 9¢ or well over two times the value it had.

Austria's Special Tie to Germany

When the Germans annexed Austria in 1938, the note-issuing privilege of the Austrian central bank was withdrawn, and for the next seven years Austria became a mere monetary appendage to Hitler's Germany. That regime ended in 1945, but Austria has spent the postwar period continuing to follow Germany's monetary lead.

The vastly inflated German (and Austrian) reichsmark collapsed soon after war's end. Germany adopted the new deutsche mark, and Austria went back to the schilling. Fortunately for both countries, German chancellor Ludwig Erhard—greatly influenced by those titans of the so-called "Austrian school" of economics, Eugen von Boehm-Bawerk and Ludwig von Mises—instituted the hard-money policy that helped create Germany's recent "economic miracle."

With a few brief interruptions this policy has been fol-

AUSTRIAN SCHILLING

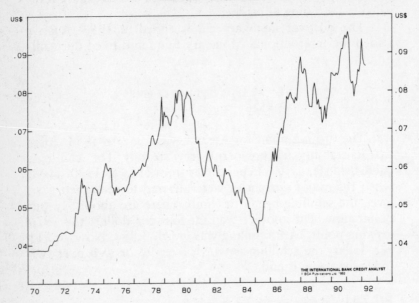

New champ of European currencies? The Austrian schilling has had an awesome rise against the dollar in recent years. It also offered investors the highest total return (rise plus interest) of any currency. As icing on the cake, it's ideally poised to gain from the rebuilding of Eastern Europe.

lowed by both countries ever since—particularly after 1973, when currencies were allowed to float. In fact, one of the few departures from a hard-currency regime occurred in both countries just before that, when Germany and Austria—along with Switzerland—inflated their currencies in an unsuccessful attempt to keep the dollar's rate artificially high.

When the dollar ceased to be the absolute standard by which all currencies were measured, Austria decided in effect to tie both its exchange rate and its monetary policy to the deutsche mark. Germany was, after all, its largest trading partner by far. Between 1971 and 1981 the mark's value stood virtually unchanged against the schilling in Vienna's foreign exchange markets, and it has moved very little since.

How Austria Kept the Schilling Strong

Austrian central bank monetary policy has not only used the exchange rate to bring stability, it has also employed a consistent interest-rate policy to support it. To ensure that Austrian capital wouldn't drain out into Germany's much larger capital markets—especially as there would be no foreign exchange risk in doing so—the decision was made to keep Austrian interest rates a bit above German rates. On average, rates on schillings are between 0.5% and 1% higher than deutsche mark interest rates. And since the schilling has appreciated against the dollar to the same extent as the mark, the overall return on schilling deposits has been much better than both mark and Swiss franc deposits.

This is why the overall return on schilling deposits has been over 750% since 1970, compared to 500% for Swiss francs.

Absent from the foregoing discussion has been much mention of the Swiss franc. Yet to almost the same degree Austria ties its exchange rate to Germany, its largest trading partner, so too does Switzerland. Germany is also Switzerland's largest trading partner, and it would hurt the Swiss economy to allow the franc to rise too much above the mark, and by extension, the schilling.

This means there is every reason to believe that the schilling and the Swiss franc will continue to enjoy fairly stable currency cross-rates. And so long as the German and Swiss central banks keep to low-inflation policies, so too will the Austrians.

We've seen how the Swiss made their franc so sound. Now let's turn the same spotlight on the Austrians.

"Let Others Wage Wars, Let You, Happy Austria, Marry"

This saying well describes the very rapid and peaceful growth of the small House of Hapsburg from the twelfth century to the point where, in the sixteenth, it ruled most of the Old and New Worlds (the latter because Spain was at one point ruled by the Austrian Hapsburgs). Few wars were waged to achieve this; rather the family married into nearly every royal house of Europe.

In the nineteenth century, the Austro-Hungarian Empire included all or parts of what are now Italy, Poland, Czechoslovakia, Yugoslavia, and Romania. This empire brought with it a level of culture that has never been surpassed. Think of any field of knowledge or art, and in the late nineteenth and early twentieth centuries, Austrians were the world's pathbreakers.

After World War I the empire ended, and Austria took the tiny geographic shape we know today. But that war's blow was felt in more than just lost territory. A period of decline set in, which reached its nadir in 1938, when the Nazis invaded.

That year 1 million people left Austria, including the intellectual lifeblood of the country: everyone from von Mises to Freud.

The Seeds of Austria's Remarkable Currency

Austria's economic fortunes paralleled its cultural experience: growth through much of the nineteenth century was followed by hardship through much of the twentieth.

Austria has had a central bank since 1816. It was established to try to provide stability in the wake of the wild inflation and devaluation that came with the Napoleonic wars. Throughout the latter nineteenth century and very early twentieth, this goal was fairly well achieved: Austria was known as a hard-currency, low-inflation nation during most of this time. The 1863 Banking Act set strict laws against, among other things, issuing too much unbacked paper money. At that time, Austria was on a silver coin standard. In 1900, in large part at the urging of its finance minister von Boehm-Bawerk, Austria embraced a gold standard.

A gold standard alone, however, will not ensure a country's monetary stability forever. There must exist the underlying will to hue to its strictures. A mere fourteen years into the gold standard's life, it was abandoned. Faced with the need to finance World War I, Austria closed the gold-redemption window and shifted the printing presses into high gear. As in Germany, the results of this monetary creation did not make themselves fully felt until just after the war. But unlike German inflation, which completely destroyed the currency in 1923, Austrian inflation was stopped before total havoc was reached.

Modern Austria's economic history is the story of one long, hard road to recovery. World War I, then the inflation of the early twenties, and the Great Depression. Moreover, Austria experienced the Great Depression more deeply and bitterly than any other country. Then came Hitler, National Socialism, war, and desperation. In 1946 Austria's gross national product (GNP) was less than two-thirds of its level before Hitler invaded in 1938. And the 1938 GNP had itself been less than that of 1914.

On the Edge of the Iron Curtain

It is generally agreed that what turned Austria around was American economic aid in the form of the Marshall Plan. The Soviets, of course, opposed this program, so support went to the western part of Austria, which is still in general the richest part. This area benefited even more by a development that was to be a precursor of the new Austria: the country became a haven. While not yet the financial haven it is now, it provided a new home for Czech and Hungarian refugees fleeing communism, as well as the ethnic Germans leaving gerrymandered Czechoslovakia.

These anticommunist refugees breathed new life into the Austrian economy. They were, not surprisingly, among the most entrepreneurial, creative, and innovative individuals of their societies. They felt comfortable in Austria, not just because of the freedom but also because of ties of culture, history, and language. They still do; as the Iron Curtain fell, Austria found itself perfectly placed to take advantage of these age-old ties.

Hard Choices Ensure a Hard Currency—Prosperity

How Austria faced and solved its only postwar economic crisis could be a lesson for all countries.

The crisis came in the early fifties, with inflation soaring at a 30% clip. But in 1952 the hard choices were made: bank-credit inflation was abruptly stopped, government spending cut, and prices for public services raised. At the cost of only a one-year economic stagnation, steady Austrian economic growth began and has now lasted two generations.

Its economic problems were far from over, however. In the midfifties Austria was still a poor country. Per-capita income was only three-quarters of the Western European average, which itself was very low by American standards. In fact, it would not be until the seventies that Austria—for the first time since 1918—would enjoy a standard of living higher than the European average.

By a rare combination of low inflation, hard work, tolerance, and ingenuity, Austria pulled off an economic miracle that was in its way even more impressive than Germany's and Japan's. The big payoff came in the seventies. A quarter-century of growth with two decades of low inflation allowed Austria first to catch up and then to surpass most of Europe by the end of the decade. This process has continued into the nineties.

Austria's Incredible Social Partnership

Austria's government, businesspeople, and labor unions work together in extraordinary harmony. It is a system that many other countries would love to copy, but none has succeeded in doing so.

This is the Social Partnership. It is an agreement between government, labor unions, and business to work together and compromise to ensure the smoothest possible economy. While there is an official commission designed to meet and work things out, no mere commission could have brought off the successful Austrian experience. Rather, the seeds of success are found by looking at Austria's history.

For the partnership to work, government promises not to inflate too much, business promises not to fire workers except when absolutely necessary, and labor promises not to strike. Of the three, unions have probably lived up to the agreement more than the others. Austria beats even Switzerland in terms of labor peace.

3. The Japanese Yen: Star of the Eighties

While Japan's yen takes second place to the Swiss franc in overall appreciation since 1970 (182% for the yen vs. 247% for the franc), no other currency performed better than the yen during the eighties. The yen rose 74.5% from 1980 to 1991. The franc rose only about 20% over that entire period, since it fell back from 1980 to 1985 and only then soared. The yen just kept going up and up during the eighties and never looked back.

The Key to Japan's Economic Powerhouse

There are many stories about how Japan gained its tremendous economic strength during the eighties. One story speaks volumes. Late in the decade, Toyota introduced its first true luxury car, the Lexus LS400, into the U.S. market. Three months later, disaster seemed to strike. Toyota announced that it was recalling all eight thousand of the cars it had sold by that point—about a third of a billion dollars' worth of cars.

Why? Because, incredible as it may seem, of all those eight thousand cars, Toyota had received two consumer complaints. One had to do with a defective brake light. The other concerned a sticky cruise control mechanism.

Two consumers out of eight thousand complained, and all the cars were taken in and thoroughly reexamined. And never was any single Lexus buyer inconvenienced by having to take his car to the dealership, as would have been the case for American cars. The cars were picked up and returned to them all within a few weeks.

The cars of ten owners in Grand Rapids, Michigan, were serviced by technicians flying in from Detroit, 150 miles away, who picked up the cars and checked, fixed, washed, and returned them.

That this particular Toyota dealership was in Detroit is ironic. That, of course, was the birthplace of the American automobile industry. For decades American cars were unquestionably the best-made and -serviced cars around. But these days, could you imagine a U.S. car company doing what Toyota did?

By many measures Japan bestrode the world like a colossus in the eighties. Industrial production soared 170% over the decade, compared to 49% for the United States, for instance. But these are just statistics. For the reason behind them, stories like how Lexus handled adversity can illustrate more.

In so many ways Japan began by copying the United States and then gradually bringing out a product that was superior. Everyone knows how true this has been of things like cars and cameras and VCRs. What is not well-known is that it is equally true of the Japanese yen itself.

One Yen = One Dollar: What a Way to Start

The yen was born in June 1871, when it was established as a virtual copy of the U.S. dollar. It had the exact same gold value, and one yen equaled one dollar.

Japan sat World War I out and so did not inflate its currency as the belligerent nations did, including the United States. Thus the yen actually rose above $1.00, reaching $1.06 in 1918.

But thereafter the yen began a half-century rough patch. In the twenties Japan uncoupled the yen from the dollar, and the yen promptly sank from $1.06 to about 40¢, or ¥2.5 per dollar. In 1933 Japan tied the yen to the pound, but in the thirties the pound sank, so the yen sank too. At war's start in 1939, Japan switched again and tied itself to the Nazi German reichsmark. When it did, the yen had dropped to 23.4¢, or ¥4.267 per dollar.

The wartime link with the German mark did not strengthen the yen. By February 1946, with Japan's infrastructure smashed, the yen had plunged to 875 per dollar. This meant that in twenty years the yen had lost 99.9% of the dollar value it once had. But that was the nadir, the very lowest point. Since then the yen has fought its way back up, and there's no telling how high it will go.

In 1949, with the foundations again in place for economic growth, the yen was fixed firmly at 360 per dollar. It stayed at that exact level for twenty-one years, until 1970. In the twenty-one years since—free of international controls and allowed to float to its own level—it has risen to 120 per dollar. This means that since 1946 the yen has risen 629% against the U.S. dollar.

While We Worry, the Japanese Gloat

The United States worries whenever its dollar rises even a little. "It will make our products too expensive to export"

JAPANESE YEN

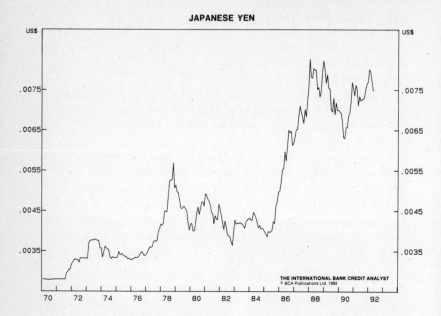

The rising currency of the rising sun: Reflecting the world's most impressive post-war economy, the yen has risen and risen, making the dollar look powerless before it. No other currency can say this.

goes the lament. In recent years this is the reaction even if the dollar rises by 10% to 20%. Our government finds a way to knock it back down, amid cheers and sighs of relief.

Japan's yen has soared 629% since World War II. It rose over 100% during the last few years alone. And yet the world's demand for Japanese exports has not been dampened at all; the exports have, in fact, flooded the world. And even with a dollar that has lost so much of its value against the yen, people in Japan don't seem to want much of what we have to offer.

The Japanese realize something American politicians do

not. Far from being afraid of a high currency, they are proud of it. They realize that it represents the world's vote of confidence in their economy. Instead of trying to manipulate their currency down to make their goods cheaper, they just concentrate on making the best good for the price—for any price, be it in yen, dollars, or pesos. Not surprisingly, the world has responded. The next time you hear on your car radio about how a strong currency hurts an economy or how a weak currency helps it, just think of Japan and its septupling yen as you maneuver around all the other Toyotas.

It's not that Japan or its economy is problem-free. As we'll see in chapter 28, they often like to inflate their money supply. Money and credit have grown about four times faster in Japan than they have in Switzerland since 1960. In the eighties explosive credit growth led to a huge inflation of property and stock prices. But even though stock prices in 1990 and 1991 fell by nearly 40%, and real estate prices threatened to do likewise, all the tumult and uncertainty had no unusual effect on the yen's price. And all the while, Japan kept churning out the products the world snapped up.

One intriguing thing about the yen is its consistency. There have been very few years when it fell, and then not really by much. From 1979 to 1985, the European currencies were giving back much of their prior gains against the dollar. But the yen never went through a big retrenchment phase. It fell 10% during its last recession, 1973 to 1975. It fell another 15% to 20% from 1978 to 1980. But that was all the reaction there was from the huge prior gains of the seventies.

Maybe Japan is overdue for a recession and maybe the yen is overdue for a real correction. That is always the market's fear when any asset rises in a straight line. "Trees don't grow to the sky" is what you usually hear about a great performer on its way up in the commodity or security markets. And while that saying is a truism, it is also undeniably true. So the yen may have its comeuppance. Still, those who have in the past bet money on a yen fall have lost their bets.

4. The German Mark

When Germans think seriously about their currency (and they seem to think about all things seriously), there is one specter that lurks never far from the surface of their minds. It is the specter of runaway inflation, and in their reveries it looks something like this: ragged and penniless billionaires pushing wheelbarrows (it's always wheelbarrows) that contain billions of marks, hoping that they can get to the grocery store before the price of a loaf of bread has risen to trillions of marks.

Where does this vision come from and why does it die so hard in Germany? From 1920 to 1923 the German mark collapsed in the most bizarre hyperinflation of all time. Savings accounts that would have let one retire in style in 1914 could not buy a third-class postage stamp a few years later.

As money lost its value, all other values were thrown into chaos. Into that chaos stepped the false order of Nazism.

Just as the economic nightmare still haunting American memories is the Great Depression, Germans are still affected by the runaway inflation that destroyed the currency and the fortunes of millions of families. So it is not so surprising that for decades, protecting their mark has become a national mania. The German central bank, the Bundesbank, has a legal duty to defend the mark. It takes that duty seriously.

How the Mark Began

The mark began almost a thousand years ago as a unit of weight: half a pound of silver. Had it kept to its original value, one mark would now be worth about $25. By a remarkable coincidence the modern German mark was born a few weeks after the yen, in 1871. The newly united Germany needed a new country-wide currency. At that time the mark's value was M4.2 per dollar, or 23.8¢ per mark.

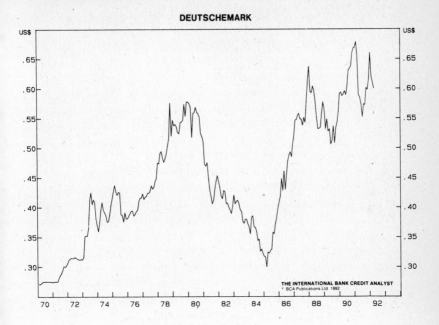

DEUTSCHEMARK

Founding member of "Inflation Anonymous": Still psyched-out by the currency-destroying inflation of the 1920s, the German central bank seems willing to do anything to avoid that happening again. As a result, the mark often makes new highs against the dollar.

Exactly one hundred years later, the mark was worth 27¢. But, oh, the changes it had to go through in between.

For the first forty-odd years of its life, the mark held its value of M4.2 per dollar. But then came World War I in 1914. Germany, like all the combatants, went off the gold standard and simply printed paper marks to pay bills. Those bills ballooned after Germany lost and was forced to pay for all the war's expenses, for everyone.

The Mark Goes Up in Smoke, Not Once but Twice

It is hard to use terms lurid enough terms when describing the utter collapse of the mark that ensued. Let's keep our comparison to the dollar. In 1914 one dollar bought M4.2. In late 1923 one dollar bought M4.2 trillion (M4,200,000,000,000). The mark actually kept falling, but after that no one even bothered to measure its exact value. It no longer had any value, and the economy descended to the most primitive form of exchange: barter.

A new reichsmark was established in 1924 at the rate of 1 trillion old marks for one new one. This was to be Hitler's currency, and he used the most barbarous methods in modern currency history to keep it from falling in value. After he came to power in 1933, marks began to flee Germany, usually into Switzerland. This dramatic outflow began to depress the mark's value, so Hitler declared a moratorium on all mark outflows in 1934. Although it was accompanied by strict jail sentences, it was not enough deterrent. So on December 1, 1936, the death penalty was announced.

The mark still fell, and when Hitler's reign collapsed, the reichsmark lost virtually all its purchasing power. Thus for the second time in twenty-three years, Germans saw their currency become worthless.

"Never Again!"

They vowed that it would never again happen. Backed by American capital, a new mark was born on June 20, 1948. This was the deutsche mark we know today.

The D-mark started with high hopes, but it soon began to lose value in an all too familiar way. From its original 1948 value of DM3.33 per dollar, the value slid a year later to DM4.2 per dollar. It fell to an all-time low in 1951 of DM8.06 per dollar (that is, each mark was worth 12.4¢). After that the mark worked its way up, as the German economic miracle took hold. It doubled in ten years. In 1961 the value was fixed at DM4.00 per dollar (25¢); in 1969 it was DM3.66 (27.3¢). Soon after, the fixed-rate system of currency exchange between the major nations collapsed altogether, but this basically good currency kept rising. By 1991 it had reached DM1.44 per dollar, or 69.44¢. The only interruption in this forty-year rise was the five-year period from 1980 to 1985, the early years of the Reagan administration, when the dollar rose above its true value.

Many thought the July 1, 1990, unification of the strong West German deutsche mark to the worthless East German ostmark would bring down the D-mark. The two were joined at a one-to-one conversion rate, a value that was much more than the East German mark was truly worth. But such is the mark's basic strength that this overvalued conversion caused no problem at all: within months the mark was at its all-time high against the U.S. dollar.

As Europe grows closer together and gains in power, the mark is acknowledged by all to be the single most important European currency. Former residents of the Iron Curtain countries, who long viewed the dollar as their strong standard of value, are now looking to the D-mark.

Germany is not a perfect model of economic freedom. Much of its industry holds sway in giant cartels; competition and entrepreneurship are discouraged in favor of order and stability. In fact, in many ways the German economy resembles the corporate state system that Mussolini first envisioned for Italy. As foreign as that setup appears for Americans, no one can deny that it has worked well for Germany.

The mark turned 120 years old in December 1991. Looking back over its life, it has had three almost equal stages:

• In its first forty years, from unification to World War I, the mark stayed exactly stable. Tied as it was to gold, its value never varied.
• From World War I until December 1951, the second forty years of life saw the mark collapse into nothingness once, collapse into virtual nothingness once again, and start

yet a third time down that same road, when from 1948 to 1951 it lost 59% of its dollar value.

• Just when no one would have given much for the mark's future, its third forty years began. It has been a golden era for the mark. From its weakness in 1951 to its strength in 1991, the deutsche mark has risen against the dollar by 460%.

As it starts its fourth forty years of life, Germany dominates the new Europe, as it twice did the old. But this time it does not dominate through force of arms, or ideology. Both of these are in fact almost completely absent from today's Germany. It dominates instead through hard work and sheer economic muscle.

5. The Dutch Guilder

The Dutch guilder rounds out the Fabulous Five, those currencies that in recent years have more than doubled against the dollar.

The guilder is also called the florin, and Swiss banks, for instance, usually abbreviate it to "Fl." The reason is that the guilder got its name from one of the most extraordinary monies of history. In 1252 the Italian city-state of Florence was the intellectual, cultural, and financial center of the world, much like New York was a generation ago. In that year Florence first minted its florin, the first gold coin to appear in Western Europe since the fall of Rome.

The Dutch word for gold is *gulden; guilder* was an English modification of that word. The guilder of Florence contained 3.5 grams of gold. For three hundred years, that value remained completely stable. From 1252 to 1531 the gold value of the florin never varied. Today on the world currency markets we can't keep our dollar stable for three hundred seconds.

The glories of Florence were made possible, in no small

part, by a strong and stable currency. In the fifteen hundreds, the Renaissance faded and Europe was torn apart by bitter religious wars. When they were over, the days of the great Catholic nations of the south were over. Northern, Protestant nations began to dominate Europe, as they have ever since.

The country that succeeded Florence as the financial capital of the world was Holland. Knowing full well whose mantle they were inheriting, the Dutch named their money the florin. Where, not long before, Florence had ruled the artistic and financial worlds with its florin, by the seventeenth century the Dutch began to do the same with theirs. In both cases the flourishing nation's currency—the world's most envied currency at that time—made the country's ascendency possible.

Paper Money Makes Its Debut in the West

In 1587, over four hundred years ago, the Bank of Venice came up with something entirely new in the western world. Just as Florence had given the world the concept of banks, neighboring Venice gave it paper money banknotes. Paper money had been used in ancient China, where it was inflated into worthlessness, but this was paper currency's first appearance in the West. It didn't last long in Venice, but in 1609 Amsterdam began issuing what is now the world's oldest paper currency.

Holland's paper guilder was not inflated. Each paper guilder was essentially a warehouse receipt representing a fixed weight of metal at the bank. No longer did people have to lug around physical gold. All knew that the paper guilder issued by the Bank of Amsterdam was as good as gold, and it was so much easier to carry. In fact, so sought after was the currency for just this convenience that from 1609 to 1794 the paper money almost without exception traded at a 3% to 9% premium over the gold content.

Damaged by Tyrants, the Guilder
Always Comes Back

From 1794 to 1814, Holland was ruled by France, breaking the guilder's centuries-old, near-perfect stability. After Napoleon's fall, however, Holland once again established a guilder that held firm and stable for another century.

Remaining neutral in World War I, Holland was spared the ruin that hit most other European economies and currencies. The guilder's value by 1940, after years of inflation and depression all around it, was only 17.7% below the gold standard value it had had at its height in 1875, in a more stable century. By contrast, the currencies of Britain, France, and Germany had lost much more of their gold values.

Unfortunately, in May 1940 Hitler invaded, shut down the free gold market, and outlawed export of all guilders. The Nazis also looted and destroyed much of Holland.

From 1940 to 1949, the guilder fell by 53%, losing more than half of its prewar gold value. By 1949 the guilder was worth Fl3.8 per dollar, or 26.3¢ per guilder. It has never fallen below this since.

It recovered several years before Germany's mark. In fact, throughout the fifties and sixties the guilder traded at a premium to the mark; i.e., one guilder was worth more than one mark. But as chart 6 shows, beginning in 1970 this changed. Just as the guilder began to rise dramatically against the dollar, it began a virtually unprecedented fall against the mark. This went on throughout the seventies.

Ever since 1980, however, the guilder has stayed steady at almost exactly 90% of the mark's value. The mark and the guilder were the first to show that there could be stability among the major European currencies. As the same chart shows, the mark value of the guilder has remained completely steady for over a decade. They showed that strong European currencies could act as a stable block against the gyrating dollar.

Before we leave the guilder, there's one more thing you

DUTCH GUILDER

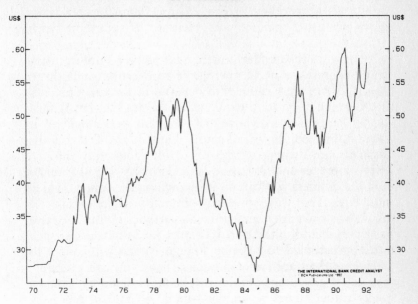

In Germany's shadow: Over the past decade, the guilder has remained exactly steady against the mark, at about 90% of the mark's value. If Germany runs into unexpected trouble trying to absorb the former East, it is possible that the guilder could come out of the mark's shadow and rise.

might find interesting. Many investors believe that a big fall in a country's interest rate automatically means a fall in that currency's price. For them, we'd like to draw attention to what happened to the Dutch guilder from 1985 to 1988. Deposit rates on the guilder fell by half, from 8% to 4%. Yet during that time the guilder doubled in value against the dollar, from 27¢ to 55¢.

The Dutch are just as hardworking as the Germans, but quieter and lower-keyed. The guilder is a fine currency, often

overlooked. It certainly has a longer record of strength and
stability than any other currency existing today. In a few years
the paper Dutch guilder will celebrate its four hundredth
birthday.

But since the guilder's interest rates and its price remain
steady against the mark, there isn't an overriding reason to
own it. There were those who believed in the early nineties
that German unification would cause the mark to fall against
the guilder, which had none of Germany's new liabilities. It
hasn't happened, though of course it still might. For now the
Germans are turning what seemed like a liability into an
asset—a bigger and more powerful Germany. If you want to
own the guilder, you can do it by owning the ecu, of which
more later. That way, you own both mark and guilder in one
(as well as owning other European currencies). But Holland
has a rich financial tradition. Its banks, for instance, are much
more accustomed to offering foreign currency accounts to
foreigners than are German banks. Thus you can probably
take better advantage of the strengths of Holland by using its
banks rather than the guilder—until, of course, the ever-
changing story of Europe makes it again worthwhile to single
out the never-changing guilder.

▼

CHAPTER 6

Three Promising Europeans

6. The French Franc

Aside from Italy with its lira, few nations have so transformed themselves and their currencies in the last few years as has France. Not so long ago it was viewed as a place heavy on charm but short on efficiency, and cursed with what seemed like an eternally sick currency. But seasoned visitors there are now obliged to shake their heads in wonder. France has all the style and charm it ever did, and yet has become in many ways more efficient than Germany.

Who would have believed just fifteen years ago that one day France would have a lower inflation rate, stronger currency, and more profitable government bonds than Germany. And who could have guessed that today the French would enjoy faster, safer, more punctual trains and a superior overall phone system than the Germans do. Yet all these things are true.

You can compare France's change to the change that has happened in Italy. But in one vital way France's progress has been even better. Virtually all of France's regions have participated in its betterment, but vast parts of southern Italy are still too mired in the mistakes of the past.

A fundamental change could be noticed as recently as the early eighties. No longer anti-American, France had in fact become a place that was intrigued by America's free market successes and wanted to emulate them. Ronald Reagan was popular in France in a way he never was in Germany.

In any case, since that time an investor who had the savvy to buy French government bonds would have done amazingly well, as interest rates, though still high, have declined (making those bonds worth more). And the franc has equaled or bested the German mark.

Americans who bought French bonds in the last few years pocketed a triple whammy:

1. They earned high interest.
2. The value of the bonds themselves went up as newer interest rates declined.
3. Since the bonds were denominated in French francs, which had gone up against the dollar, American investors can now redeem them for many more dollars than it took to buy them in the first place.

The History of a Grand Old Currency

The French franc is the granddaddy of all francs. It was born in 1360 as a one-franc coin of 3.877388 grams of gold (.1241 troy ounces). Today this amount of gold—and thus the original franc—would be worth $44.68.

It would take about 225 modern-day French francs to equal the gold value of 1 original French franc. So instead of being worth $44.68, the franc today is worth less than 20¢.

Soon after its birth, the franc suffered a familiar fate at the hands of its government. The kings of France devalued the franc almost immediately, by issuing coins called "one-francs" but nonetheless containing ever less metal. In fact, they often shaved gold from existing coins, kept it, and released the lighter coins as one-francs. The people were thus habitually cheated, and the kings enriched themselves at their subjects' expense.

From its official value of 3.88 grams of gold in 1360, the franc's value was lowered in 1365 to 3.82 grams, in 1423 to 3.06 grams. Then in 1577 gold was abandoned altogether, and the franc was defined as 14.07 silver grams.

Every French king and government until Napoleon debased the franc, with one honorable exception, Henry IV. The first (and perhaps still the most beloved) of the Bourbon dynasty, King Henry not only did not debase the franc, he gave the French people more value by increasing its silver content at one fell swoop by 64% (from 14 to 23 silver grams).

Unfortunately, his son, Louis XIII, began another period of franc debasement that continued under Louis XIV, XV, and XVI. In fact, this inflation of the franc resulted in the pauperization of many, if not most, Frenchmen, and was not the least cause of the French Revolution. More unfortunately, the revolutionaries were even greater inflationists, totally destroying the French currency.

Napoleon finally stabilized the franc in 1803. He defined it in terms of both silver and gold—4.5 grams of silver or 290.3 milligrams of fine gold—and made it convertible into either. This was to be a highly influential move. As the nineteenth century continued, other countries defined the value of their currencies (the Swiss franc, Belgian franc, and Italian lira) as the exact same weight of silver.

In 1803 the franc had an exchange value of Fr5.182 per dollar. The surprising thing is that today, after two hundred years of all the ups and downs, the French franc is now exchanged at Fr5.8 per dollar—not much different from its 1803 value. France and America were rough equals back then; France went into a tailspin but came back, and America soared, then slipped. The two are rough equals again.

When Napoleon stabilized the French franc, it took Fr25.221 to buy one British pound; today there are about Fr10 per pound, not Fr25. Surely that is a clear commentary on how the pound has fallen and how the franc has come back.

From World War I until the sixties, the franc's value was ravaged. From its value of 290.3 milligrams of gold in 1803 (and 1913), it fell to 59 milligrams worth of gold in 1928, 39 in 1937, 25 in 1938, and 21 when the Nazis marched in in 1940. Then it really fell, from 7.5 milligrams in 1945 to 2.5 in 1950 and 1.8 in 1958.

The franc's dollar value fell from Fr5.2 (1913) to Fr26 (1928), Fr44 (1939), Fr119 (1945), Fr350 (1949), and finally, a record of Fr494 in 1958. This was the year Charles de Gaulle took over and soon did something about the French currency.

He rigorously tied the franc to gold and set it at Fr4.94 per dollar, exchanging Fr100 of the old currency for 1 new, gold-pegged franc. It has roughly stayed in this range of Fr4 to Fr6 per dollar ever since, with one exception: in the early eighties the markets reacted angrily to François Mitterand's election as president, pushing the dollar up until it reached Fr10 per dollar by 1985. A socialist, Mitterand at first practiced government takeover of industries, to the dismay of investors. By 1985 he was pursuing more realistic policies, and France prospered. By 1987 the franc was back in its old Fr4-to-Fr6 range against the dollar.

From 1913 to 1958, the depreciation of the franc was almost legendary. Even today, many people look upon it as a weak currency. Yet, in fact, the thirty-four years since 1958 have seen a fairly stable French franc. In 1991 France had a lower inflation rate (3.3%) than either Germany (4.5%) or Switzerland (6.6%). This is something that could never have been dreamed of a generation ago.

Since 1986 the franc has done an admirable job of keeping its value completely steady against the German mark. Also, French interest rates have been higher than German ones, so holders of French francs have actually fared better than mark holders, further bolstering the franc.

The future looks promising as well. France is strongly committed to currency stability. Its leaders have become fervent supporters of a European Currency Unit (ecu) to which the franc would be linked.

7. The Italian Lira

In 1972 a secret White House tape caught Richard Nixon saying, "I don't give a [expletive deleted] about the Italian lira."

Today Italy is no longer the butt of such derision. Its prime minister sits as an equal partner with other major world leaders, and its economy and the lira draw respect approaching awe from bankers and investors everywhere.

If you travel to the more exclusive resorts in Europe now, chances are you'll see at least as many Italians as Swiss or Germans. (You won't see too many Americans, unfortunately. It's too expensive for us after the long fall of the dollar.) The Italian tourists are all benefiting from a currency that has become truly world-class.

The transformation of Italy's image is rather recent. In the late seventies, Italy was profoundly troubled with strikes and general inefficiency and malaise, and with that came a currency that packed no power. The dollar was much stronger. So for the American tourist Italy was cheap. Our dollars bought a lot there.

Now the exact opposite is true. Italian entrepreneurial flair (which goes back to the days of the Medicis and beyond) has combined with a stylistic elegance that rivals that of Paris. Together they have raised the value of Italian goods and services to heights few could have imagined just a few years ago.

Local governments, delighted by the rise of industry, have done their part too. They have enacted flexible policies

ITALIAN LIRA

Two born-again currencies great for American investors: Long scorned, the Italian lira has become done well against the dollar—doubling in value while paying interest rates in double digits. The French franc has also doubled quickly against the dollar while paying hefty interest rates. What's more, France's economy is now more efficient even than the Germans' and boasts an even lower inflation rate than inflation-spooked Germany. All this makes the franc a currency to reckon with.

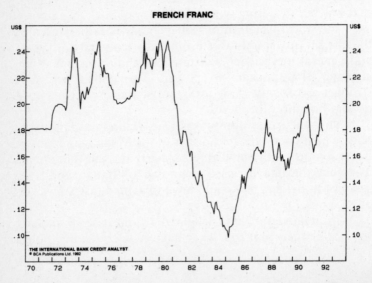

FRENCH FRANC

that encourage businesses to work around the central government's hodge-podge of taxes and worn-out restrictions. Italian business now enjoys a relatively clear field in which to run and grow.

A Currency's Long, Painful Decline

The Italian lira was born in 1861, just before modern united Italy itself was. Its value at that time was fixed at 4.5 grams of silver. That weight of silver is now worth about 58¢, which is what the lira would be worth if it was still pegged to the current value of 4.5 grams of silver. In other words, it would take only L1.74 to buy $1.

That, of course, is laughably untrue.

Today Italians have to pony up over eight hundred times the value of 4.5 grams of silver—or L1400, to buy 1 not-so-strong dollar. And in 1985, when the lira was really hanging onto the ropes, it took almost twelve hundred times the value of 4.5 grams of silver, or close to L2,500, to buy a dollar.

Losing Value in Either Silver or Gold

Until it stabilized just a few years ago, the lira had been losing value for eight hundred years. In 1192 Venice's lira coin (the Italian lira's predecessor) was worth 20 silver grams, only 16 by 1282, 10 by 1379, 5 by 1527, and 2.5 when Napoleon finally ended independent Venice in 1797.

It would be hard to weigh the amount of silver the lira now represents.

The promise of stability held out at the lira's birth just before 1862 didn't last long. Its decline mirrored the unfulfilled promise of Italy itself. By the 1920s the lira was valued at L19 per dollar (each lira worth about 5.25¢). After 1945 it was fixed at L225 per dollar but, within a few months, had collapsed to L800. It never really recovered, but from 1960 to 1970, when all major currencies were nominally fixed, the lira was pegged at L625 per dollar.

Another way of putting all this was that while the lira in 1862 was worth 290.3 milligrams of gold, in 1962 it was worth only 1.4 milligrams. And in mid-1991 it was worth only 0.2 milligrams. Thus in the past thirty years, the lira has lost 85% of its value in gold. Since 1862 it has lost over 99.9% of its gold value.

The lira fell against the dollar, even in the 1970s, when the dollar itself was falling. From L625 per dollar in 1970, it reached an all-time low of L2,250 in 1985.

But then something extraordinary happened.

The Worm Turns

During the last half of the eighties, the lira rose by nearly 100% against the dollar. It reached a high of about L1,200 per dollar, still historically low, but nonetheless the first time since its birth that the lira had really risen against the dollar.

And what a time it was for those Americans who were wise enough to put their savings into lira time deposits in a bank or bought Italian government short-term paper. They saw the dollar value of their lira deposits double in five years. And during that time, their lira deposits never earned less than 10% interest; sometimes such deposits earned 20%.

The rise of the lira mirrors the rebirth of Italy itself. Incredible as it may seem, by many measures Italy is now a richer nation than Great Britain.

Some Clouds Still Hover, However

Northern Italy (i.e., Rome and above), were it detached from the rest of Italy, would perhaps enjoy a higher living standard than *any* other European country. So talk of separation keeps popping up. And it could be more than just talk.

Modern Italy was cobbled together in the 1860s by joining parts that often did not and do not yet get along; they scarcely even understand each other's dialects. Northerners feel that the south produces far less and drains far more from the north than is justified. The south has the political power, which it uses to drain too much of the north's economic power, or so the north charges.

There are separatist groups active today in Lombardy, powerhouse of the north. So Italy may have a rocky political future.

And while Italy has become an economic giant, its political system is still fairly primitive. It has also not been able to claim a role on the world geopolitical stage in keeping with its newly gained wealth. Its public deficit remains enormous, tying future generations down. At the same time, Italy's birthrate is now among the world's lowest. Women have an average of fewer than two children, which puts a shadow on the country's ability to keep growing at the same lively pace it has in recent years.

Still, as Italy enjoys an economic stature it has not held since the Renaissance, the lira has become a currency to be taken seriously.

8. The Ecu

Europe has become today's biggest success story. While the United States languishes and even Japan stumbles, a newly rejuvenated Europe roars on. Fueled by the new Germany, Europe is poised for big things in the nineties. If it is true that currency values follow leading and growing economies, the European Common Market currencies may be as strong in the nineties as the dollar was in the fifties and sixties, the yen was in the eighties and the Swiss franc was in the seventies (though even Switzerland has applied to join the European Community).

One problem for an investor is exactly how to tie part of his cash holdings to the new Europe. After all, the European Community comprises eleven different currencies. (There are 12 countries in the EC, but only 11 currencies: Luxembourg uses the same franc as Belgium does). And while Germany may be strongest in the long run, it has taken on a tremendous—but probably temporary—burden in the formerly communist East Germany. A single investment in the mark alone may not always be the best course.

Happily, however, there is a single currency few Americans know about that encompasses all the EC currencies. This is the European Currency Unit, known as the ecu. While the mark makes up the largest single component (30%), the ecu is proportionally spread among the ten others as well. As we'll see, interest rate yields on ecu CDs are excellent, and the price of the currency itself has been rising smartly. We'll see how as little as $5,000 can be put into an ecu CD at the best banks. This means that for almost everyone who wants to tie his wealth to the new Europe of the nineties, there is an extremely practical way to do it.

While most people in the United States have barely heard of the ecu, it has been around since 1979. And while the European Currency Unit is of relatively recent origin, the name *ecu* has a long and colorful history in Europe. This is one reason why so many Europeans are now plotting to make the ecu the single currency for most of Europe before the end of the century.

Although the fact is little known in the United States, for much of this past millennium (that is, from 1266 to about 1850), *ecu* was probably the most common name for money in Europe. Those now pushing the ecu are doubtless aware of the romantic visions the name conjures up for history-conscious Europeans.

The Romantic History of the Ecu

The first ecu was minted by King Louis IX of France (1226–1270), now known as St. Louis. Under him France became the first nation in modern Europe to enjoy peace, prosperity, and progress. He stamped out private feudal warfare, simplified and reduced taxes, built the first French navy, built the cathedrals of Chartres and Sainte-Chapelle, and founded the Sorbonne. St. Louis was regarded as the ideal Christian monarch. Pious and ascetic, he was also a manly warrior, leading two of the Crusades. His humanity, charity, and justice brought him the love and respect not only of the Christian world but also of the Moslem world against which he fought. A generation after he died, he was declared a saint, a distinction accorded to no other ruler.

The French benefited most from two specific acts by King Louis: the establishment of Roman law as the uniform system of justice for all classes, and on August 15, 1266, the establishment of the gold ecu as the uniform currency. The coin was imprinted with a shield (*ecu* in French) bearing the coat of arms of France. Established at 4.19 grams of gold, the gold ecu held its value to the extent that in 1422, about 150 years later, King Henry V of England copied the French coin and minted his own ecu. Before that, the rulers of Lausanne, Savoy, Flanders, Brabant, and Holland had all established the ecu as their money. Spain and Portugal each had their escudo (still the currency of Portugal), the Italian states their scudi. Naples actually called it the ecu. Finally, in the Swiss cantons, ecus were silver coins minted until about 1850, and in Basel the ecu was the unit of account, as it had been previously for so many other European capitals.

Even the Sainted Ecu Is Debased

The ecu ultimately suffered from political debasement. In France the ecu coin went from 375 years as a gold coin (1266–1641) to 74 years as silver (1642–1716) to a mere 4 years as paper (1716–1720). In fact, the first paper money inflationist, John Law, chose the name ecu for his first paper money, which soon after became the first paper money to collapse in runaway inflation, in 1720.

Had the history of the ecu stopped there, it would have been an ignominious end; but it was reconstituted as a silver coin and maintained its value until the French Revolution several years later. Then another paper money inflation caused the revolutionary government to prohibit silver ecus for three years. While the ecu was abolished in 1834, throughout the nineteenth century people still used the word *ecu* to designate the sum of three francs.

When modern European money managers chose the name ecu (now meaning European Currency Unit, not shield), they knew that twentieth-century Europeans retained a sense of what the ecu had stood for over the centuries—stability and prosperity through international trade. The fact that during most of this century Europe's currencies were unstable and parochial must have made the old ecu even more attractive to postwar visionaries who began dreaming of a new European currency.

What Makes Up Today's Ecu

These visionaries eventually came up with a weighted "basket" of all European currencies, and the ecu was born on March 13, 1979. In 1992 it became the unit of account of the Common Market (EC) as well as the currency in which all EC bonds and loans are denominated.

Table 2 gives the composition of the ecu in three stages— at its inception and as updated twice since (after each five-year period the weighting is changed).

As you can see from the table on page 83, the deutsche mark has always been by far the largest single component of the ecu. In a world of volatile currency swings, where the mark can rise and fall mightily against even its fellow EC currency, the pound, it is good to see how little the relative weights of the ecu have changed in ten years. It makes the ecu an attractive choice for those desiring currency stability.

For Americans, an Attractive and Little-Known Investment

This is not to say that the ecu has been stable against the dollar—far from it. In the last five years, as the European

TABLE 2

Composite Currencies of the European Currency Unit

Currency	March 1979	1984	1989 (and current)
German mark	33.0%	32.6%	30.1%
French franc	19.8%	19.4%	19.0%
British pound	13.3%	14.9%	13.0%
Dutch guilder	10.5%	10.3%	9.4%
Italian lira	9.5%	9.4%	10.15%
Belgian franc*	9.6%	8.6%	7.9%
Danish krone	3.1%	2.7%	2.45%
Irish pound	1.2%	1.2%	1.1%
Greek drachma	NA	0.9%	0.8%
Portuguese escudo	NA	NA	0.8%
Spanish peseta	NA	NA	5.3%
Total	100.0%	100.0%	100.0%

*includes Luxembourg franc.

currencies have risen against the dollar, so too has the ecu. On average it has risen over 10% per year since 1985. Add to this the attractive interest rates on ecu deposits, which are also a weighted amalgam of the various currencies' rates, and the return in dollar terms has been substantial. In addition, when one factors in the 10 + % yields of the ecu during much of this time, the rise or total return on money invested becomes over 25% per year.

Interest rates on the ecu reflect the weighted averages of all the EC member interest rates. For instance, ecu yields have recently been about 200 to 300 basis points (2% to 3%) higher than yields on German mark instruments of similar maturities.

European investors can now look on the ecu as just another European currency; yields and exchange rates versus

ECU RATE

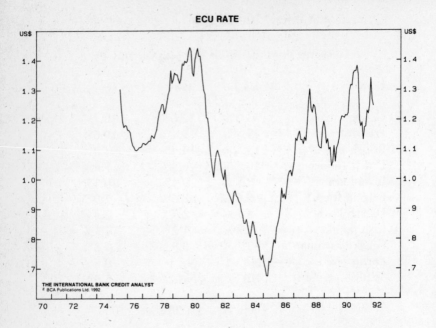

THE INTERNATIONAL BANK CREDIT ANALYST
£ BCA Publications Ltd. 1992

If a united Europe really takes off, the ecu may leave its steady rise and begin to soar. Until then—as a weighted basket of European currencies—it provides an easy choice for investors who believe in Europe but don't want to pick and choose the best currency. Also, ecu interest rates are generous; they tend to be even higher than Germany's.

the dollar fluctuate daily. But it is still not legal tender anywhere, and no single monetary authority stands behind it. There are also no ecu banknotes. But support for making the ecu more universal is coming—not so much from Europe's governments as from Europe's businessmen. Seventy percent of European businesses surveyed believed a single ecu would help their exports; over half thought it would help marketing and distribution. Virtually none believed a common ecu would hurt them.

It is a safe bet that the ecu will continue to appreciate against the major non-European currencies as long as Europe bids to become a major world economic power in the nineties.

Should We Be Betting on the Ecu in Hopes of a United Europe?

It is by no means certain that the ecu will become the single European currency, because there would have to be only one central bank. And that would mean that the eleven different EC central banks today would need to give up power. This may not happen. A common central bank would have to satisfy everyone from the Germans, who'll tolerate little or no inflation, to the Greeks and Italians, who aren't so bothered by higher inflation.

There are other things that separate the European countries. One of the acknowledged reasons for the economic success of the United States is the fact that it is united. The fifty states have one culture, one currency, one language, and complete freedom for people, capital, and goods to move from one state to another.

But Europe lacks many of these unifying forces, starting with the language. People are not likely to vote with their feet and relocate in another country with better opportunities if they cannot speak its language. Moreover, unlike the mobile Americans, Europeans are very deeply rooted.

Living in Another Land Is Quite Different Than in Another State

For several years there have been no obstacles to citizens in one EC land living and working in another. But it really hasn't happened. In all but three nations, less than 2% of the residents come from other EC countries. (The three exceptions are Luxembourg; Belgium, where many "Eurocrats" reside; and Ireland, home to many Britons).

Certainly one reason for this immobility is language.

There are no less than nine official languages in the EC; fully one-third of all community funds and employees are used just in translating from one to another.

There exist computers that can translate; even the best of them however, stumble over word order in long German sentences, and at best they render flat, machine-like prose.

So for the EC's 320 million people there is still no substitute for learning each others' languages in order to make the one-market ideal work as well as it can. To do this, European teachers are now stressing fluency in a language over grammar, considering it more important for one to learn to get a point across than to be grammatically correct.

Which foreign languages are the most popular among students? Overwhelmingly, English is the most-studied language. There are only a few exceptions. French-speaking Belgians mostly study Dutch. Dutch-speaking Belgians study French; Luxembourgers, German and French; and French is the most popular foreign language in Portugal. But English is gaining in all countries, and students are as likely to speak English as anything else. Ironically, this is the most common language in Europe.

They Not Only Speak Differently, They Think Differently

The French government is not happy about this English hegemony. Thirty years ago the French backed the idea of a unified Europe, in part to advance French culture and language. It has not turned out that way. They have complained to the EC, which has tried to placate them by now suggesting to EC students that they learn *two* languages (translation: French as well as English).

Yet the community is very far from its goal of fluency in even one language. English is still spoken mainly by the business classes in most nations. But as *The Economist* recently pointed out, "A British businessman need only have his car break down 20 miles outside Milan to see how far his English doesn't get him at the garage."

The fact that the English still speak of "20 miles" rather than, say, "32 kilometers," as the rest of Europe does brings up another obstacle. The British have for centuries considered themselves outside of Europe. They drive on the left side of the road, use different measurements, and show no enthusiasm for changing. More specifically, Britons enjoy special economic relationships with many of their former colonies that will be hard to reconcile into current thinking about a one-market Europe. For example, they can import excellent New Zealand lamb for much less than they could buy lower-quality European lamb. To the extent that the EC wants to pull down barriers among its members only to erect a giant wall around them against the rest of the world, there will be problems.

Other Barriers to a Single Currency

As said before, it is no sure thing that there will be a common currency actually used by everyone in Europe. To have a truly strong currency means a common central bank, ideally independent of any or all political governments. At present only the Swiss, Dutch, and German central banks are really politically independent. The German Bundesbank pledges never to give up that independence even to German politicians, much less to politicians from countries lacking their bone-deep fear of inflation.

But the cost of having eleven different currencies is high. Just how high was recently demonstrated by the Bureau of European Consumer Organizations in Brussels. In a survey, the Bureau began with a sum of BF40,000 (about $1,100) and took it to ten other EC countries, spending nothing but changing it into the local currency each time. By the time it got back to Belgium, only BF21,000 francs remained. Forty-seven percent of the value had been wiped out in exchange fees. The survey found the average cost to change money was 2.5% to 3%. However, it cost 14% to turn Portuguese escudos into Italian lire, and 21% to turn Greek drachmas into German marks.

This is perhaps an extreme example. One can cut down exchange costs by using traveler's checks or traveling with just one strong currency. But Europe is definitely the poorer for lacking a single currency.

A Single Tax for All: Maybe the Biggest Obstacle

The absence of a single tax rate is causing trouble too. The total tax level as a percent of a country's production ranges from 29% in Spain to 50% in Denmark. Income taxes vary even more. Sales taxes, called Value Added Taxes, are a real hodge-podge. Standard rates range from 12% (Spain and Luxembourg) to 25% in Ireland. Italy charges a 38% luxury rate on such items as video cameras; the United Kingdom and Holland have no such luxury tax. And Britain has no tax at all on such items as food, books, and children's clothes.

Chances of all these countries bringing their entire tax systems into harmony are very small when you realize that even where a flat standard exists, it has failed. All EC citizens are supposed to be able to bring back about $400 worth of goods across each other's borders exempt from sales tax. But high-tax Ireland and Denmark have acted illegally to impose arbitrary conditions on their citizens: they must be out of the country for a certain period; the item must fit in a suitcase to be tax-exempt; etc. Much will need to happen for there to be free borders in Europe.

Freeing the Banks: Easier Said Than Done

The proposal to free banks in the EC is also problematic. The idea is to allow any bank of any EC nation to expand into any other EC nation. The banks will still be supervised by their home-country banking authorities. But how free will the branches really be? How easy would it be for a British bank—used to lending mortgage money easily to would-be U.K. home owners—to do business in the strict German market, where variable-rate mortgages are practically unheard of and potential home owners have traditionally saved about a third of what they hope to borrow before they can qualify for a loan?

Also, the various nations have different bank standards. To cite just one example, what if a Taiwanese bank opened a subsidiary in liberal Luxembourg? Would it then be able to spread as it pleased within the other eleven countries? Some countries say no; others yes.

Further, no one has even tried to mandate a harmonization of withholding tax rates on interest. It is assumed that if all nations allow free flow of capital, money will find its way to the low-tax areas, leading the others to naturally lower their taxes. Again, we shall see if high-tax Denmark and France reduce their withholding taxes to Luxembourg's level. If they do, it will be a powerful portent of United Europe's chances of success.

Codes of Law Must Be Addressed

There are powerful national state monopolies that must be broken if telecommunications are to be freed in Europe. Seven different digital switching systems exist in the EC. Five operate only because of their national governments. The cost of an installed phone line, depending on the country, ranges from $225 to $500 (in the United States it is $100).

Social legislation varies widely among the twelve nations. One of the most controversial proposals is to have worker-consultation boards, where companies of more than 250 employees can organize worker committees to be consulted on every major management decision. Germany already has them; it would like to see the other eleven nations likewise encumbered.

To adjudicate differences of opinion, the European Court

of Justice was formed in Luxembourg. The thirteen judges (one from each nation plus one to break ties) are now hearing almost five hundred cases each year, nearly triple the number of a decade ago. Anyone can appeal to it: EC individuals or states, or any foreign business that feels discriminated against by the EC.

Although some national courts still yield their power to it grudgingly, they have nearly always accepted its rulings, but the court itself has so far been careful not to take any real power away from the national governments. When confronted with an issue involving ultimate sovereignty, the court has stated that, in effect, no decision can be made unless both the EC counsel and the particular national government agree. The implication is that if the issue is important enough, the rebel EC nation can go its own way.

We'll see how this disparate group of twelve nations will hang together the first time the national interests of one are threatened. It takes unanimous agreement to make new policy. What will happen if one or two hang back? And what if one or more chose to secede? Will the rest send in troops to force them back into unity? Not likely.

Many knowledgeable people just don't think a United Europe will come about. And even if it does, it will not necessarily mean a stronger Europe. It may mean a Europe with a far more centralized and powerful bureaucracy. But that is no recipe for economic strength. In short, the specter of a new, united, and strong Europe may be overblown.

United Europe or Not—The Ecu Could Be a Sound Investment

One can believe a unified Europe improbable and still see a place for the ecu in an investor's currency portfolio. Remember, the ecu has existed since 1979, long before any real plans for a united Europe.

It arose from a need to deal in one common European currency. It may be just a bookkeeping entry rather than a real flesh-and-blood currency, but you can still own bank accounts in it, buy bonds and CDs in it, and even borrow it. This has a tremendous advantage for investors who want to diversify into several currencies at one swoop, if for any reason they don't want to put all their eggs in the mark. Europe doesn't have to be united for the ecu to rise against the dollar. The component countries just have to be strong and productive compared to the United States. And many believe that is what is in the cards.

CHAPTER 7

Currencies of Other English-Speaking Countries

9. The British Pound

If you polled Americans and asked them which foreign currencies they've actually ever had in their pockets, high on the list
would be the Canadian dollar and the British pound. Those
are the foreign currencies that are least foreign to us.

And yet nowhere do these two appear on even the list of
the best twenty-five currencies of our generation, let alone
in the top ten. In fact, these two currencies have routinely
performed worse than the U.S. dollar. In the case of the British
pound, this has been going on for at least half a century. If
you want to see a sad tale of a once strong currency falling
apart against the U.S. dollar, look at chart 9 on page 93.
That describes what has happened to the pound with more
eloquence than we could muster.

It should also be a warning of what could be in store for
the dollar itself. Because before the United States was the
world superpower, with the dollar as the world key currency,
Britain and its pound sterling played these roles. Throughout

BRITISH POUND

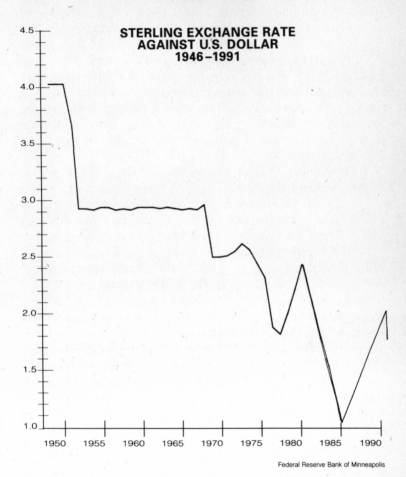

STERLING EXCHANGE RATE
AGAINST U.S. DOLLAR
1946–1991

Federal Reserve Bank of Minneapolis

How the once-mighty pound has fallen (so, too, the dollar?): The British pound's long, sickening fall (a reflection of its diminishing world power) shows what may also be happening to the dollar. The dollar, too, has been having big falls followed by weak rallies. Is there any reason to believe that either currency will become powerful again?

both the eighteenth and nineteenth centuries—two hundred years—Britannia's ships ruled the world's waves as the pound ruled its financial markets.

It is certainly the granddaddy of all of today's currencies. Even before the Norman conquest of England in 1066, the unit of account was the livre, first established around 800 by Charlemagne and introduced to Saxon England by Norman traders. (This livre was itself the French version of the ancient Roman libra, which, as a pound of first copper and then cheaper bronze, was the Roman unit of account from 600 B.C. to 200 A.D.)

Livre means pound in English, and the original pound sterling was exactly that, a pound (12 troy ounces) of sterling silver. Today 12 ounces of silver at about $4 per ounce is worth nearly $50. Instead, the pound sterling is worth about $1.70. Thus, the pound has lost 96.9% of its original value.

Like the Roman pound before it, the English pound's value started off in glory and then gradually disintegrated. William the Conqueror put England's finances on a sound footing, and for almost three hundred years the value of a pound was actually worth over a pound of silver. Then began a terrible series of wars, both foreign (the Hundred Years War with France) and internal (the War of the Roses). Because these wars were costly, and because they drained productive energy, the pound lost value. From 1350 to 1551, the silver value of the pound plunged from 342 grams to only 26 grams, losing over 92% of its value in two hundred years.

A Strong Currency Twice Saved by Strong Women

Britain was clearly in trouble. But both nation and pound were saved by that strong woman and excellent queen, Elizabeth I. She ruled from 1558 to 1603, and by the time she died, England had not only gained unprecedented glory, wealth, and culture, but the pound had risen from 26 to 111 silver grams, a gain of 327%.

Moreover, this value held steady from the sixteenth to

the twentieth century. In 1821 the pound was fixed at 123.3 grams of silver, and this was to last until World War II. Then, as chart 9 shows, the pound's value plunged, along with Britain's strength and place in the world. By the end of the seventies, Britain was in bad shape. But in 1979 another strong woman began to turn things around. By the time Margaret Thatcher left power in 1990, Britain's economy had greatly improved, and the pound, firmly tied to the strongest European currency, the German mark, had doubled against the dollar in just six years.

A Sickening Decline and Then a Glimmer of Hope

We no longer define a pound sterling in terms of silver. We use the dollar instead. From the early days of the United States, the British pound was worth $4.87 cents. By the end of World War I, as America gradually replaced Britain as the world's great power, the pound was still at that old level and therefore had become overvalued. At the beginning of World War II, Britain finally devalued the pound 17% to $4.03. This was not nearly enough; sterling was still overvalued. So in 1949, nine years later, a big 30% devaluation came, from $4.03 to $2.80. In 1967 another devaluation put the pound at $2.40. Currency floating arrived five years later, and the pound sank as low as $1.05 in 1985. This meant that in less than fifty years, the once-proud pound had lost over 78% of its value against the U.S. dollar, itself not the strongest currency in recent decades.

There has been, we repeat, a dramatic turnaround for Britain and the pound since then. Britain has made so much progress that in 1991 the finance minister could proclaim that the nation had become a "permanent low-inflation country." And while one might question this statement, no one could laugh at it. It is still too early to say that the pound has once again become a strong currency—after all, in 1990 it was still 25% lower versus the dollar than it had been in 1980. Against the mark the pound was often bumping along at the lower end of its allowed range, until it abruptly fell out of it. Under rules of the European Monetary System, currencies are allowed to fluctuate against other EMS currencies by only a preset percent before a devaluation must take place. A dozen years of Conservative government had caused that party's popularity to wear thin, and there's no assurance the Labour party won't return Britain to the failed policies of the past. By some measures (see chapter 22 on finding currency bargains) the pound is still overvalued against the dollar. Also, the currency crisis of September 1992 caused the pound to withdraw from the EMS system and cut its tie to the mark. It quickly plunged.

All this is true. But these days it is possible to feel a glimmer of real optimism about the pound for probably the first time in living memory.

Let's now look at some currencies of countries that once used the pound. Having become independent or just discouraged by the pound's awful slide, these countries struck out on their own. Like the pound, however, their currencies all have usually performed badly against the U.S. dollar.

10. The Canadian Dollar

Before 1880 the Canadian dollar was loosely tied to the British pound. Thereafter it was tied to the U.S. dollar on a one-to-one basis. It shadowed the greenback's every move. When in 1933 the U.S. dollar was devalued against gold, so too was the Canadian dollar, and by the same amount.

But when the pound had its big 30% overnight devaluation in 1949, Canada, which still had strong ties to Britain, felt it had to devalue too. The northern dollar dropped to U.S. 91¢. The markets regarded this as too low and judged that Canada needn't have devalued at all. Within three years the Canadian dollar rose back to equal the U.S. dollar and then, lo and behold, even went above the U.S. dollar. Throughout the rest of the fifties, the Canadian dollar was usually above the greenback, reaching an 8% premium over it by 1959. This decade can be called a golden age for the currency.

In 1962 the Canadian dollar was devalued to US92.5¢. This was kept steady until fixed exchange rates collapsed in the early seventies. At this time the Canadian dollar sharply rose above one U.S. dollar again, and for a while it looked like Canada was joining the ranks of Germany, Switzerland, and Japan as a strong currency country.

Alas, it was not to be. The brief premium of the Canadian dollar over the U.S. dollar was not to last. The big turning point in the Canadian dollar came in November 1975, when the Parti Québécois won power in Quebec. So shocked was the rest of Canada that a fundamental sense of confidence about the country was lost and has never truly been regained. The Canadian dollar fell below the U.S. dollar and has never gone back above it. During more than nine years the price kept falling, hitting an all-time low in early 1985 when it briefly touched US71¢. Since then there's been a steady rise, and in 1991 it reached US89¢. Though cause for celebration, this level is still below the average level of the sixties, to say nothing of the fifties.

Canada has not fulfilled the promise it held back then. The economy is weaker than America's. Inflation, taxes, unemployment, and debt levels are all higher; productivity is lower. Underscoring all this is the uncertainty about the future of Canada itself. These fears are probably exaggerated. Most French speakers are not convinced they'd be so much better off on their own. But one can't be sure what the future holds. Canada has more than its share of problems, even this one aside. The Canadian monetary authorities know this; that's why they've had to keep interest rates high on the Canadian dollar. During most of the past decade, rates have been over 10%. It is about the only way they can attract money and keep the value of the currency up. However, even high interest rates will not permanently boost the currency of a country whose policies are not conducive to thrift and production.

So if you are interested in investing in Canadian CDs, bonds, or stocks, you'll want to be aware of what is happening to the Canadian Dollar. Watch the fundamental changes the government is making there. If those changes tilt the country closer to Switzerland, Austria, and Germany, you can move ahead with more confidence.

11. The New Zealand Dollar

This is a country—and a currency—with a disappointing past, but a future that holds out tremendous promise.

At the turn of the century, if one were to choose two countries that would be emerging stars of the new twentieth century, Argentina and New Zealand would have likely been chosen. With its English system of law and culture and its tremendous natural resources, great things were expected from New Zealand.

Instead, there was mainly disappointment. High taxes crippled productivity, and inflation crippled the currency. As is so often true, the story of a country is found in the story of its currency value.

In 1907, New Zealand was transformed from a British colony into a dominion—in effect giving it independence. The British pound was replaced by the New Zealand pound on a one-to-one basis. The Kiwi pound thus started out life at $4.87. Unfortunately, within a generation it fell 25% against the British pound, itself no pillar of strength. Because World War II hurt Britain tremendously more than New Zealand, in 1948 both pounds were tied together, and both sank together. The New Zealand pound sank faster during the sixties. In 1966 the British pound was worth $2.80, the New Zealand pound only $1.90. The next year, New Zealand replaced the pound with the dollar, perhaps hoping that the name change would turn the currency around. It didn't. By July 1968 the N.Z. dollar fell to only US87¢, a decline of nearly 50% in less than two years.

Over the next decade the N.Z. dollar made a weak comeback. By 1979 it was worth U.S. $1.07. Then came another sickening period of decline. By 1985 it was worth just over US45¢. In ninety years the New Zealand currency had thus lost 90% of its value against the U.S. dollar.

Where in 1900, people were flocking to move to New Zealand, by the mideighties people were flocking to leave it. Pessimism ran deep.

The Seeds of a Big Turnaround?

Something had to be done, and something was. The Labour party began radically to privatize the economy and brush away the decades of cumbersome state controls. In the monetary realm the central bank now has a zero-inflation policy. Alone among central banks, it has pledged virtually not to inflate at all. If this pledge is kept, it could make the New Zealand dollar stronger than the Swiss franc. But it will be a hard pledge to keep. If the N.Z. dollar experiences several years of stability and if people stop expecting inflation, it will be especially tempting to inflate. The government can get lots of benefits at the beginning of inflation, with few of the drawbacks. The United States was able to inflate in the sixties, but the bad effects did not begin to become clear until the seventies and eighties.

In any event, it is not certain that political considerations will let the zero-inflation pledge stand. Unemployment remains stubbornly high at over 10%, and there's always the danger that if the economy does not improve fast enough people will lose patience and clamor for the old policies.

Are the new free market reforms beginning to boost the New Zealand dollar? Not yet. After its fall to US45¢, it bounced back to US65¢ at the end of 1987, partially in response to the belief that something new was to be tried. Since then, the N.Z. dollar has fallen every year: to US63¢ in 1988, US60¢ in 1989, US59¢ in 1990, and near the end of 1991, only US56¢ (thus falling 14% against the U.S. dollar since 1987).

But if even half of New Zealand's reforms take hold and work, this could be a coming currency, finally reversing decades of decline. Events here will bear watching closely.

12. The Australian Dollar

Australia is one of America's favorite foreign countries, and the Aussie dollar one of our favorite foreign currencies. It is one of only six traded on the Chicago and New York futures markets, where most Americans follows currency values. Of the six it is the one with the least clear reason for being included. The yen, mark, Swiss franc, pound, and Canadian dollar are either very mighty in their own right or are currencies of our largest trading partners, or both. But as the Australian dollar is neither strong in trade nor a large trading partner, much of its popularity must be as a sentimental favorite with Americans.

And yet there have also been very practical explanations for the Australian dollar's appeal. During the late eighties the Australian dollar was the closest thing to a dream currency investment we have ever seen. From a low of US63¢ in late 1986, the Australian dollar soared to nearly US90¢ in early 1989. It has held its value fairly well since; it was at US78¢ in December 1991. But there's more: Americans love high-interest yields, and no major currency offered higher interest rates during this time than the Down Under dollar. Rarely under 15%, it earned as high as 20%. Seldom do investors have a chance to earn 15% to 20% annual interest in a currency whose exchange rate also is rising 15% to 20% per year against the dollar. In fact, we've never seen anything like it.

But going on the sound principle that "the last shall be first," maybe this shouldn't have been a surprise. When the Australian dollar began its stellar performance in 1986, that currency, as well as the country itself, had been falling for decades from very great heights. It's a little-known fact that

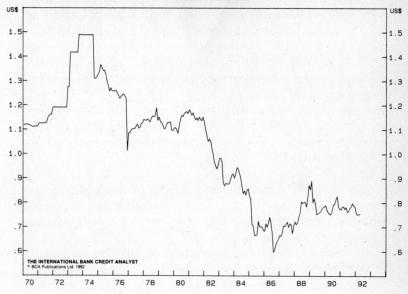

Whither the down-under dollar? Few currencies have so richly rewarded U.S. investors willing to bet on a turnaround. After falling for decades against the dollar, the Aussie dollar rose 50% while paying interest rates as high as 18% year after year. In the 1990s, however, interest rates dropped and government reforms merely struggled. As a result the currency stalled for a while but recently has given off some faint hints of a new uptrend.

in 1900 Australia was the world's richest nation per person. Today it is barely able to stay in the top thirty. By 1910, fixed at one-to-one to the world's then-strongest currency, the British pound, the Australian pound (as it was then called) was worth US$4.84. Then the fall began. By 1940 it was worth only US$3.22; by 1952, US$1.84. In 1966 the Australian pound became the Australian dollar and fixed at US$1.12.

This change of names didn't radically change the trend; twenty years later the value had fallen to about US60¢. So the Australian currency had lost over 80% of its 1910 value by 1986. And that was lost against the U.S. dollar, which itself had hardly been a rock during this time! So the dream currency of the last few years is recovering from a decades-long nightmare.

There are refreshing signs that the Australian government is changing the policies that brought the country to its earlier sad state. In 1990 alone, the Aussie government took these giant steps:

1. Abolished the decade-old right of the jobless to receive unemployment benefits for the rest of their lives, a right that not surprisingly had made it pay to forget work and just barbecue on the beach.

2. Announced the privatization of the Commonwealth Bank. This is very symbolic. Not only was this bank the country's first step into public ownership in 1921, this was the bank that, from 1921 to 1960, had the sole right to issue the Australian dollar itself and keep up its value. It didn't do a great job.

3. Decided to sell the state-owned airline companies. A strike in 1989 shut down all domestic routes during the tourist season, doing great harm to the industry.

4. Allowed limited competition with the state-owned telecommunications industry.

They've been able to do this mainly because the hard left wing, so powerful in Australia for so long, has collapsed intellectually. "If you want to get a good belly laugh," the then Prime Minister Robert Hawke has said to the socialist holdouts, "go to Eastern Europe, look their citizens in the eye, and tell them that their welfare systems depends on maintenance of state ownership and absence of competition."

The proposed solution to many of the country's problems, which we in the United States would do well to copy, is to sell off state-owned industries and use the proceeds either to repair Australia's aging infrastructure or retire part of its huge foreign debt—one of the largest, per capita, in the world.

This is not to say that Australia is now problem-free. Far from it. Who knows how popular these reforms will remain? It would be a mistake to place all of your money in the Aussie dollar. It has gained new respect, but one must still be wary and wait until it can be said that it has become one of the world's strongest currencies.

▼

CHAPTER 8

The Four Asian Tigers

All of the other currencies we've seen have had at least a glorious past, even if more recent times haven't been so happy. But the currencies of the four Asian tigers—Singapore, Hong Kong, South Korea, and Taiwan—don't have much of a pedigree. Their recent past and present have been excellent, and their futures look even better. Together, these four countries have forged the fastest industrial revolutions in world history.

We've got to say at the outset that only two of these four have currencies that can be held outside the home country. South Korea and Taiwan still do not. But since you might soon be able to hold them as well, it is worth taking a look at them. First, however, to the ones already available.

13. The Hong Kong Dollar

This is the only major Asian currency that has not spent the past few years rising against the U.S. dollar. That's because since 1983 it has been tied to the dollar. This is rather ironic. No other nation is so free market oriented. And yet no other international currency does not float freely on the world currency markets. How did it get this way?

The Hong Kong dollar is almost a hundred years old, born in 1895 as a silver coin. Weighing just under one ounce, the Hong Kong dollar's value fluctuated with the silver price. (It would today be worth almost US$4 instead of under US13¢.) The silver standard kept the Hong Kong dollar stable until the Great Depression and trade wars of the thirties brought on a period of instability, which was worsened when Japan occupied Hong Kong and substituted its yen for the local dollar.

Since World War II the Hong Kong dollar has been very strong and stable, as befits its vibrant economy. From the fifties on, the value usually fluctuated between HK$5.80 and HK$7.80 per U.S. dollar, or between about US13¢ and US17¢ per Hong Kong dollar. Even though the U.S. dollar was climbing at that time around the world, the Hong Kong dollar was still fairly strong. Nonetheless, it had begun to be subject to speculative volatility due to political factors, as it became apparent that Britain would turn over its colony to China in 1997.

In October 1983 the Hong Kong dollar was fixed to the U.S. dollar. Not only did this put an end to currency speculation, it also boosted Hong Kong's exports. Because as chart 11 on page 110 shows, this peg to the U.S. dollar cheapened the Hong Kong dollar from just over US17¢ to just under US13¢. Hong Kong's goods thus became cheaper overnight. And as the U.S. dollar weakened, starting in 1985, so too did the Hong Kong dollar against all the other major nations, again helping its exports.

The peg has kept the value stable; even during the T'ienamen Square crisis of 1989, the tie to the U.S. dollar held. Some locals question the wisdom of putting their monetary policy in the hands of politicians in Washington, D.C. And yet the peg has worked. It is popular, inflation is low, and production and exports remain high.

The big question, of course, is what exactly will happen

in 1997, when Hong Kong reverts back to China. One thing is certain: China will be getting a jewel. If growth keeps up as it has, by 2000 the average Hong Konger will be richer than the average Briton, whose country will have just given Hong Kong up. A Hong Konger born today is so healthy that he can expect to live seventy-eight years—two years longer than the average American born today. (In all the world only the Japanese now have longer life expectancies.)

Will China destroy this? It is of course the conventional wisdom to be pessimistic. After all, China remains a repressive state. And though Peking has pledged not to change the way of life for fifty years, Communist governments have broken pledges before. But there is real reason to be optimistic. Already, that part of China nearest Hong Kong is being transformed into a kind of new Hong Kong. This is Canton province, now called Guangdong.

To quote from *The Economist* of November 16, 1991:

> If it were not part of China, Guangdong province would be a decent-sized country with a population of 63m. As an economic unit, it has two advantages over the rest of China, and is about to acquire a third. First, its people, the Cantonese, have traded with the outside world for centuries. In Hong Kong and the other outposts of the Chinese world, they are world-class businessmen. Secondly, Beijing's control over its southern provinces has always been haphazard. The main benefit to Guangdong is an ironic one—it was starved of investment during the 1960s and 1970s, which means that today it has far fewer of the grotesquely inefficient state-owned enterprises that are bleeding the rest of China white. Thirdly, in 1997 the remaining artificial barriers will fall between Guangdong and one of the world's best natural harbors, which comes equipped with highly sophisticated trading and financial services: Hong Kong.
>
> Guangdong's emergence began in 1979, when Deng Ziaoping launched reforms which returned control of the land to the peasants. In the next six years, rural income

more than doubled in the whole of China. More importantly for Guangdong, Mr. Deng made China as open to world trade as any other large developing economy. He created 14 open coastal cities, relaxing restrictions on foreign investment. In addition (and using Singaporean advice), he established five "special economic zones" (sezs) with added incentives for investors. Three of the sezs are in Guangdong.

The fuel for Guangdong's boom has been investment by foreign companies. By June this year they had started over 15,000 ventures in the province, at a cost of over $20 billion. Four-fifths of this money came from Hong Kong companies, enticed by the fact that building a new factory in Guangdong costs one-fifth what it would in Hong Kong. It is also cheaper than it would be in the two obvious alternative sites in Southeast Asia. While manufacturing employment in Hong Kong has fallen from 900,000 jobs in the early 1980s to 720,000 now, Hong Kong companies have created over 2m new jobs in Guangdong.

The Hong Kong dollar is an intriguing currency investment of the future. It has upside potential. Aside from the possibility that it will become the currency of a future larger country (or province of one) that is poised on the verge of tremendous growth in productivity, it may be undervalued even today. When you look at the price charts to see how the currencies of Singapore, Taiwan, and South Korea have all risen against the U.S. dollar while Hong Kong has been tied steadily to it, you have to believe that if the peg were removed, the Hong Kong dollar would rise, if not soar.

The downside risk can be seen by remembering what happened in T'ienamen Square. China may have a good degree of economic freedom, but it is still politically repressive. The best one can hope for is that China goes the way of the Soviet Union—politically at least—and breaks up. Then the more Western-oriented parts like Guangdong can really come into their own. If that happens, and the Hong Kong dollar becomes the Canton dollar, then watch out: the sky would be the limit.

14. The Singaporean Dollar: A Steady Star

Do you remember our Fabulous Five currencies from Europe and Japan that have more than doubled against the U.S. dollar just since 1970? Well, the Singaporean dollar was sixth on the list, rising over 75 % from 1970 to 1991. But the amazing thing about the Singaporean dollar is that during all this time it has never really fallen much against the U.S. dollar. When the U.S. dollar falls, the Singaporean dollar rises. When the U.S. dollar rallies and rises, soaring against the European currencies, the Singaporean dollar stays steady or only slightly falls.

During the big dollar fall of the seventies, the Singaporean dollar rose nicely, from US32¢ to US49¢, a 50% increase. Then from 1980 to 1985, when the major European currencies were taking it on the chin, the Singaporean dollar only fell back from US49¢ to US46¢, a loss of just over 6%.

How About When the U.S. Dollar Fell?

When the U.S. dollar began plunging again in 1985, the European and Japanese currencies doubled in just a couple of years. But none of them are now appreciably higher than they were in 1988, though they are all near their record highs.

The Singaporean dollar, by contrast, has since 1985 quietly and steadily gone from strength to strength. It didn't rise nearly as much as the others from 1985 to 1988. In fact, it stayed roughly steady. But from 1988 to the present there has been one record high after another. Against most currencies the U.S. dollar had two impressive (but temporary) 20 + % rallies from 1988 to 1992, but not against the Singaporean dollar: even when the U.S. dollar has risen, it has still fallen against the Singaporean dollar. Chart 12 on page 110 shows the very steady recent rise in the Singaporean dollar's value: US46¢ at 1986's end; US50¢ at 1987's; US51.4¢ at 1988's; US52.8¢ at 1989's; US57.3¢ at 1990's; and US60.6¢ in December 1991. No other currency has done this—the Taiwanese dollar comes close, but you can't hold that currency internationally.

The fact that the Singaporean dollar has usually made new record highs every day for years now has gone unremarked. That's probably because it inches up each day to new highs, and when the year is over, the rise is only 6% to 8%—before adding interest rates, that is.

Singapore's interest rates on its dollar have been on the low side. But if your currency were such a steady riser, you wouldn't need to pay high interest rates to get people to take it.

The island nation of Hong Kong, it has been said, sits geographically like a little pimple on the backside of China (particularly Canton). Singapore is also a little island, which sits at the bottom of Malaysia. Both these smaller countries have become far wealthier than their giant neighbors, though it didn't start out that way. Three generations ago Hong Kong was just as run-down as China. And in the mid-1960s, when Singapore was tied politically to Malaysia and monetarily to the Malaysian dollar, no one could have suspected that just a quarter of a century later, tiny, independent Singapore (238 square miles compared to Malaysia's 50,000 square miles) would be so much wealthier. A population one-sixth of Malaysia's produces a GNP per capita six times that of Malaysia.

Before 1963 Singapore and Malaysia had been British colonies for a century. In 1965 a mere two years after being joined together, Singapore decided to become independent. Two years after that, the Singaporean dollar was created, at par (one-to-one) value with the Malaysian dollar. Now called the ringgit, the Malaysian currency has risen against the U.S. dollar in the past generation. It comes in twenty-fourth on the list of top twenty-five world currencies since 1970. But it has only risen about 14% since then, a far cry from Singapore's 75% (not including interest). Incidentally, the ringgit can be traded internationally, and several European banks, notably ABN-AMRO in Amsterdam, offer accounts in it.

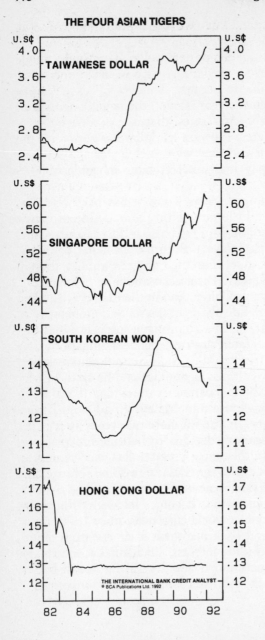

THE FOUR ASIAN TIGERS

TAIWANESE DOLLAR

SINGAPORE DOLLAR

SOUTH KOREAN WON

HONG KONG DOLLAR

THE INTERNATIONAL BANK CREDIT ANALYST
© BCA Publications Ltd. 1992

Understanding the Four Asian Tigers: The slow steady rise of the Taiwanese and Singapore dollars reflects healthy, growing economies and well-managed government policy. South Korea has recently run into some problems and its currency reflects this. The Hong Kong dollar has the most interesting and potentially profitable story. The forced drop from 1982 to 1984 shows what Hong Kong had to do to link its currency to the weaker dollar. That linking has made the two dollars mirror images. In time, a growing Hong Kong economy may force its dollar free and its value could soar.

Singapore's small size can work against it. Its small labor pool (1.3 million) is not growing and there is no unemployment. So that means missed opportunities. That's why Singapore is looking at Malaysia for the purpose of shifting some low-wage jobs.

A more ticklish problem is the government. Singapore has been a one-party, authoritarian state ever since independence. In fact, until 1990 it was ruled by the same man for thirty-one years, Lee Kuan Yew. Lee is still a "senior minister without portfolio," a power behind the throne, and is grooming his son, Lee Hsien Loong, now deputy prime minister, to take over. There has been some crude censorship: the *Wall Street Journal* was banned for years because of an article deemed not supportive enough of the Lee government. More recently, chewing gum was banned for reasons of public cleanliness.

This kind of high-handed government is a warning flag; it could lead to a decline in motivation and eventually law and order.

It would be good to point out, however, that none of these "tigers" has a modern government. Hong Kong is a colony, and Taiwan and South Korea are as authoritarian as Singapore. It wouldn't work for us, but it seems to work for the population in those countries.

Stability is deemed more important than liberty. Singapore in particular has remarkably stable government policies. With no real opposition the Lee government has been able to do whatever is believed necessary for a strong economy. Unlike those in the United States, economic policies in Singapore have been predictable and promotive of growth and productivity. The infrastructure is excellent. Unlike that in all the rest of Asia, Singapore's traffic moves quickly on modern, efficient roads and rails. The airport is so efficient it is almost unnerving—it sometimes seems as if it is run by robots.

If Singapore can find room both to grow and liberalize, its future looks bright. Indeed, even with its drawbacks, Singapore and its dollar have enjoyed remarkable success.

15 and 16. The South Korean Won and Taiwanese Dollar

The South Korean won and Taiwanese dollar are not yet available for trade outside their respective countries. Their authoritarian governments are still too wary of the outside world. While secure in power, they are insecure about their relationships to foreigners. This is a shame, because both these currencies, like the Singaporean dollar, have shown steady rises for years, whether the U.S. dollar goes up or down.

Both governments are politically repressive, and although both have begun to liberalize, the same groups remain in power in each country as they have for decades. The infrastructures of both countries are dreadful. (It can take all day to cross Seoul by private car, and Taiwan's air is five times as dirty as Los Angeles's.)

Both have primitive financial systems. South Korea's government poured artificially cheap debt into a few favored industries. But this excessive debt has caused problems, and some industries are now in real trouble: too much debt and not enough cash.

Taiwan has the opposite problem. Chinese traditionally hate debt and love cash. But there was too much cash floating around with too few places to go (strict rules prevent it from leaving the country). It cascaded into the small Taipei stock market with a vengeance. At times in 1990, daily turnover was greater than the New York and Tokyo markets combined. All this cash produced the classic bubble. When it burst, the Taiwan financial system was shaken to its core, its institutions revealed to be, as the saying goes, "not ready for prime time."

So both countries continue to enjoy extremely successful economies with strong and rising currencies that, because of primitive political and financial systems, are not yet available internationally. It is only a matter of time before they are, however.

PART III

▼

Earning High Returns with Low Risk in the World's Best CDs

▲

CHAPTER 9

▼

Interest Rates: When to Love Them, When to Leave Them

To some degree, we all use the interest that we earn on our savings to help support the way we live. You may make a lot of your income that way or only a little, but it's money all the same. The more you know about interest, the more money you should be able to earn that way.

For example, you should know that, at its heart, the word *interest* means risk. And high interest means high risk. If we go back to the beginnings of the use of interest, it will be clearer why this is so.

Let's go *way* back—to the caveman.

How Thrifty Cavemen Got Richer on "Seed Money"

During the spring a thrifty caveman who hadn't used up all his seeds at the end of the previous year could lend his unused seeds to another caveman—that is, to someone who hadn't bothered to conserve his seeds and now needed more. In exchange for the seeds he was able to lend out, the thrifty caveman was paid back not just an equal amount of seeds but, in addition, a portion of the vegetables the seeds had produced. He got this food not by doing the dirty work of planting it, but by having seeds that an unthrifty neighbor needed desperately. The thrifty caveman could have used up or lost his seeds the season before. But he chose to save some of them, knowing that he could use this saved "capital" to make money (vegetables) with it.

Interest paid in vegetables or money no doubt continued through Greek and Roman times. But if we jump to the Middle Ages, we get a better idea of how bank interest developed into its present form.

Early Bank Interest

Banks as we know them came into existence in twelfth-century Italy. They accepted deposits and they made loans very much as we do today. A smart banker of one of the great twelfth-century Italian banking houses could probably come back today and, with very little brushing up, find a place for himself in one of our large banks.

He'd still have to figure out how to attract deposits (so he could later lend that money out at a profit), and he'd have to decide how much interest to pay to his depositors in order to attract them. There would, though, be one minor difference. This difference illustrates—through words from the early Italian language, Latin—why *interest* means risk.

The Italian Renaissance world was ruled by the Catholic Church. The church provided the legal structure, and just as modern governments protect their citizens against being charged exorbitant rates of interest, the church of that day had strict laws against usury.

The word *usury* came into our language through the Latin *usura,* which means a situation in which more is asked in return than is given. When we say that someone is "using" someone else, it has the same implication: taking advantage of the person. In the Latin world, if a lender took little or no risk of getting paid back but charged a high rate for his loan, he was taking advantage. And the church called that a no-no.

Interest is something else. *Intereo* is Latin for "to be lost," and *interisse,* a substantive, developed into our modern *interest,* or "that which is lost." So to those early Italian bankers interest must have been looked upon not so much as a chance for profit, but rather the risk of loss. Interest was to bankers the just compensation that they, as borrowers from the public, paid to depositors for the risk they ran of not getting their money back. The depositors took some risk of not getting paid back and were paid by the bankers for taking the risk—in the form of interest.

A ruthless moneylender charging unusually high rates to a temporarily needy widow was a usurer (transgressing church law) because the interest he charged was not related to the risk he took. On the other hand, a merchant banker charging the same rate of interest to a prince with a bad reputation for getting rid of the people who lent him money was merely charging fair interest because he was taking a substantial risk ... to both his money and his continued existence.

When *You* Charge Interest

When you make a bank deposit or buy a bond, you are lending money to someone who will pay you interest for the temporary use of it. In doing so, you are taking some risks. The bank or bond issuer may go broke, or the money he does pay back may have lost its buying power through inflation or currency devaluation. You *deserve* to be paid for taking those risks.

That's why the most creditworthy and least risky borrowers (governments, banks, corporations) easily get our money. They pose the least risk, so we are willing to lend them our money at a lower rate of interest. The government's T-bills and Treasury bonds typically pay the lowest rates of interest because the government can always repay its debts, even if it means printing new dollar bills to do it.

The obligations of big corporations and banks represent more of a risk. These lenders may be bailed out by the government if they are in danger of going bankrupt and reneging on their debts, but they are not certain of being saved. And unlike the government, they can't print money. So corporations have to pay higher rates of interest than the government does in order to attract buyers of their bonds.

Farther down the line, highly leveraged borrowers like Donald Trump or Carl Icahn, who would not be bailed out by the government if they ran into big trouble, have to offer very high rates (like those on junk bonds) in order to get people to lend them money. They might have had to offer as much as 15% when the government was offering half that to buyers of its T-bills and Treasury bonds.

Why Some Countries Pay Higher Interest Than Others

When you consider that riskier borrowers have to pay higher rates of interest in order to attract money, it's easier to see why different countries pay different interest rates.

All government paper is theoretically "safe." When you buy a U.S. Treasury bill, you know there is absolutely no risk of default because the government can print money. The same goes for people who buy Japanese, Swiss, or British government paper.

But interest rates on all government "paper" are not the same. Recently, for example, the ninety-day British T-bill paid 10%, while the general Swiss equivalent paid 8%, and U.S. T-bills paid only 3.5%.

Why?

The short answer is that the currency is different in each country. People who deposit their money or buy bonds are willing to accept a lower rate of interest if they are sure that the money they get back will not have lost some of its value. For example, investors have generally accepted a lower rate of interest from Swiss CDs and Swiss bonds than from the British CDs and British Gilts. That is because, for a long time now, they have had more faith in the future of the franc than in the future of the pound. And rightly so.

But a more complete answer involves looking at what might be called the personality, or character, of the country issuing the bills and bonds. We are simply more willing to buy the bonds of a country we respect, a country with good habits. Short-term U.S. rates, like T-bills, were very low in 1991–92. But this was not a result of a respectable U.S. financial situation. It was rather a calculated attempt to push down interest rates due to a number of things: a political attempt to help President Bush, to try to jump start the economy, and because business loan demand was low. Governments can *temporarily* manipulate short-term rates—but not long-term bond rates, and U.S. bond rates were far higher than CD or T-bill rates throughout this time.

Just remind yourself about the caveman and how his good habit of saving seeds from one season to the next enabled him to earn interest in the form of vegetables—and with it probably the respect of his community. It's the inability to save that causes a country to lose the respect of the world community and forces it to pay out a higher rate of interest to bank depositors and to the buyers of its bonds.

Countries that, like the thrifty caveman, are mindful of the future and are willing to consume less now in order to provide more for tomorrow will have less need to borrow and, other things being equal, will be blessed by low interest rates. And that won't be their only reward. Typically, countries that save a lot enjoy higher productivity, a higher standard of living, and generally lower prices. Conversely, a society that lives for the present and doesn't bother to save and invest for the future will generally be cursed by higher interest rates, higher prices, lower productivity, and a lower standard of living.

We Americans need only look at our declining savings rate over the past generation to understand what's been happening to the dollar and to our standard of living. And when we seek to earn interest on our savings—either in a bank or through the purchase of bonds—we'd be wise to consider in what currency we are best off earning that interest.

In the long run, interest we earn in the most respected currencies will best ensure the purchasing power of our savings. Do you remember the interest rates offered on money market accounts in the early eighties? Did you get 14%? More?

As those rates dropped, some Americans felt hunger pangs for the rich yields they had recently enjoyed. They looked overseas. They saw that one could get quite a bit more interest by depositing savings in a top-rated European bank— say, in British pounds or Swiss francs. The more they had counted on earning high interest, the harder they looked for it outside the United States. And that's what they found overseas.

For example, in 1989 here's what rates were being offered in five major currencies:

Swiss franc: 4%
U.S. dollar: 8%
Canadian dollar: 12%
British pound: 16%
Australian dollar: 18%

And that is in major currencies for which runaway inflation is not a daily peril. At the same time, if you deposited your money in a bank in Managua, in Nicaraguan cordobas—hold your breath—you might have gotten 500% annual rates of interest. Lots of luck!

Unless you're looking for thrills, forget about putting

your money in a Nicaraguan bank. And consider why. If you are offered a very high rate of interest in any currency, be advised that when your deposit is mature, the bank will pay you back in *that* currency, not in dollars. So, if you earn 30% interest on Mexican peso deposits, your payoff is in Mexican pesos. If you put down enough U.S. dollars to buy a M$100,000 CD paying 30%, what you get at the end of the year is M$130,000.

Not bad if the peso's value holds its own against the dollar—in fact, found money. Common sense, however, tells you that if the peso had that ability, Mexican banks would not have to offer you 30%. There have been times when the peso was not only unable to maintain its value against the dollar but actually lost more than 30% against the dollar, which would have wiped out the apparent advantage in those high interest rates. When your pesos were converted back into dollars, you might even have ended up poorer than you were at the start. The recent strength in the Mexican economy may have lowered the risk quite a bit. Still, at the start of your search for higher yields on your savings, you will probably sleep better earning your interest in a currency that doesn't have to pay outlandish rates of interest.

We don't mean to imply that Americans should stay away from interest rates offered overseas simply because they're higher than the dollar. While it is true that high interest rates *often* mean that something is rotten in the economy and probably in the country's currency, too—that is not *always* the case. Sometimes you can get high interest rates in the currency of a country that is turning things around in its economy and whose currency is firming and about to rise. It is these exceptions that are worth your time and study because the rewards of earning interest in them can be very high indeed.

England under Margaret Thatcher created such an opportunity. So let's see what would have happened if you put $10,000 of your savings into a British pound deposit account in 1985.

Higher Interest Rates *Plus* a Currency Bonus

From 1985 to 1991 your bank deposits in the pound would have paid you interest of from 10% to 15% each year. A fine rate of interest but chicken feed compared to what you would have made in the form of a currency bonus when you turned your pounds back into dollars.

In 1985, when you took out a British pound CD, each pound you bought cost you little more than a dollar, actually $1.05. But in 1991 each pound you converted back into dollars got you $1.97—almost double what you paid.

Just by stuffing a wad of pound notes into your mattress during this period and forgetting about interest altogether, you would nearly have doubled your money. But by depositing your money in an interest-bearing pound account, your gains would be truly incredible. You would have almost quadrupled your money—in a bank, in a safe currency.

Let's see what actually happens to $10,000 of your money, starting in February 1985, when put into a one-year pound bank deposit (CD) with instructions to the bank to roll it over every year at the then-current rate of interest. When you opened the account, the pound was worth $1.05. Ten thousand dollars got you £9,523.81, which we'll round off at £9,524.

Your $10,000, which you turned into £9,524 in February 1985 and saw increase by varying rates of interest over the next six years, ended up as £18,970—virtually *double*. Over that period your money grew by 16.5% a year, after compounding, or higher than the actual interest rate of any of those years. That demonstrates the awesome power of compounded interest.

And in 1991, when you converted your £18,970 back into dollars (money that you could spend at home), you were in for another pleasant surprise. The pounds you were exchanging were no longer worth $1.05 each, the price at which you bought them in 1985, but $1.97 for each pound—or almost *double* again.

TABLE 3

Growth of a British Pound Account

Date	Account Value	Interest Rate	Interest Earned
February 1985	£9,524	13.6%	£1,295
February 1986	£10,819	12.6%	£1,363
February 1987	£12,182	10.8%	£1,316
February 1988	£13,498	9.1%	£1,228
February 1989	£14,726	13%	£1,914
February 1990	£16,640	14%	£2,330
February 1991	£18,970		

Multiply the £18,970 that you converted in February 1991 by the then-current rate of exchange of $1.97 to the pound. You'll find that your $10,000 deposit had grown to $37,371. You almost *quadrupled* your money in only six years.

You made $27,371 in profit. And only about a third of that came from interest earned. The rest came the rise in the pound against the dollar (or the fall in the dollar).

Quadrupling one's money is something we all dream about. What makes this case especially noteworthy is that is was so easy and so safe. It was easy because all you had to do was to buy a British pound one-year time deposit (CD) and tell your bank to roll it over every year. It was safe because your money was always sleeping snug in a great bank and was held in a great currency.

And you always had control of it. As long as things were going well, you could let your instructions to the bank stand. When you sensed that the pound was no longer rising (the dollar no longer falling), you could have asked your bank to switch your deposit into another stronger currency, even back into dollars. You could have done it even in the middle of the year because, in Europe, penalties for early withdrawal of a CD are minimal compared to this country.

In this period (when the value of currencies were changing so rapidly), by simply looking for the currency offering the highest bank interest rate and staying with that currency, you weren't sure to end up with the best profits. The pound, for example, did not give the highest interest rates in that period. The Australian and New Zealand dollars—along with the Italian lira—paid even more interest. At times their interest rates got as high as 20%. And while these currencies did rise (or hold their own) against the dollar during this period—thus giving Americans who took out deposit accounts in these currencies all the benefit of those high interest rates and more—the Australian and the New Zealand dollars and the Italian lira were just not as strong as the pound. So Americans who chose those currencies for their bank accounts did well, but not as well as those who chose deposits in British pounds.

Strongest Currency Brings Highest Profits

Look at what happened to Americans who chose to keep their deposits in Swiss francs. In the early part of the same time period, Swiss franc interest rates were almost laughably low compared the British pound rates. They were even lower than interest rates in the United States.

In February 1985 (which hindsight tells us was the absolute best time to switch out of the dollar), here are the rates of interest you could have gotten: British pound, 13.7%; U.S. dollar, 9%; and Swiss franc, 5.5%. Looking at these three choices, you'd have to be very foolish about money to pass up the 13.7% rate of interest in a British pound deposit account in favor the 5.5% interest that the Swiss franc accounts were paying. Or you'd have to be *very wise about currencies.*

Americans who chose to keep their money in Swiss francs in the first three years of this period saw the interest rate drop and drop. Their money earned 5.5% in 1985. The following year, all they could get was 3.9%; the next year, 3.5%. And in February 1988 their interest rate went to a ridiculous 1.3%.

TABLE 4

Growth of a Swiss Franc Account

Date	Account Value	Interest Rate	Interest Earned
February 1985	SFr28,571	5.5%	SFr1,571
February 1986	SFr30,142	3.9%	SFr1,176
February 1987	SFr31,318	3.5%	SFr1,096
February 1988	SFr32,414		

At the time that Swiss franc accounts were paying this measly 1.3%, British pound accounts paid a much lustier 9.1%. And even U.S. dollar accounts paid almost 7%. But there was no reason for the Americans who kept their money in Swiss francs to cry over the low interest rates. They could, in fact, laugh all the way to the bank.

If you had put $10,000 in a Swiss franc CD in 1985 with instructions to the bank to simply roll it over every February, here's what would have happened to your money. First, the bank would have converted your dollars into francs. In February 1985 each Swiss franc was worth 35¢, so each dollar bought SFr2.85. And $10,000 bought SFr28,571. That was your opening balance. Table 4 shows how it would have grown.

Compared to an American who kept his money in British pounds during this period, your account hasn't grown nearly as much. Even with the power of compounded interest, it has barely grown 13% in three years! The British pound account grew three and half times faster—for a rise of 47% in the same three years.

Still, in February 1988, as a holder of a Swiss franc account, you could turn your balance into U.S. dollars and end up with about the same amount in dollars as the holder of a British pound account, even though his account seemed to have grown so much faster than yours. That's because the Swiss franc really took off in those years, beating the pound's performance against the dollar by a wide margin.

In February 1988, had you been in British pounds, your balance would have been worth a shade over $20,000. And in Swiss francs it would have been worth about $19,500.

When a Country's Interest Rates Go Up and the Currency Weakens

The advantage of being in the strongest currency becomes clearer when we take your Swiss franc account from February 1988 down to February 1991. In that period the rate of interest paid on Swiss franc accounts bounced around quite a bit, going from 1.33% in 1987 to near 10% in 1990, which gave your account balance an extra thrust in Swiss francs. Your final balance, which had started out with SFr28,571 in 1985 and grew to SFr32,414 in February 1988, went on to become SFr37,676 by February 1991.

If the Swiss franc had continued to rise in value too, you would have been a very rich person indeed. But that was not the case. In the first half of the six years we are describing, Swiss franc interest rates went down dramatically, so you earned meager interest. In the second half of that period, Swiss interest rates came closer to (and briefly even exceeded) U.S. interest rates. So your balance grew more rapidly.

The currency itself, however, traced an entirely different line. The Swiss franc soared against the dollar in the first half of the period. In the second half of the period it had its ups and downs, at one point even *falling* against the dollar. So even though you were earning more *interest* in that part of the period in Swiss francs, your bottom line, so to speak, wasn't growing as fast as it had been earlier.

Your final 1991 balance of SFr36,676 was convertible at the rate of 81¢ for each franc. So you ended up with $30,518, tripling your investment of $10,000 six years earlier.

You may remember that the British pound account did even better over the six years (almost quadrupling the original investment). This was because the pound rose more steadily against the dollar.

Choosing Between the Best Interest and the Best Currency

The low rate of interest that Swiss franc accounts paid in the early part of the period we've described suggests that investors found Swiss francs very attractive, so attractive in fact that they were willing to accept a paltry rate of interest. So we can only surmise that if Swiss interest rates had stayed low over all six years, your Swiss franc balance in 1991 would surely have been lower than the SFr37,676 you ended up with. But the number of dollars you could get for it might certainly have been higher.

The idea that lower interest rates can be better than higher ones goes against the gut. Most people believe instinctively that, given a choice between 14% and 5%, it is better to choose the 14%.

If you are determined to get the highest rates of interest on your money, almost no matter what, you may be encouraged by the experience of a man we call Max Yield. You can read his story in the next chapter.

▼

CHAPTER 10

Max Yield Stalks the Highest Interest (and averages 66% per year)

You are about to read a fable. It tells about an average American investor who ignored all the advice of the previous chapter (about not overfocusing on rates of interest being offered and, instead, staying with the currency that is showing the best performance against the dollar). The hero of this chapter just went for highest yields offered in foreign currencies at the beginning of each year and fairly consistently made out like a bandit.

Let's call our hypothetical investor Max Yield, because he's compulsive about getting the highest yield, or rate of interest, possible. And starting in 1970, let's follow him through twenty years of investing in foreign currency accounts.

Ground Rules of the Game

These are the ground rules Max will follow. He starts with $10,000 on New Year's Day, 1970. He surveys the *major* world currencies and then invests his $10,000 in the currency that is paying the very highest rate of interest. Then on each succeeding New Year's Day he will switch to another currency if a better yield is available; if there is no higher interest rate around, he simply rolls over his new balance into another one-year CD or government paper in the same currency.

On that first day of 1970, U.S. dollar yields were 10%. This was higher than those anywhere else, so Max kept his money in dollars, which turned out just fine. No currency rose in value enough to negate the better U.S. yields. His first decision was a good one.

Top Interest Also Brings Currency Gain

A year later, the situation changed. U.S. yields were now only 6%, but British were 7.25% and German 7.50%. So Max converted his funds, now $11,000 (it had earned 10%, remember?) into DM40,000, as this was how many marks $11,000 would buy in January 1971. A year later, he had earned the annual yield of 7.50% and ended the year with DM43,000.

So far, so good. But it gets better. During that year the mark rose from 27.5¢ to 31¢, so if converted back to dollars, his DM43,000 was now worth over $13,200. Once again, choosing the highest-yielding currency was the wisest choice. He was up 32% in two years. With his money snug in a bank.

1972: No Clear Choice

In January 1972 Max faced a tough choice. There was no yield clearly higher than any other. The three highest were virtually equal: the yen (5.5%), the dollar (5.375%), and the D-mark (also 5.375%).

This was a situation you will sometimes find in the world—all rates roughly equal. Was it worth the extra

0.125% in interest to switch from marks to yen? Max realized that the bank's fees to convert one currency into another might be greater than 0.125%, so switching wouldn't have gotten him any more money (*he thought*).

So he decided to stay in marks: his first poor decision. The mark rose just under 1% that year against the dollar, but the yen rose by nearly 4%. Max kicked himself for losing out on more than 3% extra profit, so he resolved to go back to his original plan: switch into the best-yielding currency *every* time, no matter what.

As he read the results of his venture to date, the highest yields meant the biggest gains after conversion back into dollars. They had, consistently, for three years. The handwriting was on the wall. So why not read it?

1973: Was That Handwriting or Just Graffiti?

Happy and feeling cocky with his newfound knowledge, Max Yield scanned the world for the highest yields again in January 1973. No major currency, not dollars (6%), D-marks (7.75%), Swiss francs (4.25%), or yen (5.875%) could equal British pound rates at 9%. So Max switched his marks into pounds.

But here he stumbled. While the pound was worth $2.36 at the start of 1973, at year's end it was only $2.22, thus losing 6.8% of its value in dollar terms. This meant that a 9% yield ended up yielding merely 2.2% more in dollar terms (9 − 6.8 = 2.2). He'd have been better off staying in dollars even though the dollar yield was only 6%.

But that would have been peanuts compared to what he would have made if he had stayed in D-marks. Remember he gave up the D-mark for the pound's promise of an extra 1.25% yield? So while he was ahead in interest earned by being in the pound, the pound lost value against the dollar. At the same time the mark increased in value by no less than 20% during 1973 (31.3¢ to 37.6¢). Adding 7.75% German interest, Max would have increased his nest egg by almost 28% that year, had he stayed in marks, instead of by the 2.2% he was ahead in the pound.

1974—A Chance to Earn 16%

At the beginning of 1974, U.S. yields were only 9.25%, and German rates were 12%. But pound rates were just under 16%. Max had never had such rates, so he decided to stay with the pound again. They were just too good to pass up.

Sure enough, 1974 saw the pound increase by 4.7%, for a total annual return of 20.7%. The system was working again.

1975

The only major currency yielding anywhere close to 16% in 1975 was the Italian lira (15.1%). But while the lira is now quite a respectable currency, in the midseventies it was not. Moreover, one could not easily buy a lira deposit outside Italy. For these reasons we will assume that Max chose the next highest yielding, the yen, at 13.75%. Unfortunately, the yen lost 2% of its value against the dollar during the year, but left with an 11.75% effective yield, Max was not totally defeated by what his money earned that year.

As 1975 ended, he could be pleased with how his system of always seeking the maximum rate of interest had worked for him. *In six years, from 1970 through 1975, his $10,000 had increased by 94%, an average annual yield of 15.67% over that time.*

Max Rides a Roller Coaster

In 1976 the British pound was Max's clear choice. It paid 10%, compared to 8.25% on the yen, 5.5% for the dollar,

3.875% for the mark, and 1.5% for the Swiss franc. But the pound plunged that year from $2.03 to $1.68: a 17.3% decline. Max, for the first time since 1970, saw all the interest he earned completely wiped out—and his principal reduced by 7.3%—when his pound balance was converted back into dollars.

Figuring he'd just been the victim of a seven-year itch, Max disregarded that year's loss and pressed on using the same system. On New Year's Day, 1977, the pound was the clear favorite again: yielding 13.5%, compared to 5% in dollars, 4.67% in marks, 1.25% in francs, and 7.5% in yen. Max stayed in pounds, and the pound rose 10.5%, for a total return of 24%, his best ever.

The only double-digit yield available in 1978 was the lira (11%), which was still not all that widely available. The French franc (9.25%) and Belgian franc (8.875%) were only somewhat more so. U.S. yields (7.25%) were well above British, German, Swiss, and Japanese. But they didn't beckon to Max; after all his foreign gains he couldn't bear to return to the U.S. dollar.

Max decided to put his money in French francs. It was a good choice. The franc rose by another 9.33%, for a total return of almost 19% for the year.

18% a Year So Far—Then Even More

After nine years of chasing the highest yields, Max was feeling just great. He'd made over 160%, or an average of 18% a year. What's more, he had lost money just one year. So he kept pursuing the top yield.

In 1979 the pound was yielding the highest at 12.5%. (Second best was the U.S. dollar, at 11%.) Switching across the Channel, figuratively speaking, from France to Britain, Max saw the pound soar by 10% from $2.00 to $2.20. A total return of 22.5% for the year. This brought Max, after ten years, to a profit of 223%, or an average of 22.3% per year.

A New Decade Dawns and Interest Rates Go Bonkers

The eighties started with a world interest rate bonanza. Most currencies were sporting very high yields (even the dollar was 14.33%). But once again, the best was the pound, at a lofty 17.33%. And once again the pound rose. The rise was only by 3.6%, but enough to bring Max's yield to 20.9% and to convince him that high yields would go on forever.

New Year's Day, 1981, provided a sweet dilemma. The best yield, at 18%, was on Eurodollar deposits, that is, on U.S. dollars held at foreign banks. Canadian dollars (17%) were next best; pounds yielded only 14.125%. Max was sorely tempted to stay in a foreign currency, having tasted big exchange rate gains for years. But he finally decided to keep going for the top yields, come what may. He went back to the greenback and collected his 18%.

At year's end he was mighty glad he did. Because had he stayed in the pound, he'd have lost 6% of his principal, as the pound fell 21% against the dollar that year. Max thanked his lucky stars he'd stuck to his strategy.

Max Tastes Some Italian Wine and Isn't Sure He Likes It

Yields on the Italian lira were an amazing 21.375% as 1982 dawned. British rates at 15.125% were the only thing as close, though U.S. yields were at 14.25%, nearly as high. Still, Max couldn't resist the idea of earning over 20% in bank interest. So he found a Swiss bank in the Italian-speaking Ticino area

of Switzerland, near the Italian-Swiss border, and converted
all his funds into lira.

Alas, the lira fell that year from L1,228 per dollar to
L1,399. Max's currency loss was a stinging 13.9%. But the
21.375% interest he earned was high enough to cover that
unwelcome loss and still raise his hoard for the year by another 7.5%. He'd clearly have done better just by being in
the dollar, but at least he hadn't actually lost.

In 1983 the lira again paid the highest interest rate, 19%.
The pound was a poor second at 11%, with the dollar at 9%.
So Max remained in lira. But the lira not only fell in value
again, losing another 21.3% against the dollar, the loss was
large enough to overwhelm the 19% yield, and it gave Max
his second decrease in principal in fourteen years. He tried to
console himself with the fact that he only lost 2.3% and that,
further, he'd have also lost 1% had he been in the pound.

But he suddenly realized that for the third year in a row
he'd have been best off had he opted to be in the U.S. dollar.
What was happening to the strategy that had proved so right
during the seventies? Max preferred not to be confused by
the new facts. All he knew were high yields, and that was all
he wanted to know. So he stayed the course.

More Italian Wine: Good and Bad Vintages

The pattern continued in 1984. Once again the lira (17.75%)
was the best interest rate by far. The French franc (12.25%),
the dollar (9.75%) and the pound (9.375%) followed. Once
again Max chose the lira, and once again the lira fell against
the dollar—this time by 14.75%. A small 3% gain was left.
Still he'd have done even worse had he taken the second
choice (the franc fell by 10.5%, leaving 1.75%) or the pound,
which fell 17%, completely erasing its yield.

In short, he had chosen about the best of the nondollar
currencies, but once again he'd have done much better had
he just left his money in dollars that year, earning nearly 10%.

For four years in a row, the rise of the U.S. dollar against often better-yielding currencies was making Max's system look foolish. Although there was a new trend afoot, Max neither understood nor liked it. So he pressed on, once again picking the lira in order to earn its 15.7% yield.

That worked better. The dollar finally fell against all currencies in 1985—and fell big. The lira gained 12.1%, making a fabulous total return of 27.8%. Of course, those who chose the pound watched it soar from $1.12 to $1.45— a 29.2% exchange-rate return, which, tacked on to a 11.67% yield, totaled a stunning 40.9% annual return!

As the dollar slid, happy days were here again for those Americans who, like Max, kept going for high yields and found them outside the dollar.

As 1986 dawned, Max was sorely tempted to switch into the pound. Suddenly 27.8% was not good enough. Hungry to make up for lost years, he eyed the 41% annual return that his friends got in 1985. And the 12.75% pound interest rates for 1986 seemed plenty high enough.

But as he made his ritual New Year's Day scan of world interest rates, he saw a currency new to him; the Australian dollar was paying 18%. So for the first time in four years, he switched out of the lira and put his money in Australian dollars.

The yield was big on the Aussie dollar all right, but the currency lost 2.4% against the dollar in 1986. Max was left with a pretty good 14.6% profit. Still, he felt a little bitter because had he stayed with the lira, his total return that year would have been nearly 35% (the lira rose 20% in 1986). He felt only marginally better when he figured that had he switched to the pound, he'd be only 13.375% richer.

Patience Is Rewarded

You may think it was churlish of Max to feel bad about accepting a 14.6% return. But, no doubt about it, it is hard to see a currency you've just switched out of do better than the currency you gave it up for. Still, if your strategy has proven a good one over time—which Max's certainly had been—it might be best for you to be patient. In Max's case patience was about to be well rewarded.

In 1987 the Australian dollar once again offered the best yield, 16% versus 11.375% for the lira and 11% for the pound. This time the Aussie dollar rose by 8.7%, for a 24.6% total, a little better than the lira's return.

New Year's 1988 saw the Aussie dollar still the best yielder, at 12.875%. (The lira was at 10.5%; the pound at 8.875%.) This year the Aussie dollar soared in value by 18.4% for a grand total of 31.3%. This was also the year when Max's original $10,000 vaulted past the $100,000 mark (to $120,270). Thus, in nineteen years, following his high-yield strategy was good for a profit of 1,100%, or an average annual yield of 58%. Incredible.

But the good news was not over. As 1989 began, Aussie dollar rates were still the best, at 16.875%. Even a 7.3% loss in the currency's value that year still resulted in a 9.6% increase. Staying with the Down Under dollar in 1990 yielded a nominal 15.75%, but the currency fell again, by 2.2%, which thus still resulted in 13.6% profits. By the start of 1991, the original $10,000 had become the equivalent of $149,750. This was a fantastic 1,397.5% growth over 21 years, or a 66.5% average rise each year.

Had Max just stayed in the U.S. dollar all those years, as most Americans did, his compounded interest would have turned $10,000 into $58,900. A 489% gain is not bad, but 1,398% is much better.

Only Nine Switches in Twenty-one Years

In this example we did not deduct any fees for currency conversion. These can add up if one is switching currencies madly. But note that all this great return was made by switching into another currency only nine times in twenty-one years, from January 1970 to January 1991. This is an average switch of once every two years four months, certainly not churning one's account.

In 1991 and 1992 the Dollar Goes Up but Max Still Does Well—*Outside* the Dollar

During 1991 Max Yield was in the Spanish peseta, buying one-year Spanish Treasury bills, which at the beginning of 1991 yielded 14.49%, the highest yield he could find.

During 1991 the Spanish peseta fell 5.45% against the U.S. dollar. (Most currencies fell a little against the dollar in 1991.) But even allowing for this, Max's overall yield was 9%, still more than he would have gotten had he stayed in the U.S. dollar.

As 1992 opened, Max faced a tantalizing choice. He could roll over his peseta T-bills, but he'd only get 12.21%. This was still higher than all the other currencies he knew. He saw two currencies new to him paying even more, however. Looking north, the Swedish krone was paying 13.75%, and, looking south, the South African rand offered 18.1%.

South African interest rates had been high for years. The government had to offer them to attract capital that would otherwise be frightened off by the political situation. But as 1992 opened, things were seeming to look up; Apartheid was being repealed, and many countries were ending their trade sanctions. The place was coming in from the fringes of the world economy.

Max remembered the experience he had had with Italy a decade before: he'd bought lire while Italy was still on the fringes of being a major economic power. He'd taken a chance, and if you remember, he's paid dearly for it. Because the lira was not yet backed as a major and respected currency, it fell, sometimes more than the interest rate it paid.

Max Yield decided to heed this lesson and stick to major, respected economies. So he chose Sweden's 13.6% rate.

Before long, he was very glad that he had. By the end of October, the South African rand had fallen 26% against the dollar, overwhelming any interest payment he would have received. South Africa, though making strides, was still not yet in the major leagues.

Over the same period, the Swedish krone also fell against the dollar; all currencies did in 1992—but only by 3%, much lower than the annual 13.6% he was getting in interest. Max was still far ahead of the game, and much better off than if he had stayed in the U.S. dollar's measly 4%. He was also glad he'd switched out of the peseta; it had fallen 9% against the dollar over the first ten months of 1992.

Max had had a near catastrophe. Other "Maxes" could, and did, fall for the siren call of 18% South African rates. Remember, you can always get fantastic interest rates if you want to, but you are taking a chance on the country. In a global search for the highest yield, you have to draw the line somewhere. All investors would reject 400% rates on a Yugoslavian dinar inflating at a 1,000% rate, and with its country breaking up before our eyes. However, many could be swayed into 18% on the rand. Max had learned his lesson on the lira: he would wait until South Africa or any other high-paying nation had truly entered the ranks of the stable, major industrialized countries.

When we last saw him, Max was kicking himself and saying, "If only I'd put in fifty thousand dollars in nineteen seventy, I'd have three-quarters of a million dollars today."

Max did not always choose the currencies with the best overall performance, only the highest-yielding ones. We'll see in a later chapter how much he could have made just by buying currencies that may not have yielded the most but rose the most in value against the dollar.

Let's now leave Max Yield to enjoy his fabulous, 1,400%

gains made over those twenty-one years (as well as the very healthy profits he made the next two years, even when the dollar was rising), and consider what all his experience means.

Remember that at the root of the notion of interest has always been risk. Why then has the last generation turned that traditional idea on its head? No longer is it always "the higher the interest, the higher the risk." Investors like Max have been well rewarded—and fairly consistently so over the past generation—for choosing high yields. The risk doesn't seem to have been there for him.

High Yields without the Risk of Default

Of course, not all high-yielding instruments have done well. The infamous junk bonds of the eighties were so named because the borrower's poor credit standing meant that he had to offer higher interest, sometimes a lot higher in order to attract investors. The interest rates might have seemed very attractive, but many who reached for them got their fingers badly burned. Many "junky" borrowers—mostly corporations—were forced to default on their bonds, leaving those who "invested" in them with big losses.

The recent experience of junk bonds reminds us that the highest yield often is *not* the highest yield. Corporate borrowers who issue junk bonds are, of course, a lot different than government borrowers, like Australia, Italy, France, and Britain, whose Treasury bills Max always tried to buy.

Like all governments, the government of Australia has the power to print money to bail itself out if it ever finds itself short of cash on hand to repay its bond and note holders. No government would ever choose to default on its obligations so long as a little credit creation could pay off creditors.

As long as American investors like Max Yield stayed with the highest-quality government or bank paper, they could enjoy the high interest they earned abroad without any risk of default. This is something new under the sun. And something totally different from high-yield "junk" bonds.

High Yields with Very Little Risk of Currency Loss

What's also been new under the sun is the fairly small risk for Americans like Max of seeing their high-yielding foreign currency deposits fall in value against the dollar. In the twenty-one years from January 1970 to January 1991, Max's chase after the highest yield kept him in the dollar only two years, 1970 and 1981. The other nineteen years were in other major world currencies. In nine of those years—roughly half the time—the foreign currencies Max held declined in value against the U.S. dollar. And yet this was no real tragedy because in all but two of those years the overwhelming interest-rate superiority was enough to ensure that an investor did not lose any of his money. Indeed, in four of those nine years, he still watched his holdings increase by (actual or virtual) *double-digit* rates!

In just two of those twenty-one years did he ever lose money, once by 7.3% and once by only 2.3%. And for the whole of the period, he saw his original investment zoom in value by nearly 1,400%.

The experience of this generation has been extraordinary. There have been roughly 180 generations since that day around 2000 B.C. when the first recorded interest rate was offered. In not one of them was it so easy for the average person to pick from the highest rates offered anywhere on the planet and make so much money at so little risk.

In a sense the world's currency markets have become perverted. For Americans this is especially true, watching their dollar plunge in value over the last twenty years. The smartest ones have realized that since it was such a safe bet that the dollar will fall, going into other currencies was actually less risky than staying in the declining dollar. Moreover, they earned a lot more interest.

No one likes to pay high interest. Yet that's what some governments have been forced to do. Traditionally they'd only do this if inflation, instability, or a spendthrift population made the country's currency and its bonds seem unsafe. But to lure investors from overseas, the Australian and Italian governments have often had to provide higher-than-normal interest rates. It was the price they paid for excesses in their past. Governments of low inflation—stable and thrifty countries like Switzerland—rarely have to offer high rates.

Yet as the world has become more prosperous and the United States has found itself wrestling with a mountain of problems, the currencies that offer high rates of interest because they *have to* still have performed better than the U.S. dollar. For American investors this is a chance to profit two ways at once: they have been able to earn higher than stateside interest rates, and when they convert their pounds, marks, francs, and yen back into American money, they have sometimes found that they have earned another 25% to 50% through currency conversion.

No one can say how long this phenomenon will last. Since it is an historical anomaly, we can't expect the easy profits to last forever. On the other hand, if the weakness in the dollar mirrors our new, less powerful role in world affairs, what has happened in the last twenty years or so may be with us for a long, long time.

The Right Currency Almost Assures the Most Profit

People around the world have long been able to pick and switch from their own currency into a higher-yielding major currency. But total return (total interest earned plus total currency appreciation) depends on the staying power of the currency they use.

The 1,400% profit that Max made was earned by *getting out* of the dollar. Now let's see how a Swiss Max Yield who was already outside the dollar would have made out doing the same thing. A Swiss making the same moves that Max made over the same twenty-one-year period would have had a very different result.

Had a Swiss Max Yield invested SFr10,000 on January 1, 1970—and made all the same moves that the American Max made over the twenty-one-year period and then turned his funds back into Swiss francs again—he'd have ended up with SFr59,670. This is only an increase of 497% against an American's 1,400% increase. The American Max would have made almost three times as much in percentage terms because the dollar had fallen so much while he was largely in other currencies. Not so the Swiss franc.

But let's see how much of an increase was made in their purchasing powers.

Let's say the American and the Swiss both start out with the same amount in dollar terms in January 1970. The American invests $10,000; the Swiss, SFr43,730 (which equaled $10,000 at that time). We've already seen how in January 1991 the American would have $149,750. The Swiss would have had a gain of only 497% on his francs, turning SFr43,730 into SFr261,068. But in January 1991 SFr261,068 was worth $202,378. This is an increase of 1,924% in dollar terms. So the Swiss made a lower percentage profit but ended up with more money to spend.

To understand this seeming anomaly better, imagine that the American Max and the Swiss Max had been friends in 1991 and went on a trip together. The Swiss brought his Swiss francs and the American Max brought his dollars. It wouldn't have made any difference whether they traveled in the United States or in Switzerland or Japan for that matter. Their dollars or Swiss francs would have to be converted into a local currency in order to pay for hotels, restaurants, etc. And what each of them had drawn from their identical investments—once it was converted into the currency of the country they were visiting—would have given the Swiss Max about 30% more to spend than his American counterpart.

Even accepting a yield growth rate about two-thirds less than what the American got, the Swiss ended up with over one-third more money in total dollars terms. This is a painful demonstration of how much value the U.S. dollar has lost over the past generation and how much more spending power you end up with by using a strong currency as your base.

Sticking to One Currency, the Swiss Franc

Now, let's see how much a stay-at-home Swiss would have made over those years just keeping his money in Swiss francs, earning compounded interest. If in 1970 he had invested the equivalent of $10,000 in Swiss francs at regular bank interest, his deposit would have been SFr43,730. By the start of 1991, his bank balance would have shown SFr98,560. That is a 125% increase; certainly not much interest for twenty-one years. All but four of those years saw rates of just 5% or less. (Even with compounding, the average annual return was 6%. Pretty small potatoes.)

But by January 1991 SFr98,560 was worth $77,000. Because the Swiss franc rose so much (from 23¢ to 80¢), the return in dollar terms was 670% (32% annual average over the twenty-one years)—much more than *you'd* have received keeping $10,000 in an American bank earning much higher interest.

For a stay-at-home Swiss the 125% return he received in Swiss francs brought him no bonus when he converted back into his own currency. He was already in his own currency. So the 125% gain for the stay-at-home Swiss was clearly not as good as the 500% increase that the Swiss Max Yield had gotten by switching his Swiss franc holdings into the highest-yielding currency around.

The stay-at-home Swiss and the Swiss Max Yield *both* did extremely well because their base currency did extremely well.

We Americans have not had that kind of luck for a long time—and we cannot become Swiss overnight. If your income and expenses are in U.S. dollars, you are a U.S. dollar–based investor. For years now, it's meant seeing your standard of living eroded by an eroding dollar. It's not a happy thought, but it is something you can help correct.

By first denominating a portion of your savings in Swiss francs, for example, and then going after high yields, you would have benefited in two ways during the past generation. You'd have earned a lot higher than stateside interest, and on top of that, you would have ended up with money that was worth more at a checkout counter in the United States. The foreign currency you ended up with would have been convertible into a lot more dollars.

As you have seen from the example of Max Yield, earning a high rate of interest can be very nourishing to your bank balance. But for Max it was even more important to be in a strong currency—one that was appreciating the most against the dollar—because a bank balance in those currencies showed the heftiest bonus when Max converted their value back into dollars.

In the chapter that follows, you will learn what your dollars could have earned in a bank if kept in just *one* strong currency—the Swiss franc, the Austrian schilling, or the Japanese yen. And if at this moment you think that one foreign currency has a great future against the dollar, you can follow the pattern set out next.

CHAPTER 11

▼

Two Americans Sit Tight in One Strong Currency (and average 36% and 81% per year)

O ne American does absolutely nothing for twenty-one years and earns over 36% a year. His friend makes a few shrewd moves and earns 81% a year.

In the last chapter we followed the fortunes of an American investor we called Max Yield because of his approach to riches: each year, he simply picked the foreign currency that offered him the highest rate of interest. Max found that system very effective. But *we* could see that he would have made even more money by picking the strongest currency each year, not the highest yield.

In this chapter we plan to follow the financial fortunes of two American investors who don't want to go to the trouble of picking different currencies each year, even if the new currency would give them a higher rate of interest or the possibility of a better exchange rate. They prefer to have their bank accounts sit tight in one strong currency either all or most of the time. Both men understand that any currency will fluctuate in value, that it will do better against the dollar in some years but not in others.

One of them is in no hurry to see his bank balance double; he's content to let it just collect and compound interest, without touching it. He has chosen to put his money into Austrian schillings, and he's willing to let the schilling rise against the dollar on its own schedule. We'll call him Mr. Walker because he is satisfied to see his money grow at a leisurely pace . . . to walk, not run.

The other investor is less patient. He wants to see his money move a little faster—you might say, trot. So we'll call him Mr. Trotter. And we'll soon see what happens to him.

The Rewards of Leaving Your Money in One Good Currency

On January 1, 1970, Mr. Walker put $10,000 into an Austrian schilling deposit account at a good bank and then forgot about it for twenty-one years. Simple, yes, but also very profitable as it turned out.

To start with, Mr. Walker's $10,000 bought him S258,732, and here's how his schilling grew while earning a different rate of interest each year.

Year	Account Balance, Jan. 1	Interest Rate That Year
1970	S258,732 (original balance)	5.67%
1971	S273,402	4.39%
1972	S285,404	5.17%
1973	S300,160	6.94%
1974	S320,991	7.26%
1975	S344,295	5.48%
1976	S363,162	4.67%
1977	S380,122	7.49%

Year	Account Balance, Jan. 1	Interest Rate That Year
1978	S408,593	6.45%
1979	S434,947	5.59%
1980	S459,261	10.38%
1981	S506,932	10.32%
1982	S559,247	8.00%
1983	S603,987	5.36%
1984	S636,361	6.57%
1985	S678,170	6.11%
1986	S719,606	5.19%
1987	S756,954	4.35%
1988	S789,881	4.59%
1989	S826,137	5.50%
1990	S871,574	5.75%
1991	S921,690 (final balance)	

When Walker's final balance is turned back into dollars, at the then exchange rate of S10.72 to the dollar, he gets $85,979.

That's a gain of 759.79% in twenty-one years—or an average annual gain of more than 36% a year.

Mr. Walker Can Sit Tight— But Mr. Trotter Must Tinker

What Mr. Walker did was essentially to do nothing. For some people this may seem like the easiest thing in the world. But for others it is the hardest. Many people like to tinker with their investments, to squeeze out extra profits by using judgment and by timing their moves. And if that sort of involvement suits your personality, you might make more money and have more fun by getting so involved.

After all, no currency—not even the legendary Swiss franc—has gone *straight* up since 1970. As chart 2 indicates, there was a seven-year period in which the franc fell and the dollar rose. Had Mr. Walker, for example, been holding francs through the entire period we are describing, it would have been very frustrating for him from 1979 to 1985, even though he would have ended up seeing his money multiply more than five times. It was no day at the beach even in the Austrian schilling, because that currency had a bad period, too, in roughly the same time period.

But as you have seen, even though the currency he chose had a number of years in which it did not do particularly well, Walker saw his $10,000 investment multiply over eight times.

Mr. Trotter didn't have Mr. Walker's patience. He wasn't willing to stay with any currency while it was not performing up to his expectation. He was determined to stay with the schilling only as long as it was beating the dollar and then to switch to dollars when dollars got stronger than the schilling. Let's see how he made out doing that.

We start Mr. Trotter out with $10,000 in January of 1970—the same as Mr. Walker—and see what happens if he does only a small amount of tinkering: that is, if he makes just three switches in and out of the dollar in that twenty-one-year period.

Until December 1979, the schilling does well against the dollar, so Mr. Trotter is content to do the same thing that Mr. Walker does. He keeps his schillings in a bank, drawing interest. And he just forgets about them.

His $10,000, or S258,732, draws modest interest. But the value of the schilling does rise from 3.86¢ at the beginning of the period to about 8¢ per schilling at the end of ten years.

His original S258,732—by accumulating compounded interest—grows to S459,261 in ten years. And now, in dollars, it's worth $36,770.30: a gain of 268%, averaging almost 27% a year.

That's a wonderful gain for doing absolutely nothing.

Mr. Walker did the same thing from January 1970 to December 1979, gaining the same 268%, of course. And you may recall that he decided it made sense for him to stand pat until January 1991. "I'm in this for the long haul," he told his friend Mr. Trotter. And it would turn out to be a decision he'd never have to shed a tear about, because he would end the twenty-one-year period with a gain of over 750%.

Trotter Takes a Different Path

In January 1980, after ten years of doing the same thing, the two friends mentally parted company. Mr. Walker continued to walk slowly; he stayed with the same currency that had rewarded him so well. Mr. Trotter decided to reach for greater returns; he switched out of schillings and back into the dollar.

What made him decide that? Maybe he just didn't want to tempt the fates after such a spectacular gain. Maybe he thought the dollar had fallen too far in too short a time and was ready for a rebound. "What works in one decade," he told his friend Mr. Walker, "may not work in another."

In any case, on the first business day of 1980, Mr. Trotter gives his bank instructions to sell his schillings and buy dollars. His bank puts what is now $36,770 into a Eurodollar money-market account earning (in 1980) over 13% interest. Let's see how that move profited him in the next five years. In the Eurodollar money market account, his 1980 balance of $36,770 compounded its interest until the end of 1984, at which time it was worth $65,484.96. So he did more than just OK on the interest he earned.

But Mr. Trotter's story gets better because he was also right on the dollar. It had indeed gotten too cheap. Or you might say he was right about the schilling. It had gotten too expensive too fast and was due for a drop. So he was well out of it.

New Year's Day, 1985—Time to Change Again

Back on New Year's Day, 1980, when the two friends decided to take different paths to riches, the schilling was worth 8¢.

Five years later, in January 1985, when the friends met again, it was down to about 4.5¢. What an embarrassing moment for Mr. Walker to meet Mr. Trotter again—after five years of seeing his chosen currency get banged around. And what a tempting time for Mr. Trotter not only to gloat and count his gains, but perhaps also to get out of the dollar. (The schilling continued to go down against the dollar for a few more months. We are using round dates for our examples—specifically New Year's Day in 1970, 1980, and 1985—to show that you don't have to pick the exact high point or low point of a currency to make extraordinary profits. The dates we use were good turning points, to be sure, but not the exact highs or lows of any currency.)

Anyway, on New Year's Day, 1985, Mr. Trotter runs into his friend Mr. Walker at the Rose Bowl Game. And the two friends compare their investments. Mr. Walker merely reported that he sat tight, stayed in schillings, and ended 1984 with an account containing S681,250—up from S459,250 five years before. (That may have sounded like a gain. But it certainly wasn't in dollar terms. His account in 1980, was worth $36,770; five years later it was, in dollars, worth only $30,965. A paper loss of 16%, all because the schilling had not done well against the dollar.)

But—even with that paper loss—Mr. Walker was determined to keep his money in schillings. "Your dollars," he told his friend Mr. Trotter, "have gotten too strong. I just came back from a trip to Europe and I could buy everything for a song. Three Savile Row suits; I could never afford that kind of suit before. I also went on a ski vacation in Switzerland for less than it would cost me to ski in Colorado." No, he told Mr. Trotter, that just couldn't last; the schilling and other foreign currencies were now too low. He was going to keep his money in schillings; he'd see that currency rise again.

Mr. Trotter listened. It made sense to him. But first, he had to show Mr. Walker who was smarter. He pointed out that by switching to dollars in 1980, he had been able to see his original $10,000 investment (which had grown to $36,770 by the beginning of 1980) rise to fully $65,485 by January 1985. A gain of 555% for the full fifteen-year period—an average gain of 37% a year!

Still, what his friend Mr. Walker had said about the schilling being too weak (or the dollar being too strong) gave him pause. So on the first business day of 1985, he instructed his bank to turn his $65,485 back into schillings.

At S22 to the dollar (4.54¢ per schilling) the schilling balance came to S1,440,670—or about S1.5 million. Quite a change from the roughly quarter of a million schillings Mr. Trotter started with in 1970.

Mr. Trotter continued to keep his money in the bank, in schillings, earning interest from the beginning of 1985 until January of 1991. Just by earning interest, the account grew to almost S2 million in six years. But by then one could get S10.7 to the dollar; Mr. Trotter's schillings were worth 9.2¢ each. His account was now worth $180,000—a gain of 1,700% in twenty-one years, or on average, a gain of 80.9% a year.

This was accomplished with only three switches—and without picking the exact high or low of any currency.

Mr. Walker and Mr. Trotter picked the best-performing of the major currencies for that period. But they would have done extremely well in the Swiss franc or the Japanese yen too.

Let's see how Mr. Trotter would have done, for example, if he had followed his same three moves in and out of the dollar, selecting either Swiss francs or Japanese yen rather than Austrian schillings. How much difference would that make?

Suppose Mr. Trotter puts his $10,000 into a Swiss franc account on January 1, 1970. The franc is worth 23.17¢, and he earns 2% interest.

A year later the franc is about the same. It's worth 23.23¢. So Mr. Trotter is 2% richer. That's enough to give anyone doubts. But Mr. Trotter is convinced that the dollar is too high and must someday drop (for all the reasons chronicled earlier in this book). So he decides to stick with his plan, and until 1980 he never looks back. He makes the right decision. Eventually, the franc rises from 23¢ in 1971 to 67¢ in November 1978, the high for the franc in this period.

Of course, Mr. Trotter couldn't have known that 1978 would have been the high for the franc in this period; so he sticks with the franc for another year and two months—until his meeting with his friend Mr. Walker at the Rose Bowl Game in 1980. By then, the franc had dropped to 62.5¢. So he decides to switch to the dollar and content himself with a gain of 170% over the $10,000 he started with in 1970, or a respectable 17% a year.

By switching to a Eurodollar money-market account from 1980 (not the high for the franc) until 1985, Trotter was able to see his dollar account grow beautifully for five years as the dollar not only earned high interest but also appreciated against the franc. In those five years his account rose from $32,627 to $58,106.76.

In January 1985 Mr. Trotter switched his dollar account back into francs, getting SFr153,932.91. Then in six years of earning interest and watching the franc grow in value as the value of the dollar fell, Mr. Trotter could, by January 1991, value his account at a heart-warming $154,010.46. That's a gain of 1,440% for the period or an average gain of 71.5% a year. Not as good as the gain he had made in Austrian schillings, but an unbelievable gain nonetheless to anyone accustomed to ordinary compound interest in a bank. (Incidentally, had Mr. Walker invested his $10,000 in Swiss francs and just stayed there for the same twenty-one years, his gain would have been 513% or an annual gain of 24.4% a year.)

Let's do another example—with Mr. Trotter making his switches from the dollar to another currency in 1970, back to the dollar in 1980, and back to that other currency in 1985. Only this time, let's see how he does in Japanese yen.

His $10,000 buys ¥3.6 million in January 1970. After drawing interest for ten years, he now has ¥7.23 million, which in 1980 is worth $30,081.60. Going into dollars for the next five years was a small advantage. By being in dollars until 1985, his account rose to $53,573, just slightly more than what it would have been if he had stayed in yen. But switching back to yen in 1985 brought rich rewards because it enabled Mr. Trotter to be in yen when it was making its biggest move—when, in fact, it doubled in dollar value in just five years. By January 1991 Trotter, by adding interest earned, would have in his account almost ¥18 million. And at the rate of ¥125 to the dollar, the account that started with $10,000 in 1970 was worth about $140,000 by 1991. An average gain of 62% a year.

In all the cases we have just described—Mr. Trotter in Swiss francs, in Austrian schillings, in Japanese yen—we have purposely picked New Year's Day in 1970, 1980, and 1985 to avoid giving the impression that Mr. Trotter was smart enough to pick the peaks and troughs of the currencies he was investing in.

He wasn't smart enough. Almost nobody is.

All he needed was a feel for what was "too high" for a currency or "too low." And that is something *you* can develop. Later in this book we will give you some touchstones to use when you are deciding the best time to get out of dollars or back into them. We'll also help you evaluate which alternate currencies to favor when you get out of the dollar.

If you watch major turning points both in the world news and the world's markets, if you sense what is making various currencies rise and fall, if you see where you can get higher-than-average interest rates and/or a very promising currency—you can do very, very well. Maybe not as well as Mr. Trotter. But quite well, all the same. Probably better than you could do as easily on Wall Street—and with much less risk.

Are You Ready to Earn High Interest in Another Currency?

You now know that there are times to seek high interest rates in another currency and times to stay in the dollar. You've also learned how an investor like Max Yield went after the highest yield he could get and managed to make a yearly gain of 65% even though his approach took him through a number of difficult years. And you watched Mr. Walker and Mr. Trotter, who limited themselves either to Austrian schillings alone or to a combination of the dollar and the schilling. Mr. Walker gained 36% a year giving the matter no thought at all; Mr. Trotter, using a minimum of thought, did a lot better. With an average yearly gain of more than 80%, he even did better than Max Yield.

Now, if you are in a mood to compete with these gentlemen, you should learn how to open a foreign currency account in a good bank.

In the next two chapters, we will show you how easy this can be.

CHAPTER 12

▼

Opening a Foreign Bank Account: Easier Than You Think

If you have shied away from the advantages of a foreign bank account because you think that banking overseas would be a hassle, put that notion out of your mind.

In fact, if you know how to do it, banking with safe, strong, and flexible foreign banks is actually easier than staying only with domestic banks. You can easily learn to use your foreign and domestic banks together to accomplish all you wish: deposits, withdrawals, buying, selling, or borrowing any currency. Moreover, you can, if you want, do it all at home, traveling only as far as your local ATM machine.

The First Step

Before putting money into a currency of your choice, you have to open a bank account. But in this age of instant worldwide communications by fax or phone, this can be just as easy as opening a bank account down the street.

The ease of opening an account depends on the laws of the country in which the bank is located and the policies of the particular bank.

For instance, by Swiss law, you must have your signature notarized before you can open an account at any Swiss bank, even a U.S. bank branch operating in Switzerland. (The same goes for Austrian banks.) But that's no big deal. Your local bank will probably notarize for you without charge. So will someone you know who is a real estate agent; they do it all the time. Some banks that cater to the very wealthy may also require that you be recommended by a current client. But there are many more that are glad to get your business just on your own request.

Sometimes the bank requires a copy of your passport. This is to ensure that you are a non-resident of that country and thus entitled to the tax benefits non-residents get. On any case, it is very easy to fill the forms out, giving your name, address, and your beneficiary in case of death. Fill these out, sign your name to a signature card, and enclose a check with instructions (such as, "Please buy deutsche marks with this check") to open an account in any major currency, and you're in business.

Get to Know Your Bank First

Before committing funds, it's wise to write any bank you choose and ask them to send you information on opening an account, as well as the number of currencies they offer. From their response you'll see how good their English is, and how prompt, courteous, and personal their service may be. How you are treated in your initial correspondence often shows how well you'll be treated if you open an account there. (See the next chapter for addresses and fax numbers of several excellent banks that are accustomed to doing business with Americans.)

With the availability of fax machines, the time difference

can actually work in your favor if you bank in Europe. Here's how: if you fax your request in the evening, when you wake up you'll usually get the bank's response. This holds true at the best banks for normal requests or questions about any investment you have or are interested in or whatever transaction you want the bank to perform. In this way, European banks are even more convenient than most U.S. banks.

Note: banks prefer your letters or faxes to be typed. If this is not possible, please print carefully. Later on you may get an officer who knows you and becomes familiar with your handwriting. Knowing him or her will make you feel more part of the bank's family than you are likely to feel in most large American banks.

The Easy Way to Transfer Money

Once your overseas bank account is opened, getting money to and from it is easier than you might think. You can actually have your own local bank wire funds to a New York (or Los Angeles) correspondent bank of the foreign bank you choose.

All foreign banks have correspondent banks in all major countries. When opening your account, just ask them to send you a list of their correspondent banks in the United States, or whichever country you live in. By asking your local bank to transfer money to these accounts at the big U.S. bank, you are actually depositing money into your foreign bank account, identifying yourself either by your name and account number or just by account number for privacy.

For example, you can instruct your local bank to transfer a certain amount of your money to the Chase Manhattan Bank in New York, account number 100-000-00-1 (which is the account your foreign bank has at Chase) and add "for the further credit of John Doe, account number 100-010-1," which would be your own account in the bank you've chosen overseas. You then notify the foreign bank itself into which currency account you want your money changed. This may sound complicated, but it's not. After you do it the first time, you'll wonder why you ever thought it was difficult.

Getting your money home is equally easy. You can fax your foreign bank, giving them wire transfer instructions to your American bank, saying how much to send. Be sure to get your local bank's correct routing instructions. Tell your bank you are expecting an amount of money from a bank in whatever country your bank is in. Ask the customer service rep to write down the *precise* wire instructions, so you can send them to your foreign bank. Your American bank will know how to do that.

Fax this routing information to your foreign bank. They will then instruct their correspondent bank to have the sum wired directly to your local bank. The whole process usually takes a day, or two at the very most.

If you request it, your bank overseas can send you the money in the currency you've bought. Otherwise, they'll convert it into dollars.

More accurately, it will convert the sum you've asked for into the currency of the country of the receiving bank, which will give it to you. If you are traveling in a third country, you'll get that third country's currency.

When your local account is credited, you will be able to withdraw the money with your ATM card at a local ATM machine.

If your foreign account is large enough, you can get a major credit card tied to your account. These will actually be debit cards. They'll be VISA or EuroCard cards, but when you use them, the bills will come to the bank and the bank will debit your account for the sum you've spent, plus a small fee. Besides being able to use your card for purchases, you can also request a PIN (personal identification number) and use, for example, your VISA card to get cash from any ATM machine accepting VISA cards.

These are all over the world. Of course, you'll only be able to get the cash of the country you are in. If you are traveling in Australia, you'll get Australian dollars, for example.

As a rule, it is cheaper to go the route of bank-to-bank wire transfers. But if you are stuck and your only recourse is to use your credit card to get cash fast, then the convenience can be worth any extra fee.

How much has to be in your foreign account before that bank will issue you a credit card? That depends on the bank. In general you'll need at least $30,000 or its equivalent in total assets. In other words, it need not be all in liquid cash. It can be in bonds, stocks, metal, etc. The bank may of course have to sell enough to pay the bill. Or it could make you a loan and take the money it's loaned to pay for the bill. The bank, if it knows you well enough, can waive a minimum. But this should not be expected.

In sum, whether you choose to wire your funds home to your local bank or use a credit card to get cash, your foreign funds can be as close as your local ATM machine.

Of course, we've glossed over the cheapest way to withdraw money. Simply ask the foreign bank to debit your account and send you a check. It will be mailed from the bank and drawn upon the bank's account at its correspondent bank closest to you. You can either deposit the check into your account, or take it to the correspondent bank and cash it, just as you would any other check.

Taxes, Yes—But They Don't Have to Be a Hassle

You can see that properly approached, foreign banks can be dealt with just as you would deal with your local bank. This also goes for paying taxes, though there are a few differences of which you should be aware.

Even in so-called tax havens like Switzerland and Austria, be aware that there are withholding taxes on interest. Swiss banks are obliged to withhold 35% of interest payments and Austrian banks 20%. (Luxembourg and Dutch banks have no such tax.)

But there are ways around this.

There is a method for U.S. taxpayers to get credit from the IRS for the taxes that have been withheld by the foreign bank, but it is a time-consuming process. It is better to avoid the tax altogether, which you can do by buying CDs or other instruments actually booked at the bank's subsidiary in a jurisdiction with no such tax. Most Swiss banks book their CDs in their subsidiaries outside Switzerland.

Austrian banks offering tax-free CDs do so at their Channel Island affiliates, and so far, they (unlike Swiss banks) charge nothing extra for doing this. So this causes the unusual situation of being able to get more Swiss francs for your money in Austria than in Switzerland.

If your bank does have extra charges for CDs, you can save this money by buying fiduciaries. These are instruments that are placed by your bank at another bank. You will be in effect loaning money to that second bank; but that's just a technicality.

That bank will be in a country like Luxembourg or Holland that has no withholding tax or interest. It should be a bank of the highest quality. This is because the liability to repay interest and principal will be on that second bank. Your bank, however, will probably make good on a fiduciary in the very unlikely event the second bank becomes insolvent. These banks are chosen by your bank expressly for their safety.

Must You Pay Taxes in the United States on Interest Earned Overseas?

If you are a U.S. citizen, you are obligated to pay taxes on all interest income you receive, from whatever source. The United States taxes interest income just as it does any other type of income. This takes away an incentive for Americans to save and has indirectly led to the decline of the dollar—one of the reasons you want to be in different currencies to begin with.

So wise or not, U.S. citizens must declare interest income on their foreign accounts, just the same as similar income from their domestic bank accounts. But there is a difference. U.S. banks send their information directly to the IRS, but foreign banks don't. It is your responsibility to declare the information yourself.

When tax time comes, remember that you'll have to translate your currency profits into U.S. dollars. This is the only currency the IRS deals in.

In fact, this is one reason why so very few U.S. banks offer foreign currency accounts. U.S. banks have to supply and file 1099 forms with the IRS. If they offered foreign currency accounts, then they'd have to make the conversions on the 1099s. They wouldn't do it by hand, of course. They'd use computers, and since most American banks have so few foreign currency accounts, this would be expensive.

European banks have been dealing in many different currencies for decades, if not centuries. Their computer systems are already programmed to keep track of holdings in various currencies. The best of these banks will supply your statement of account as often as you wish it, all denominated in the currency of your choice, usually your home currency. They'll be able to update all your holdings daily, all at the push of a button or two.

Some people think that having foreign accounts raises "red flags" with the IRS, and thus stay away from them, but they are missing out on legitimate profit by doing this. There is nothing illegal about having a foreign account. Declare it, pay the taxes on what we hope are huge profits, and generally treat it just as you would your domestic bank or brokerage accounts. In reality, it is the same.

Investment income is investment income regardless of the country it comes from. View foreign banks as places you can use to profit in ways you can't in the United States—not because it is illegal, but because provincial U.S. banks don't usually make these accounts available. You won't be harassed in any way by the IRS so long as you treat your foreign account like a domestic one. The wealthiest people and corporations have used foreign accounts for years to reap advantages. There is no reason you can't as well.

Getting the Best Currency Price

When you buy a foreign currency, you don't pay a commission on the sale. Instead, you'll pay the bank's selling price for that currency that day. The currency exchange rates you see quoted in the newspapers or on TV are the interbank or "wholesale" rates for the currency. Don't expect to pay these prices. These are the prices the banks use to trade among themselves, in amounts of over $1 million.

Individuals buying or selling lesser sums pay what amounts to the "retail" rate. There will be a difference, or spread, between the bank's buying (bid) and selling (ask) price to you. The best foreign banks normally charge a rate of about 1.4% above or below the interbank rate for fairly small (below $50) amounts.

Say you want to buy $3,000 worth of deutsche marks on a day the TV tells you the well-publicized interbank rate is DM1.90 (or 52.60¢ per mark). Using 1.4% as a guide, you should not have to pay more than 53.37¢ per mark (DM1.87 to the dollar) to buy those smaller amounts of German marks. Conversely, had you sold that day, you should expect to receive about 51.86¢ for your marks.

This 1.4% rule of thumb applies only to the best-priced banks, which have decades of experience in the retail foreign exchange trade. There are banks with spreads considerably worse than this, especially for amounts under $100,000. We have seen spreads as bad as 5% each way! Keep this in mind when you approach any bank to open an account. You can get lower spreads by shopping around. And once you get to the $100,000 level, spreads can fall tremendously—to one third of one percent or so.

Watch the Interest Rates

Every currency has its own interest rate, which varies from bank to bank. Among major currencies, those rates have ranged during the past two decades from 0.1% on the Swiss franc to 24% on the New Zealand dollar. Moreover, there are differences within the same currency, depending on how long you hold your account (for terms ranging from twenty-four hours to twelve months) and the type of savings accounts (available-on-demand or fixed-time deposits). It is wise to compare bank interest rates to the published Euro-currency rates found on the last page of the weekly *Economist* magazine or the daily *Financial Times* (two leading British publications that are available at newsstands in many U.S. cities).

But don't assume that the interest rates you see posted in these publications are the ones you'll get. The actual rate will depend on the amount of your deposit, as well as how you hold your currency.

Each bank's exact policy is different, but in general the more you deposit and the more time restrictions on withdrawal you accept, the higher the rate. But interest rates don't begin to approximate newspaper rates until you buy a large CD, time deposit, or fiduciary. Many foreign banks won't even sell you one of these for under $50,000 or its equivalent in another currency. The bank with the lowest CD minimum is Royal Trust Bank (Austria), which offers CDs in twelve currencies for as little as $5,000 or its equivalent. At a time when U.S. money market rates are 8% for CDs of $5,000 to $50,000, you'll get perhaps 7.25%. Above $50,000, tack on another 0.125%, and above $100,000, another 0.125%. CDs over $200,000 will get you a higher rate, which may be near, or even at, the newspaper rates.

Each bank has different rates for different currencies at

different times. Austria's Royal Trust Bank may have the best rates if you've only got $5,000 to invest. But if you've got $15,000, another bank (for example, ABN-AMRO in Amsterdam) may have slightly better rates. And if you have $500,000, you may find the best rates that day at still a third bank, perhaps a good Swiss bank.

Rates can vary up to 1% on the same amount for the same term. But if you're happy with the general service you are getting, then keeping that relationship is in the long run more important than going from bank to bank in search of the best yield. As long as the offered yield is reasonable, be content. A good relationship with your banker pays its own long-term dividends.

Keep in mind you can often buy CDs, time deposits, and fiduciaries with only a portion of the principal as down payment. It is possible to buy, say, a $100,000 CD and put down only $20,000, borrowing the rest in your choice of currency. You can get the better rate for the $100,000 CD while borrowing money in another currency to finance the purchase.

The interest rate on your deposit can depend on its term. There is usually not a big difference between a twenty-four-hour CD and a twelve-month CD. Incidentally, short-term deposits make sense if you see a period of sharply higher short-term interest rates ahead. You don't want to be locked in for too long a term. When your term expires and the deposit rolls over, you'll get the higher rate if rates have risen.

If you believe rates are currently high and will likely drop, then you want to lock in the high yields for as long a term as you can.

We've thrown a lot at you in this chapter. But taken a step at a time, dealing with a great foreign bank is easy. In the next chapter we'll introduce you to some of these banks.

▼

CHAPTER 13

Overseas Banks That Love to Do Business with Americans (Plus a Few American Banks with Foreign Currency Accounts)

Thus here are many reasons knowledgeable Americans have, for years, chosen to put some of their money in banks located overseas. For one thing, they know that in the greatest banks abroad, the details of their business dealings will remain *their* business and nobody else's. The overseas banks we discuss in this chapter respect and protect a depositor's privacy. They report nothing to the IRS. Account details are even unknown, in most cases, to any but a few trusted employees of the bank. And they do other things for you that you may come to value even more. They enable you to invest profitably in ways no American bank even approaches. Many of those ways are described or touched on in the following brief descriptions.

Austria

Royal Trust Bank (Austria)

Rathaustrasse 20
P.O. Box 306
A-1011 Vienna
Telephone: 43-1-43-61-61
Fax: 43-42-81-42
Telex: 11 49 11 rtba

Services offered: currencies, securities, metals, portfolio management, etc.
Currencies available: 13 (Australia, Austria, Canada, ecu, France, Germany, Hong Kong, Japan, the Netherlands, New Zealand, Switzerland, United Kingdom, United States)
Minimum to open account: none
Minimum to open CD: $5,000
English literature available: yes
Contact: Peter Zipper

The Austrian bank now known as Royal Trust Bank (Austria), established in 1890, has had several other names in just the past decade. Through it all, the same group of bankers has remained; many of the same people have been there for twenty years or more.

No other bank we surveyed makes it possible to do so much with so little money. There is no real account opening minimum, but CD rates start with amounts of $5,000 or their equivalent in eleven other currencies. Thus, for about $20,000 it is possible to have fully paid (that is, non-leveraged) CDs in Swiss francs, yen, ecus, or Australian dollars if you wish. That will be giving you a very wide basket. Moreover, the CD terms can be broken anytime with only very small penalties, and not many banks do this.

But be aware that this bank can charge higher fees and

offer lower interest rates than many other banks that don't offer as many alternatives. That is the price one must pay, especially if you only have $5,000 or $10,000 to invest. (Note: For those interested in leverage, or at least in getting their toes wet, Royal Trust Bank (Austria) allows a minimum 25% down payment. This means that it is possible to open an account with $1,250 and buy a CD worth $5,000 in any major currency with the loan in the currency of your choice.)

During the gestation period of this book, the credit rating of this bank's Canadian parent, Royal Trustco, fell drastically, from the top-rated AAA to only BB. It is not yet clear how this has affected the Austrian bank; we urge you to check with us for updates.

Denmark

Each of the other banks recommended in this section is in a country with a currency that we spotlighted in chapter 5. The Jyske Bank of Copenhagen, Denmark, is the exception.

Jyske Bank

Private Banking (Int.)
Vesterbrogade 9, Post Box 298
DK-1501 Copenhagen V
Telephone: 45-31-21-2222
Fax: 45-31-21-4205

Services offered: all except precious metals
Currencies available: 14 (Australia, Canada, Denmark, ecu, Finland, Germany, the Netherlands, New Zealand, Norway, Spain, Sweden, Switzerland, United Kingdom, United States)
Minimum to open account: none
Minimum to open CD: $15,000 or rough equivalent

English literature available: yes
Contact: Martin Hansen, François Kunzli

The Danish krone is a member of the European monetary system, so it is one of the eleven currencies in the ecu. It enjoys a strong, confident economy, in the top rank of European countries.

Denmark has come a long way since the early eighties. Back then, inflation, deficits, and indebtedness were so high that many despaired of Denmark's future. In mid-1982 government bond yields reached an almost hyperinflationary 23%. (At that time, U.S. Treasury bond yields only rose as high as 14%.)

This scared the Danes and they took radical measures. They put in vast savings incentives, cut inflation, fixed the krone exchange rate close to the mark, and cut spending. By 1991 the economy was transformed. Inflation, at 1.9%, was the lowest of any industrial country. High-quality exports have been snapped up by the rest of the world, to the extent that the trade balance, which had shown such a deficit ten years before, had such a large surplus that it was, relative to the size of the economy, larger even than Germany and Japan!

Danish banks escaped the problems that in the nineties have beset banks in Sweden and especially Norway (where so many banks made such poor loans that they became insolvent, the largest ones being nationalized). Denmark has had an efficient bank supervisory system for over a century. Supervisors regularly visit banks and examine their loan portfolios against rather strict standards. Perhaps as a result, relatively few loans made by Danish banks in the eighties have gone bad in the nineties.

The Bank for International Settlements (BIS) is the "central banker's bank." One of its responsibilities is to try to make sure the world's banks don't get irresponsible by making too many loans as a percent of capital base. Because the BIS has been worried about the eroding capital base of so many banks, they have made new rules to require all banks to have minimum equity ratio of 8% of total loans. But Danish banks have long been required to exceed this. Since the depression of the thirties, they have had to keep a minimum capital base of 11%. This is largely why no Danish bank has failed since the thirties. Bank earnings can suffer from this conservative policy, and indeed Danish banks earn a generally lower average annual return on equity than most other banks. But the number of Danish banks, seventy-two, has remained stable for years.

In the unlikely event of bank failure, there is a Danish-style FDIC that insures each depositor for up to DKr250,000. This is about $40,000 at 1991 exchange rates.

Jyske Bank is the Bank of Jutland, but their head office for foreigners is in downtown Copenhagen. Jyske Bank's origins can be traced to the nineteenth century, but the modern name dates from 1967, when the present-day Jyske was formed as a result of a merger of several smaller banks. Depending on how it is measured, this is either the third-or fourth-largest bank in Denmark.

The bank has been offering foreign currency deposits for over a quarter century. There is no minimum opening deposit, but under DKr10,000 (about $1,700) you don't get interest. This applies just to kroner accounts. For any other currency it takes a minimum of $15,000 or its approximate equivalent in any major currency. Their interest rates are quite competitive.

With a minimum of $20,000 you can buy a deposit of $100,000 in any currency (that is a five-to-one margin) and denominate the loan in any major currency. (They'll actually charge 1% of the loan fee off the top.) They call this the Invest Loan Program. You can put your investment in a single currency, but the bank advises that you spread it out between two, three, or four different ones to better spread the exchange rate risk.

The drawback is that $20,000 minimum—and that's for five-to-one leverage. If you want to go to two to one, for example, you'll need about $58,000 to put down. Compare that to Austria's Royal Trust Bank, where the margin program requires as small an investment as $1,250.

The Netherlands

ABN-AMRO

Private Banking Non-Residents
Amsterdam Main Branch
Herengracht 595
P.O. Box 1220
1000 EH Amsterdam
Telephone: 31-206-282764
Fax: 31-206-623-9940

Services offered: all normal
Currencies available: 25 (Australia, Austria, Belgium, Canada, Denmark, ecu, France, Finland, Germany, Greece, Hong Kong, Ireland, Italy, Japan, Malaysia, the Netherlands, New Zealand, Norway, Portugal, Singapore, Spain, Sweden, Switzerland, United Kingdom, United States)
Minimum to open account: Fl25,000 (about $14,000 at 1991 exchange rates)
Minimum to open CD: same as above
English literature available: yes
Contact: Erich van Tongeren

You'll recall from our section on the Dutch guilder just how rich and strong a financial tradition Holland has. Its banks have been used to dealing with foreign currencies (as well as foreigners) for centuries. Further, we've always found the Dutch easy to deal with. Perhaps because of the limited global application of the Dutch language, it is a rare Hollander who does not speak English. They are also great travelers, and so, for instance, Dutch bankers are usually aware of the banking practices in your own country. This is a boon when you are trying to describe something familiar to you that either is not available in the same form or goes by another name outside your own country.

Fortunately, it is not hard to recommend a great Dutch bank suited to your needs. *The* Dutch bank is ABN-AMRO. Until the late eighties this was two banks, the Algemene Bank Nederland (ABN) and Amsterdam-Rotterdam Bank (AMRO). These two already-large banks joined into one, and with over $200 billion in assets, it is now the largest bank in Holland, the sixth- or seventh-largest bank in Europe, and the sixteenth-largest bank in the world.

But don't let the great size put you off. Because tucked away within the behemoth structure is the Non-Resident Private Banking Department at the Amsterdam Main Branch. It has been run since the sixties by Erich van Tongeren.

The list of this bank's merits is long. It starts with the range of currencies available. You'll be doing well at other European banks to find ten or twelve currencies available. ("Any major currency" usually means just ten or twelve). ABN-AMRO offers twenty-five of them, listed above. Moreover, these are just the choices offered in late 1991. If any other currency gains prominence and can be traded internationally, chances are this bank will offer it. So don't be afraid to ask about a particular currency.

The bank's account opening minimums are Fl25,000 (about $14,000 in late 1991). But AMRO stresses that you should not expect really personalized VIP service for under $300,000. They offer time deposits in any currency for one, two, or three months. Tying your money up for a month at a time is not very burdensome. If you don't mind the three-month note, you can get interest rates as much as 0.5% higher, depending on the currency. Also, the bank will give a higher rate on deposits of more than Fl250,000 ($140,000). Again, depending on the currency, this can also add half a percent.

Let's take an example to see the difference. Remember, though, that the rates quoted here may not be the same offered when you read this—you know how volatile interest rates can sometimes be. One recent day ABN was offering the Swiss franc as low as 6.60% per year on one-month time deposits

TABLE 5

Interest Rates on Swiss Franc Deposits

Term	Less Than $250,000	More Than $250,000
1 month	6.60%	6.85%
2 months	7.00%	7.25%
3 months	7.05%	7.30%

with a value under Fl250,000, and as high as 7.30% on three-month deposits with a value over Fl250,000.

Now if you don't have the equivalent of Fl250,000, ABN-AMRO is extremely flexible in another area. You need only put down as little as 20% to buy a time deposit. In other words, you can buy a Swiss franc deposit of, say, SFr200,000 and put up the equivalent of only SFr40,000. You'd borrow the rest in any currency you choose.

The bank can buy stocks or bonds anywhere in the world. They can buy the bonds of any government. The minimums are very small, as small as the smallest denomination of bond offered. Often that means only 1,000 units; that is, the smallest U.S. Treasury bond has a $1,000 face value, the smallest Dutch government bond Fl1,000, etc. And against bonds the bank will allow you to put down a little as 30% and denominate your loan in any currency. You could thus own a DM10,000 face-value government bond for as little as DM3,000 down payment.

On the other hand, Holland is more "politically correct" than Switzerland. For instance, you cannot buy Krugerrand coins or South African deposits (favored by Max Yield in 1992). This may change, though, as South Africa liberalizes.

Finally, there are no Dutch withholding taxes, capital gains taxes, or death duties on interest or on profits if you are not a resident of Holland.

Singapore

Hongkong Bank

21 Coller Quay #01-00
Hongkong Bank Building
Singapore 0104
Telephone: 65-530-5000
Fax: 65-225-01-663

Services offered: all normal services
Currencies available: all major currencies except Singaporean
    dollar
Minimum to open account: $25,000 and others (see below)
Minimum to open CD: same as above
English literature available: yes
Contact: NA

    The Hongkong Bank was formerly called Hongkong and Shanghai Bank. This bank is the Singaporean branch of this bank. It offers deposits or loans in any major currency except, ironically, Singaporean dollars. (It offers what are called Asian Currency Units (ACUs), which are basically what CDs are called in Singapore.)

    A few other sample minimums at this bank are £10,000 (US$20,000); DM100,000 (US$66,000); SFr100,000, (US$80,000); ¥10 million (US$77,000); A$25,000 (US$20,000); C$50,000 (US$43,000). As you can see, these minimums are on the high side. But one advantage of this bank is the extreme flexibility of its maturities. All currencies are available for terms of one, two, three, six, nine, or twelve months. In addition to this, the following are also available at call (*i.e.*, twenty-four-hour turnover): U.S. dollar; British pound; deutsche mark; yen; and ringgit. The dollar is also available in one-, two-, or three-week maturities, the pound at one week.

    Furthermore, these terms can be broken, but be prepared

to pay an interest rate and possible principal penalty, the exact nature of which is up to the bank at that time.

Switzerland

Overland Bank & Trust

Bellariastrasse 82, CH-
  8038,
Zurich
Telephone: 41-1-482-6688
Fax: 41-1-482-2884

3, Rue du Mont-Blanc, CH-
  1211
Geneva
Telephone: 41-22-732-7939
Fax: 41-22-732-5089

Services offered: all normal services
Currencies available: 11 (Australia, Canada, ecu, Germany, Italy, Japan, the Netherlands, New Zealand, Switzerland, United Kingdom, United States)
Minimum to open account: $50,000 officially, sometimes less.
Minimum to open CD: $20,000
English literature available: yes
Contact: J. M. Clerc (Zurich) Camille Perusset (Geneva)

This is the former Foreign Commerce Bank. Probably no other Swiss bank has more experience dealing with North Americans wanting foreign currencies. In fact, the manager of this bank's Geneva branch, Camille Perusset, has had his job since 1971, longer than any bank manager of any other bank in this book. He has unparalled experience dealing with clients large and small. And although he is not the manager of the Zurich branch, J. M. Clerc has been at the bank nearly as long. At both branches CD minimums are 20,000 units (*i.e.,* ($20,000, SFr20,000, and so on). Exceptions include £10,000, ¥2 million, and L20 million. CDs are for three, six, and twelve months but cannot be broken or sold before maturity without a penalty of 2–2 ½% of the amount.

Though the minimum to open an account here is $50,000, this needn't be all at once. You can start with a smaller amount, e.g., $10,000, and add to it gradually as long as you bring it up to $50,000 within a few months. (In fact, Overland has been known to accept $20,000 at times. It pays to question *each* bank on this.) Incidentally, you might also try this approach with other banks. Some are more flexible than others and you lose nothing by inquiring.

Interest rates on fiduciaries are higher than for CDs. But minimums to buy them are higher as well: $50,000 or its equivalent in one of nine currencies. (The two currencies offered in CDs but not as fiduciaries are ecus and Italian lira.)

More speculatively, the bank offers futures, options, and all major currencies on the forward market. For this last opportunity a minimum 20% margin is required.

You can buy all stocks and mutual funds through Overland, and bonds in most currencies. In fact, the Zurich branch is one of the few Swiss banks to be open for stock and bond orders all the way up to the closing of the New York markets, which means around 8:30 p.m. Zurich time.

Overland has a good quarter-century of experience in dealing with non-Swiss. This is long enough for each branch to develop their distinct "personality." Some clients swear by the Zurich branch; others love Geneva. Contact *both* branches if you wish; see what response you get and which seems to suit you best. Take it from the thousands who have gone before: if you do find a good banker at one of the two branches, it may be one of the best moves you've ever made.

Cambio + Valorenbank

Utoquai 55, P.O. Box 535
CH-8021, Zurich
Telephone: 41-1-252-2000
Fax: 41-1-252-2658

Services offered: all normal services
Currencies available: (Australia, Canada, ecu, Germany, Italy, Japan, the Netherlands, New Zealand, South Africa, Switzerland, United Kingdom, United States) etc.
Minimum to open account: $100,000
Minimum to open CD: $50,000
English literature available: yes
Contact: Werner Schwarz

Account opening minimums here are higher, $100,000,000. CDs are available in equivalents of $50,000 minimum. Unlike Overland's CDs, these can be sold on any business day. They are available in all the usual currencies—and most of the unusual ones. Often in the past when we've surveyed banks on whether CDs are available in a particular currency, this is the bank that would consistently answer yes. For sheer number of currencies, this bank can't be beat. In early 1992 the rand was paying the highest yield of any major currency—18.1%.

Fiduciary time deposits can be bought in any freely convertible currency. If it trades outside its country you can own it at Cambio. Minimum amounts, however, are $100,000. Cambio offers the most flexible leverage policy of any Swiss bank we know of. You can put down as little as 20% to buy any investment-currency, T-bills, stocks, bonds, funds, etc.

One big plus with this bank is Werner Schwarz. If you are fortunate enough to get him as your banker, you may well be getting the single best and most easy-to-deal-with banker in Switzerland.

Anker Bank

50, Avenue de la Gare
CH-1001, Lausanne
Telephone 41-21-204-741
Fax 41-21-239-767

Services offered: all normal services
Currencies available: 11 (Australia, Canada, ecu, Germany, Italy, Japan, the Netherlands, New Zealand, Switzerland, United Kingdom, United States)
Minimum to open account: Sfr.5,000 or US $5,000
Minimum to open CD: not available
English literature available: yes
Contact: F. Misrahi, P. A. Visinand

Minimums to open an account here are very low for Swiss banks—Sfr.5,000 (about $3,500 at current rates), or its equivalent in any major currency. However, you'll get no interest on these in any currency but the franc, and that only with restrictions on withdrawal. Good interest rates aren't forthcoming on deposits of under $25,000. These can be held in one-, two-, three-, six-, nine-, or twelve-month terms.

This bank does not offer CDs, but rather fiduciaries, time deposits in which the ultimate borrower is usually another European bank.

For those who want a Swiss franc interest-bearing account (currently paying 5½%) and who have only a small amount of money, this is worth looking at.

Ueberseebank AG

Limmatquai 2
CH-8024 Zurich
Telephone: 41-1-252-0304
Fax: 41-1-252-2002

Services offered: all normal services
Currencies available: all convertible currencies
Minimum to open account: Sfr.10,000
Minimum to open CD: same as above
English literature available: yes
Contact: Bruno Benz

Ueberseebank offers basic accounts in "almost any freely convertible currency," but interest on balance is paid only on accounts in Swiss francs, U.S. dollars, and D-marks. Market interest rates can be had with what they call Liquidity Funds. For a minimum of Sfr.10,000 (currently about $7,000) you can get these in U.S. dollars, ecus, D-marks, and Swiss francs. You can switch from one currency to another without charges and withdraw without restrictions. This is an excellent deal; the bank really doesn't make money out of this. They use it as a loss-leader to try to tempt you into their managed funds. But don't feel you have to buy them. You are free to stay in the liquidity funds. Nowhere else in Switzerland can you own so many currencies at such good rates for so little.

They do offer leverage, but not more than two to one and in general do not encourage it. Except for Anker Bank this is likely the only other Swiss bank that will accept accounts as small as $10,000. The bank's level of English is very good, perhaps because they are owned by a large American insurance company.

Be Aware of Mergers and Acquisitions

To this survey of banks a couple of notes must be added. First, we live in an era of bank mergers and acquisitions. It is possible that by the time you read this, a bank listed here may have been bought by or merged into another bank and may be known by another name. The important things to ask are: (1.) Have the policies changed? and (2.) Has the management changed?

Until the late 1980s bank policies and managements usually stayed unchanged for years, if not decades. But then the trend changed, and merger fever has too often spread into the banking sectors. It is not clear to us that the merger trend has really made better banks. Perhaps they will turn out to be a fad of the loose-credit eighties and will pass. In the meantime it will be wise to keep updated on any changes, both for better and for worse. What is a good bank today may have changed by the time you read this. Chris Weber's newsletter, for one, traces these changes, and it would be a good idea to check with it before you act.

Low-profile Blue-chip Banks

Over the years, we've dealt with some of the oldest and most exclusive banks in Europe. Some of them, even though excellent in every way, did not want to be publicized in a popular mass-market book. (There is a general tradition among the best old-line European banks not to appear too pushy or high profile.)

These banks can range from small, centuries-old private banks to the largest triple-A–rated Swiss banks. They'll often take as customers only those who've been recommended to them by people they already know.

An excellent alternative to this route is to go through a Swiss trust company specializing in fitting clients to the right blue-chip Swiss bank. Camafin Trust is operated by two long-time Swiss bankers with vast experience in dealing with North Americans. We've known these men, Roger Badet and Bruno Brodbeck, for nearly twenty years. They are able to open doors, establish accounts, and provide first-class service at the best blue-chip banks for clients who want to open accounts with as little as $50,000. To see what a tremendous advantage this is, realize that one can't normally expect decent service at a blue-chip Swiss bank for under $500,000—and not always even then.

It is also wise to have "on the spot" a trustworthy Swiss whom you can rely upon to inform you of any important changes either in general Swiss banking policy or in a particular bank.

For information on their "Blue-chip Bank Programs," contact Camafin at

Camafin Trust AG
Dept. 6
P.O. Box
8802 Kilchberg-Zurich
Switzerland
Telephone: 41-1-720-9623
Fax: 41-1-715-2253

Weber, Hartmann & Partners (WHP) was founded in 1992 by Hans Weber, for twenty-five years the President of Foreign Commerce Bank (now called Overland Bank).

WHP operates like Camafin, with the difference that they place clients in a single bank, the venerable Julius Baer. This bank is over a century old, has assets of over $20 billion, and is given the highest possible rating by Moodys'. Baer can pick and choose its clients, and if you were to approach them directly, you would need at least $1 million to be accepted. (The average client of Julius Baer has an amount far greater than that.)

But Weber has a special arrangement with the bank, and will open your account and act as your private banker at Baer for a minimum deposit of $250,000. They charge ¼% per year for this service, which is reasonable. In this way, one can get great personal service at a blue-chip Swiss bank for a fraction of the money everyone else needs.

Weber, Hartmann & Partners
Zurichstrasse 110 B
CH-8134 Adliswil-Zurich
Telephone: 41-1-709-1115
Fax: 41-1-709-1113

Buying Foreign Currencies Using Banks in the United States

Since January 2, 1990, banks doing business in the United States have been able to offer deposits in foreign currency. So far, very few have done so. One would have thought that the big foreign banks already operating in the United States would be competing strongly to lure in more deposits in their own home currencies. But this has not happened.

To dramatize what a "foreign" concept foreign currencies can be in America, we recently went through the Los Angeles yellow pages under "banks" and called the Los Angeles branches of eight large foreign banks: two of them Swiss, two German, and four Japanese. We asked if they opened for accounts at the U.S. office (not at their home offices) in their own currencies (*i.e.*, the Swiss franc, D-mark, or yen).

All but one bank said no. The exception, Japan's Sanyo Bank, said they offered yen deposits but were quite candid about their high charges—5% above the spot rate to buy or sell yen. If the yen gained 10%, you would break even. If it stayed the same, you'd lose 10%, less interest. Since these fees are as high as any airport banknote exchange we've seen, we do not recommend the Sanyo Bank. A 10% spread is absurd.

But again, Sanyo was the only foreign world-class bank that even said they'd offer American investors any currency besides the dollar. And while we called only Los Angeles branches, chances are if you live close to New York or Chicago and want to call branches there, you'd get the same response. We're sure this will change in the future, but right now this path is not the way to go.

U.S. Banks in the United States

This leaves the American banks. As a group, they have not been offering foreign currency accounts. Maybe this is because U.S. banks are now very gun-shy about any unconventional investment. In a reaction from the other extreme of the eighties, when they tried anything and tried it too much, they now don't want to try anything new.

Also, Americans (American bankers included) still see foreign currencies as too foreign and too exotic for Americans. They may be right—for now. But as more Americans become aware that there is a world beyond our borders, and that they can easily participate in it, more U.S. banks will offer foreign investment opportunities. As of today, however, the pickings are slim. In fact, until recently only the Mark Twain Bank of St. Louis offered such accounts.

Two of the biggest banks do have programs, but rather inflexible ones. Moreover, these two banks, Chase Manhattan and Citibank, are unfortunately not among the safest U.S. banks. We are not saying that if you deposit under $100,000 with them you'll lose it. You won't; the FDIC will bail them out. But in general these banks are not known for their service, as we found out when we replied to their newspaper ads. Long delays and confusing paperwork were common. Both at press time offered CD programs with $25,000 minimums in six major currencies: yen, D-mark, Swiss franc, Aussie dollar, British pound, and Canadian dollar. In the general manner of U.S. banks, you are not allowed to break the term of the CDs. You are allowed to switch into any of the other currencies offered whenever you want, however.

Both banks have been advertising their programs, but apparently they have not had big successes in drawing deposits. Talks with Chase or Citibank bankers reveal that they believe the U.S. public isn't ready for foreign currencies. But the success of the Mark Twain Bank's far more flexible program puts the lie, we believe, to the big bankers' claims.

Mark Twain Bank

1630 South Lindbergh Blvd.
St. Louis, MO 63131

Telephone: 800-926-4922 or 314-997-7444
Contact: Peggy Jourdan

The Mark Twain Bank protects your account up to $100,000, per FDIC limits. But a warning word is in order: if you put $100,000 in a foreign currency account in the U.S. and the value of your currency climbs 25%, you now have the equivalent of $125,000, whether you convert it to dollars or not. (This doesn't include interest, which would of course add more.)

In short, be aware that only in terms of U.S. dollars does the $100,000 insurance apply. And if the next few years are anything like the last few, you might reach that threshold sooner than you think. If you do, you'll have to decide whether to open another account at another bank. The FDIC may not cover two or more accounts at the same bank if the grand total is over $100,000.

The Mark Twain Bank has been quietly offering foreign currency CDs for quite some time and has without doubt the most experience in dealing with individual investors here in the United States. They offer CDs in all major currencies. The posted minimums are $20,000 or its equivalent in any currency. (The minimum for ecus is $100,000.) Maturities are at three, six, nine, or twelve months, with no premature withdrawals allowed. Interest rates are generally competitive with the best European banks.

Ask for their free informational package on various currencies and their current rate of return.

First Union National Bank

301 S. College
Charlotte, NC 28288
Telephone: 800-736-5636
Contact: Jim Brady or Cindy Morrison

First Union National Bank is the fourteenth largest commercial bank in the United States. It has branches in North and South Carolina, Florida, Tennessee, and Georgia.

Its greatest advantage is its offer of maximum liquidity with money market accounts (not CDs) in any major currency (including the French franc and Italian lira). They are based on either twenty-four- or forty-eight-hour call money, so they can be bought and sold at any time.

The disadvantages are several. First, interest rates are quite low. On the day we checked, D-mark call rate was at 8.06%, but the interest rate First Union National actually paid on $25,000 minimum accounts was 3.5% below this, or just over 4.5%. In fact, on their minimum deposits in all currencies they pay 3.5% under whatever the market call rate is. Even the largest deposit into these accounts earned no better than 1.5% below the market call rate.

First Union National has a Euro-currency deposit program that pays closer to market rates, but the minimum is $250,000, and it has to be held for the whole term of eighteen months. It is also, unlike the money market accounts, not FDIC insured.

Finally, the level of service may be suspect; faxes from them to us did not arrive on the day promised. While it may seem like a small thing, this type of inefficiency, in our experience, is a warning flag about a bank's service in general. However, those wanting maximum liquidity and freedom to buy and sell without caring too much about the interest rate may find this bank attractive.

CHAPTER 14

▼

The Safest Currencies to Invest In

Anyone who goes outside of his own country to invest is taking a calculated risk. He is hoping that the performance of that country's best in stocks, bonds, banks, or currencies will be better than what he could find if he stayed at home.

Certainly you are taking a currency risk if you buy another country's securities, because the securities are valued in that currency; just banking in the country doesn't necessarily oblige you to buy its currency. Whatever you do, however, you are exposed to the country's political, economic, and financial situation.

While you must be aware of the risk, there are ways to minimize it. You can identify countries that are less risky than your own, and investigate them.

All this raises the question: How exactly does one gauge how stable or risky a country is? There are companies that seek to do just that, helping businesspeople and investors decide where to put their capital. One of the best of them is the British-based International Business Communications, Ltd.

A U.S. division of this company puts out the *International Country Risk Guide* (*ICRG*). ICRG rates each country in three ways: political risk, financial risk, and economic risk, combining the three for a composite risk figure. (Their latest annual rankings of 129 countries has Switzerland in its usual position—as the safest country on earth.)

Which Countries Pose the Least Political Risk?

According to the *ICRG* ratings political safety is deemed most important, on the theory that if a nation is politically unstable, financial and economic conditions don't matter that much. So the variable of political risk makes up fully half of any country's overall, or composite, risk. Political risk is taken to mean not just how much popular support exists for the type of government in the country, but also factors like the degree of corruption in government, and how the government's stated goals, such as economic expectations, diverge from reality.

It is not enough for a country to have had the same form of government for centuries. The important thing is how flexible and adjustable that political system is to changes. China, for instance, had by 1910 experienced an uninterrupted three thousand years of the same imperial form of government. It had, however, grown rigid, unable to adjust to new realities, and when the Qing Empire fell in 1911, China was immediately plunged into decades of instability.

Today the nation with the oldest continuous form of government is the United States,* and while the United States remains one of the world's most politically stable countries, thoughtful Americans have pointed out that over this past generation or so, too many features of American political

---

*The U.S. constitution was enacted in 1787. Britain's current form of government, which many people believe to be longer-standing, dates from the Reform Act of 1832.

life have threatened to become inflexible. The current drive for legislative term limits reflects one such concern. Fundamental and needed reform is often stymied by incumbent lawmakers wishing to protect a status quo they've enjoyed for decades.

What Makes Switzerland Such a Safe Place to Invest In

Switzerland has had the same form of government since 1848, making it fairly old in terms of current longevity. Furthermore, unlike any other democracy, voters have held the four main parties in almost perfect equilibrium since World War I, each one of them usually getting about the same percentage of votes from election to election.

But in spite of this, political power is not concentrated in the hands of a relatively few people who remain in power for life. In fact, the president is chosen annually from a group of political leaders and can serve only one year. The turnover rate in the two legislative houses, while not that fast, is much faster than in most countries, and you will not find the powerful personalities whose primary goals are to protect their legislative fiefdoms.

Perhaps because it is a relatively small nation, Switzerland has a large measure of political power set firmly at the local level. This is the place most responsive to the desires or needs of the electorate.

But while longevity of political institutions does not necessarily make for attractive stability, younger is not necessarily better, either. The world is replete with examples of new countries founded by one person or a group of people who then rule for years with apparent stability, but ultimately cannot handle the question of leadership succession or institutional permanence when they pass from the scene. A dictator brings a certain stability (the shah of Iran, for example), but what happens when that person leaves is a key question those evaluating a country's long-term stability must ask.

Emerging Countries That Are Getting Safer

Singapore appears to be handling this potential problem well. Lee Kuan Yew—Singapore's founder and, until recently, its only leader—ruled with a dictatorial hand, which was nevertheless far more benevolent than most dictatorships. Lee recently passed from the scene, but his successors are running a smooth ship. This is true both economically, which has always been Singapore's strong suit, as well as politically, as the country is becoming less rigid. It is clearly moving in the right direction as regards political stability. This is probably why the latest *ICRG* political risk rating actually gives Singapore 79 out of a possible 100, a slightly better rating than the United States (78) or Australia and the United Kingdom (both 76).

Luxembourg and Switzerland tie for first place in the political category. Both receive a 93 rating. Because Luxembourg is judged to fall short of Switzerland in the other two categories (economic and financial risk), it gets a second-place overall composite risk rating—89 to Switzerland's 91.5.

These other two categories of risk each comprise 25% of *ICRG*'s composite score. Since sound and safe economic politics usually result in a good financial system, we'll examine economic risk first.

What Makes a Country Economically Safe

Economic risk ratings should take many things into account, most of them centering around how well a set of economic policies are being employed. But there are noneconomic factors that can also go into the equation. For instance, there should be an efficient and just legal system. Not only should the laws of a country be as clean as possible, any disagreements should be settled as quickly and inexpensively as possible. (Unfortunately, the American legal system, mired as it is in endless litigation, too often does not meet this last requirement.) Of equal importance, the legal system must allow and stimulate the growth of free markets. (The U.S. system does better than most in this area.)

For a country to possess a high degree of economic stability, it must give incentives that reward those taking risks in building productive enterprises. In other words, producers must be rewarded. Further, in event of any economic problems, the solutions should be market-oriented, be applied directly at the source of the problem, and be applied quickly, before the problem gets out of hand.

For instance, if there is unemployment and economic stagnation, the best course would be to immediately lower the taxes—especially social security taxes, which often hit unfairly at the lower income level, and capital gains taxes, which stunt economic risk-taking and growth. It would also be important to lower minimum wage rates to make it economic for employers to hire previously unemployable people. The wrong economic response would be to raise taxes or minimum wage rates, subsidize uneconomic sectors of the economy, or raise welfare and unemployment benefits so as to take away incentives for people to find productive jobs.

Of course, the above example is just one of the economic situations governments are faced with all the time. How they handle the myriad choices determines how the economy will do.

Few countries will solve all of their problems ideally; few will solve none of them. In the minds of most people, Taiwan comes the closest to meeting all the above principles of economic management, so it is no surprise that the *ICRG* study gives Taiwan 43 out of a possible 50, the second-highest country rating for economic risk. (Inexplicably, the only other country to get 43 is Malta, which is not usually listed among this rarified group of sound economies. Japan claims the top spot with a 49 rating.)

At the other extreme, perhaps Cuba comes closest in the public mind to meeting none of the principles of good economic management. It receives a 12 on the *ICRG* rating, but Uganda and Liberia each get the lowest rating.

Why a Country's Central Bank Is So Important to Its Safety Rating

Most countries will fall between the extremes of a Taiwan or a Cuba. While they'll likely have more economic sense than Cuba, political considerations or failure of will could make them fall short of an ideal economic climate. Most will be varying shades of gray, few all black or white.

To assess the exact tone of gray of a country's economic approach, analysts like to look at several factors. If the analysts can't rely on a country's strong historical or cultural bias toward stability or a long-term track record, they can examine the people in charge of making policy—particularly those at the central bank and finance ministry. They want to know whether these people are regarded as competent by their international peers as well as the local business community. You'd be surprised at the number of times even major nations put less than totally competent people in charge at the central bank or finance ministry. One conspicuous example was when Jimmy Carter named G. William Miller as "Fed" chairman. The dollar swooned, and confidence kept falling until Miller was replaced with Paul Volcker, someone the market knew and trusted.

Incidentally, analysts want to see a central bank acting with as much independence as possible from the central government. They don't like to see economic and financial decisions influenced by politicians. In this regard the German and Swiss central banks get the highest rating for independence, followed by the Bank of Japan and the U.S. Fed. (The French,

British, Canadian, Austrian, and Italian central banks are much more political creatures.)

Central banks are of vital importance because they are responsible for a nation's money supply. And the tighter they are with the money supply, the less inflation there will be. This will also mean a stronger economy and currency in the long run. Thus it is no accident that Germany and Switzerland have had the tightest monetary policies of any nations during the past generation, and have also had among the strongest economies and currencies during that same time.

While central banks are in charge of monetary policy, national legislatures and finance ministries control fiscal policy—that is, how much the government takes in and spends. Analysts don't like to see big-spending governments, especially when they spend more than they take in in revenues. And if they do run a budget deficit by doing this, markets prefer to see the shortfall made up in government borrowing, such as treasury bills and bonds, which are bought by investors, foreign and domestic, by *anyone* except the central bank. Because when the central bank buys its government debt, it inflates to do it. (This is called monetizing the debt.)

Markets are concerned about the interest costs that a government must pay to service its debt. The U.S. government now spends fully one-quarter of its total budget simply to pay the interest to holders of U.S. government short-, medium-, or long-term debt instruments—that is, bills, notes, or bonds. Compare this to Switzerland, which spends less than 5% of its budget on the same thing. In fact, the Swiss government is not even *allowed* to issue short-term debt, because this is often the way central banks monetize debt, and the Swiss have thus built in a type of safety net against institutionalized inflation. The total amount of Swiss government debt is comparatively small and is usually very much sought after as ultrasafe paper by investors inside and outside the country.

Be that as it may, in the *ICRG* ratings, economic risk is the only one of the three categories in which Switzerland does not get the highest rating of all 129 countries. It is given a

39.5 out of 50. Countries given a higher rating include Japan (49), Malta and Taiwan (43), Norway (42), the oil-rich economies of Oman and Qatar (both 42) and Brunei (41.5), and Holland (40.5).

Financial Risk: The Doomsday Factor

The final component that investment analysts look at is a country's level of financial risk. Investors will be loath to put capital into a country where the borrower they are lending to may default on the loan. They don't want to put money into a country when the risk of exchange control could make it impossible for them to get their money out again. And they don't want to invest their money in another country—and thus, usually, in another currency—if they fear that this other currency will fall in value against their own, thereby possibly losing them money even if they are able to get the money out.

All these risks—loan default, exchange control, and currency deregulation—are what make up the financial risk of investing in any country. It is not surprising that Switzerland gets a perfect 50 out of a possible 50 in this category. Virtually alone among countries, Switzerland has never had exchange controls. No investor has ever had to worry about having money trapped inside Switzerland. The Swiss franc has been the strongest currency for the past generation; since the sixties no money has appreciated more. So no one investing over the longer term in francs had to worry about getting back less in his or her own currency than was put in.

Finally, while we can't say for certain that no Swiss borrower has ever defaulted on a loan, the chances of this happening are extremely small. Such is the moral stigma attached to ever doing so that any borrower, medium-size or larger, would find it very hard to raise money ever again on Swiss capital markets. And the likelihood of the Swiss *government* ever defaulting on its obligation is so negligible as to be virtually nonexistent.

Germany, Japan, and the United Kingdom are the only other countries to score a perfect financial risk grade on the *ICRG* study. But when we take the long view, we can't help thinking that these three nations may not be in the same league as Switzerland. All three had exchange controls for much of this century. Britain's most recent experience lasted from 1939 to 1979. And while the recent past has not seen any risks of loan defaults in these three countries, during the Great Depression all were hit hard by them. Indeed, there is evidence today that some large Japanese entities are in real pain from too much debt.

We agree, however, that the risk of massive loan defaults in Japan is low. The importance to Britain's economy of its financial acumen is so great we doubt large defaults would be allowed to occur there. They would be forestalled, if the need ever arose, by bailouts that would be inflationary. This would drag down the pound, which alone among these top four financially safe nations has *not* outperformed the U.S. dollar over the past twenty years. (It fell 30% from January 1970 through November 1991.)

As for Germany, loan default risk is very low. The very word for debt in German is identical to the word for guilt, so in a sense the very idea of going into debt is a little sinful. Along these lines, one can only be redeemed when the debt is repaid.

Putting all the nearly four hundred different risk ratings for the world's nations (three measures each for 129 countries), we find Switzerland clearly the least risky nation on earth. No other country is so well regarded in all three potential types of risk. No country is viewed as safer as far as political and financial risk are concerned. And just a handful of countries score higher in economic risk, and not by much.

We can understand Switzerland's standing by taking a look at all the others in the top ten. Luxembourg comes second. As a financial risk it is rated less than perfect, but still high enough to make a solid second-place showing. Norway comes third, rating high marks for financial risk. This is a

1991 COUNTRY RISK RANKINGS

(Least risky score is 100 for political category,
50 apiece for economic and financial risk)

Country	Political Risk	Financial Risk	Economic Risk	Composite Risk
1. Switzerland	93.0	50.0	39.5	91.5
2. Luxembourg	93.0	49.0	36.0	89.0
3. Norway	87.0	47.0	42.0	88.0
4. Austria	88.0	47.0	39.5	87.5
5. Germany	83.0	50.0	38.5	86.0
5. Netherlands	85.0	46.0	40.5	86.0
7. Brunei	81.0	48.0	41.5	85.5
8. Japan	80.0	50.0	49.0	84.5
9. Singapore	79.0	48.0	39.5	83.5
9. U.S.	78.0	49.0	39.5	83.5
11. Canada	81.0	48.0	37.0	83.0
12. Belgium	82.0	45.0	36.5	82.0
12. Denmark	86.0	41.0	37.0	83.0
14. Sweden	81.0	47.0	35.0	81.5
14. Taiwan	71.0	49.0	43.0	81.5
16. United Kingdom	76.0	50.0	36.0	81.0
17. Finland	85.0	44.0	32.0	80.5
18. France	79.0	46.0	34.5	80.0
18. Ireland	80.0	42.0	37.5	80.0
20. New Zealand	78.0	46.0	35.0	79.5
21. Australia	76.0	45.0	37.0	79.0
21. Iceland	82.0	42.0	33.5	79.0
23. Malaysia	71.0	45.0	38.5	77.5
24. Italy	72.0	47.0	35.0	77.0
25. Venezuela	75.0	40.0	36.0	75.5
26. Portugal	69.0	42.0	38.5	75.0
27. South Korea	63.0	47.0	36.5	73.5
28. Botswana	70.0	34.0	42.0	73.0
38. Cyprus	69.0	39.0	38.0	73.0
30. Bahamas	66.0	39.0	36.5	71.0
30. Spain	65.0	42.0	35.0	71.0
32. Malta	64.0	34.0	43.0	70.5
32. Mexico	71.0	41.0	28.5	70.5
32. Oman	65.0	34.0	42.0	70.5
35. Chile	67.0	42.0	30.5	70.0
36. Czechoslovakia	73.0	36.0	30.0	69.5
37. Costa Rica	71.0	35.0	32.0	69.0
38. Indonesia	57.0	44.0	35.5	68.5
38. Uruguay	66.0	39.0	32.0	68.5
40. Thailand	57.0	42.0	37.0	68.0

little bit puzzling to us, however, as the Norwegian banking system is in fairly poor shape. After having made too many bad loans in the eighties, Norway's banks are now paying the price. Just recently the Oslo government was forced to take over one of the largest banks, Christiania, in effect nationalizing it, because no private entity wanted to buy it. There is likely more bad news to come.

Number four is Austria. It gets the same high financial risk rating as Norway (47), a score somewhat more justified in this case. The economic risk rating, 39.5, is the same as Switzerland's. In the political risk section Austria scores 88, making it second in political stability after Switzerland and Luxembourg.

Germany and Holland tie next. Politically Germany is rated less stable than the three above, perhaps because it is so much more exposed to the uncertainties of the new Eastern Europe. Its structural economic rigidities likewise cause this measure to slump a bit. Holland ranks a little better in political risk, as well as economic risk, but it is not regarded as quite as good a financial risk. Thus they get similar overall risk rankings.

The Sultanate of Brunei (formerly Borneo) is a special case. While not an economic power in any normal sense, it is extraordinarily wealthy because of its oil, and ruled by a man whose dynastic roots run quite deep. Its currency has risen 20% against the dollar in the past decade. Therefore, it is regarded as one of the most stable nations in the world. However, all of the above could have been said about Kuwait before August 1990. One year later Kuwait found itself with an overall ranking of 104 on the list of 129 countries, sandwiched between Yugoslavia and New Caledonia, both torn by civil war.

Rounding out the top ten are three more likely candidates for stability: Japan, Singapore, and the United States. Japan rates perfect as a financial risk and quite high in the economic arena, as can be easily imagined. But Japan's vulnerable point is that its political institutions are primitive compared to its economic and financial entities. Its ruling party is more than usually corrupt, and the nation is in essence a one-party state, with not much accountability offered either by other political parties or by the voters. If Japan only had the political stability of most Western European nations, it would be near the top of anyone's list of stable, risk-free countries.

Singapore and the United States are in a tie, according to the survey, for ninth place. Singapore is slowly becoming more politically stable, rating a 79, while the United States, at 78, unfortunately and apparently becomes ever less so. The United States, at 49, does rate a near perfect score on financial risk, perhaps the only risk being currency depreciation. Though some worry about exchange control and default as well, these fears are probably overplayed, at least at present.

The United States' Surprisingly Poor Overall Rating

One conclusion that may surprise many readers is the relatively poor overall showing of the United States. America is usually thought of as the most stable and least risky place in which to invest, especially now that there is so much turmoil in Europe. But the risk assessors do not see it this way. The six least risky countries are all in Western Europe. Moreover, the next group of ten after the top ten contains seven European countries. It is clear that this relatively small part of the world is now thought of as the safest area in which to invest.

The whole idea of putting a numerical rating to countries is admittedly subjective. The most important thing is to see how valuable the total picture of risk is. One way to check the value of these overall rankings is to see what the currencies of these best-rated countries have done.

During the past twenty-two years, since currencies began to float in the market to find their own values, which currencies have risen the most on the market? Lo and behold, we find a remarkable convergence between the two top-ten lists.

We find the same currencies popping up on both lists. Over time, the nations with the most stable, least risky ratings are those whose currencies have risen the most in value.

From 1970 to 1990, the ten currencies with the best record were:

1. Swiss franc, +291.9%
2. Japanese yen, +139.6%
3. Deutsche mark, +131.7%
4. Austrian schilling, +130.7%
5. Dutch guilder, +102.0%
6. Singaporean dollar, +71.7%
7. Belgian franc, +51.8%
8. Luxembourgian franc, +51.8%
9. Taiwanese dollar, +46.4%
10. Maltese pound, +33.9%

(Figures from Henry Browne, *The Currencies of the World*.)

Switzerland, Luxembourg, Austria, Germany, the Netherlands, Japan, and Singapore are all on the top-ten list of countries with the least risk. Moreover, Malta and Taiwan may not get the best overall country risk ratings, but you'll remember that they were at the pinnacle of all rated nations on the basis of just their economic policies. So it is not surprising that their currencies have done so well over time. Further, the currency of Brunei was not available in 1970. However, if measured from 1979, it rose 20% against the dollar. In fact, on a list of how all the world currencies have done since 1979, the Brunei dollar's 20% increase came in fifth.

Thus every country but two among the ten identified by *ICRG* as the most safe and least risky nations to invest in also had currencies that performed extremely well. And perhaps more important, *all* countries whose currencies have done the best over the long term have also been the safest countries in regard to economic risk, if not in overall risk. Belgium and Taiwan just miss the *ICRG* top-ten risk list:

Belgium is twelfth and Taiwan fourteenth. Malta is thirty-second overall but tied for first place in economic risk.

And what of the two least risky countries whose currencies didn't do all that well? Norway's krone has risen against most currencies in the past generation, but it is up in all that time by less than 10% against the U.S. dollar, compared to the stellar appreciation of over 200% for the Swiss franc.

That leaves, finally, the U.S. dollar. An optimist might say that the dollar, which has fallen so much in the past twenty years, is really undervalued, precisely because it is such a stable place when judged for country risk. That, indeed, may be true.

That said, however, we must consider the possibility that the markets have valued the dollar correctly and that the United States is perhaps not as stable as the country risk rankings would indicate, or that it is becoming a less safe place to invest as time goes by. If this is true, it does not bode well for the world. The United States is the only superpower left today, and the prospect of it becoming a more risky, less stable place is not a pleasant one. This is reason enough to hope that the U.S. dollar truly is undervalued and will rise to justify the fine view that most of the world has of American stability.

PART IV

▼

Profiting from the World's Fastest-Growing Stock Markets

▲

CHAPTER 15

▼

The Case for Investing Internationally

The economy of the world is getting bigger. The United States is becoming a smaller part of it. And more and more, it seems, the fastest-growing stocks, the highest-yielding CDs and bonds, the safest banks, and the currencies with the most promising long-term futures are turning up not in this country but overseas.

In the chapters that follow, you will discover surprising ways to make money in those remote markets (and in those currencies)—with or without the help of your broker.

How the World Is Changing

In 1970 the gross product of the world economy, as estimated by the Frank Russell Company, a leading financial adviser to institutional money managers, was slightly over $2 trillion. Of that, the United States contributed almost half. By 1989 the economies included in the Russell survey were producing goods and services each year worth over seven times that earlier figure, $14.5 trillion, with the United States contributing only about a third.

At the same rate of growth, the world could greet the year 2000 with its economy measurable at more than $50 trillion—with the United States playing a much smaller role than it now does.

There are plenty of reasons to think that the world economy will enjoy an even faster rate of growth as we move toward the turn of the millennium. Every week brings new technological developments that enable us to research, calculate, devise, produce, and communicate at a rate and to an extent that only a few years ago would have been considered so much science fiction. International cooperation to limit the dangers of war, to stabilize currencies, to assure health, to universalize education, to protect real and intellectual property, and to keep open the lanes for communication and trade between formerly remote parts of the world has reached an impressive level of success. So why should the state of the world economy not get better and better and grow at an even faster pace?

Another reason to be optimistic about the future world economy is the number of formerly backward countries that are now emerging and bringing with them a firm resolve to share in the wealth of the world. These countries now offer energies, resources, and skills they once seemed unable or disinclined to share with others.

Manmohan Singh, India's minister of finance, put it this way: "India is a new ball game. Our country is now prepared for big changes [in order to prosper]." Other formerly impoverished countries that have embraced economic reform, according to the World Bank, include Chile, Ghana, Indonesia, South Korea, Mexico, Morocco, and Turkey. Their rising economies already are a magnet for foreign investment. In time they may present attractive markets for other countries' goods, providing another thrust to a larger and larger world economy by the year 2000.

Where the Most Attractive Stocks Are Traded

The world's largest companies—Sony, Philips, Hoechst, Fiat, Procter and Gamble, Nomura Securities, Nestlé, Unilever, Toyota, Nippon Steel, Merck, and other well-known names—keep growing, spreading their influence worldwide, and predictably raising their dividends. As a result, they are the kind of companies that prudent investors like to put their money into. Yet, of the world's one hundred largest corporations, only 28% are based in the United States. The rest are located elsewhere. Shares in their profits are traded on stock exchanges, often at a great distance from Wall Street.

In 1970 the U.S. stock exchanges dominated the world; they represented 66% of its total market capitalization. In 1980 their share had declined to 50%. Then in just the next nine years it plummeted to 31%. In the same period Japan went from 15% of the world's market capitalization to an even larger share than ours—39%. Judging by the value of securities traded on our stock exchanges, we may no longer be the world's leader. Japan could be. The hot stocks are, more and more, traded in Tokyo, Seoul, Jakarta, Singapore, Frankfurt; fewer are traded on Wall Street.

If you remain solely in the U.S. stock market, you not only deprive yourself of most of the world's investments, you also give up a shot at the fastest-growing issues.

Morgan Stanley compared their worldwide index of major foreign markets to the S & P 500 for the years 1978 through 1989. In only one of those years did the U.S. market even come close to doing as well as the rest of the world. *In all of the other twelve periods,* the other world markets beat ours handily.

This helps to explain why advisers to U.S.-based pension and investment trusts—probably the largest investors in the world—are urging their clients to invest more overseas.

Why Institutions Are Investing More Overseas

At a recent presentation to pension fund managers, John M. Giles, vice-president of the Frank Russell Company, compared the riskiness and rate of return of a portfolio made up solely of domestic securities to another that included 70% domestic and 30% foreign stocks.

For a ten-year period ending in 1986, the purely domestic portfolio had an annualized rate of return of about 13.5% and an annualized risk level of 14.5%. By substituting foreign stocks in 30% of the portfolio, Giles pointed out, the annualized return goes up to nearly 17% (a gain of 4%), while the risk level actually drops a full percentage point. There is also an apparent benefit from an even smaller percentage of foreign stocks. In each year of the past decade, he said, a portfolio that had 20% of its assets in foreign stocks had a higher rate of return and lower volatility than a comparable domestic-only portfolio.

Pension funds will surely keep looking for the ideal mix of domestic and overseas investments. But for now, most are far short of the amount invested in foreign stocks that Giles and other consultants recommend. If they even approach Giles' ideal of 30% overseas, that surge in overseas investing would tend to make your investments in foreign stocks have an even higher yield and lower risk than they now offer.

"Ignore Foreign Stocks at Your Peril"

Large U.S. institutions (pension funds, insurance companies, banks, etc.) have trillions of dollars to invest. They must constantly find new ways to make their money grow, without taking inappropriate risks. This has come to mean investing more overseas.

Gary L. Bergstrom, president of Acadian Asset Management, is quoted as recommending that pension funds put fully half of their money abroad.

M. David Testa, chairman of Rowe Price-Fleming International, Inc., whose parent organizations manage over $67 *billion* for institutions and individual investors here and around the world, suggests that putting 30% to 50% of most portfolios overseas is probably right.

The *Financial Analysts Journal* said in 1991, "The international holdings of U.S. pension funds currently hover just below 4% of total assets. [That] could realistically approach 20% by the end of the decade. Globalization of portfolios may become *the* investment megatrend of the 1990s."

According to an article in *The New York Times* entitled "Ignore Foreign Stocks at Your Peril," the more than two hundred institutional clients of the Frank Russell Company are already almost halfway to being 20% invested overseas. Russell clients invested $400 million overseas in 1980; by 1990 the figure had grown to $28 billion (9% of what they were investing).

In the same article the *Times* predicted: "Despite the practical problems involved, it seems likely that American pension funds (with $2.7 trillion invested) will respond to the [Russell] research by increasing their overseas investments. Even a small shift [in their enormous funds] could feel like a tidal wave. One percent of $2.7 trillion is enough to buy the entire Austrian stock market—lock, stock and barrel."

Building Your Own Portfolio of Foreign Stocks (Not Recommended)

If you ever expressed to your broker an interest in investing overseas, chances are you got tepid encouragment in return. He or she may not understand foreign markets or have easy access to them.

If your broker *does* offer to buy some foreign securities for you through one of the firm's branch offices overseas, it may turn out to be a less profitable and more stressful experience than you hoped for. Trading on many foreign bourses is often thin and subject to volatility that could make you uncomfortable for periods of a week to several months. Also, for an American the price of admission to foreign stock markets can be high. You may have to pay as much as a 6% or more commission to buy securities on some foreign markets and another fat commission to sell them.

There are two ways to build your own portfolio of foreign investments that would not entail such high costs: closed-end single country and regional funds and American Depositary Receipts (ADRs). These are discussed at length in chapter 18.

Putting Your Overseas Portfolio in the Hands of Experts

Luckily there is no need for you to pick your own portfolio of foreign stocks. You can more quickly (and securely) diversify overseas through an international or global mutual fund based in the United States. By buying into one of those funds, you would—within a few days—hold shares in several dozen foreign companies. What's more, these stocks (and/or bonds) would have been chosen for you by an expert who has good reason to stay on top of them every day (something you can't be expected to do).

If you are now a shareholder in a major mutual fund family that also offers an international bond or stock fund, you need only call your fund's 800 number and say you want to switch some of your money to one of their international funds.

Letting Someone Manage Your Overseas Portfolio

There are now hundreds of international stock and bond mutual funds. They manage billions and billions of dollars both for big institutions and for investors like you. But their history is relatively short.

In 1978, when international mutual funds were all but unknown, the then little-known Templeton Growth Fund published the twenty-year growth of its shareholders' assets. That record put it at the very top of *all* mutual funds marketed in the United States in that period.

More surprising than the growth of its share value was the *nature* of Templeton Growth Fund's holdings. The title of the fund did not carry the word international, but that might well have been included. For twenty years John Templeton, operating out of a stately Southern-style mansion on Lyford Cay in Nassau, had quietly been putting into his fund's portfolio the most promising stocks he could find *anywhere*— even if they were listed on exchanges at the other end of the world.

Among United States–based mutual funds of that day, Templeton's was virtually alone in its willingness to go so far for an undervalued stock. For example, the Scudder International Fund, which actually started in 1953 as a Canadian corporation (becoming the first international fund available to U.S. investors), was still quite insignificant in 1978, with only about 0.1% of its current assets under investment. The T. Rowe Price International Stock Fund, which now has over a billion dollars under its management, making it just about the largest domestically based international fund, had not yet opened its doors in 1978. T. Rowe Price brought out its first international fund in 1980; they now offer American investors almost half a dozen funds through which to invest internationally.

Then in the second half of the eighties, when the pioneering international funds consistently beat the booming S & P average by about 5% annually, the mutual fund industry fell all over itself to provide funds that could be called international, global, Pacific rim, new Europe, emerging markets— anything that bespoke its foreignness. Fund companies also started a flood of new single-country, closed-end funds that now include at least one each for Chile, Brazil, Korea, Taiwan, Turkey, Singapore, Thailand, Ireland, and Malaysia,

two for Indonesia, four for Mexico, and half a dozen for
Germany.

How to Choose the Fund That's Best for You

International mutual funds come in all sizes. They charge
the whole range of sales loads: from none at all to the highest
allowed by law, 8.5%. And their charters permit them to
invest with such a wide assortment of restrictions (or lack of
them) that both conservative and aggressive investors can find
a comfortable place to bed down.

Every three months, *Barron's* publishes a survey of mutual fund activity, *Barron's/Lipper Mutual Funds Quarterly*,
based on the data that Lipper Analytical Services is constantly
compiling. The survey is roughly fifty tabloid-sized pages in
length and now comes as a pull-out section, so you can read
it at your leisure and file it for the future. The survey normally
appears in *Barron's* about the last week of January, April,
July, and October.

Each Barron's/Lipper quarterly survey provides a statistical overview of more funds than you will ever want to consider (well over two thousand). The cost is very modest—
only $2.50, including the full issue of *Barron's* in which it
appears.

Barron's/Lipper surveys contain an orderly listing of each
fund's three-month, one-year, and five-year performances,
their sales load and other fees, their dividend yield, the
amount of money they manage, the name of their portfolio
manager and how long he has been in charge, and even the
800 number to call if you want more information.

Aiming Where the Rabbit *Was*

You should be on guard when reading the "which mutual
funds did best" articles that probably appear every three
months in your favorite newspaper or financial magazine.
The remarkable performance of a quarterly winner could

tempt you to sign up on just that bit of information. And you might end up shooting "where the rabbit *was*."

The May 1991 Barron's/Lipper survey, for example, featured the top-performing fund of that quarter: the American Heritage fund, whose share price had increased 54% in only three months. But as *Barron's* was quick to point out, this spurt was not emblematic of the fund's past performance. Shareholders who'd been in the American Heritage fund for the prior five years had actually lost almost 40% of their holdings, even after that 54% rise was figured in.

You may want to go beyond the statistical information in *Barron's* to the more *qualitative* analysis provided by a set of biweekly reports that Morningstar, Inc., publishes called *Morningstar Mutual Funds* (MMF). You may find them in your library. Or you can begin a trial subscription and get surveys that cover more than a thousand domestic and international stock and bond funds. This would not only help you select a good international fund but enable you to reappraise the domestic mutual funds you now own.

MMF lays out the sort of analysis that financial planners like: the fund's major holdings, its portfolio turnover, expense ratio, the level of risk the fund embraces in order to achieve performance, its regional biases, and much more. This information is clearly, often graphically, presented; it is not at all hard to grasp. For more information about *Morningstar Mutual Funds,* call 1-800-876-5005.

Whether you use *Barron's* alone or *Barron's* in concert with *MMF,* or if you are comfortable making your initial selection based on the information we present in the next two chapters, here are a few criteria that will help you choose an international stock or bond fund that is more likely to make you richer over time.

Going Beyond Performance

The performances of the top international mutual funds generally travel along parallel lines. When foreign funds rise, they all seem to rise and by roughly the same magnitude. And as long as they take the trouble to hedge a rising dollar (and most do), they get helped and hurt by currency changes in much the same way. The largest of them, by virtue of the amount they must invest, have to be widely deployed around the world. Even though a fund may be overweighted in some markets, the fund's overall results are more likely to be akin to other funds than they are to be very different—so long as no market dominates its portfolio. If you pick a fund with a good three- to ten-year record, in the next ten-year period it will likely give you a total return on your money that keeps you happy.

So in making a fund selection, you should go beyond expected performance to the other factors that could make you glad you chose it. You should consider, for example, whether they levy a sales charge or not, how frugal the fund is likely to be in incurring expenses, how easy it is to get into the fund and out of it, whether they hedge currency changes, what kind of reports they periodically send shareholders, and so on.

Should You Pay a Sales Charge?

Most mutual funds are still sold through brokers, and for those funds you *have* to pay a sales charge (or load) that can reduce your investment by as much as 8.5% to start with. But that is no longer your only option.

In 1936 Scudder, Stevens and Clark pioneered the no-load fund. In a no-load fund you buy shares directly from the fund company and you pay only its current net asset value (what the portfolio would fetch if sold in the open market that day). No sales charge is involved. And when you leave, the fund company agrees to pay you the equivalent of the net asset value at that time for each share you are turning in. In other words, there is no redemption charge either.

Over the years, as investors increasingly questioned the need to pay a sales charge, no-load funds have gained a greater share of the mutual fund market. But there are two reasons still commonly given for avoiding no-loads and cheerfully paying a sales load of up to 8.5%:

1. Theoretically at least, if a fund organization employs salesmen and leaves the marketing to them, the fund can spend its full time managing your money to better returns. If it happened that way, you would be paying to get a better-performing fund, and that would certainly pay you back the sales charge before long.

2. Again theoretically, if your broker or investment adviser does the research needed to select a fund for you, you should end up with a better-performing fund than if you did the research yourself. The money you pay for the sales charge and then some should soon come back to you in fatter dividends, more frequent capital gains, and a higher share price.

Not everyone believes in the above reasons for paying a sales load, however. Sheldon Jacobs, publisher of *The Handbook for No-Load Investors,* contends: "There is no relationship between a fund's sales charge and its performance. In a typical year, if you look at the top 50 funds, you might find half of them were loads and half were no-loads. And there will always be a number of no-loads that are as good as any load fund. In the 20 years I have been recommending funds, I could always find a no-load fund that I felt had as much potential for the future as any load fund."

What about the guidance that brokers and financial planners provide you in selecting a fund for which, in part, you pay the sales charge? "For some people, that advice and counsel is no doubt worth something," Jacobs acknowledges. "But we have done a study since 1972 [that raises questions]. We found, in every instance, that a no-load investor (someone who made his own selection) is more likely to pick a top-performing fund than a load-fund investor assisted by a presumably knowledgeable broker. Maybe that's because the no-load fund investor has only one objective: to pick the best fund, whereas salesmen have several objectives, including the different commissions they can earn between funds."

If you decide you want to invest in a major international stock or bond fund but do not want to pay a sales charge, you'll find plenty of good choices. Harbor, Scudder, T. Rowe Price, and Vanguard all boast top-rated funds. All are resolutely committed to no sales charge either coming in or going out. They also maintain relatively low expenses for their shareholders' benefit.

The Advantages of a Mutual Fund Family

Most of the major fund families now offer at least one international stock and/or bond fund. And some go way beyond that. The largest of them—Fidelity, with about $100 billion under management—offers five major international equity funds, a global bond fund, an overseas annuity portfolio, and several foreign currency portfolios. T. Rowe Price offers six international stock and bond funds; Scudder, five. Vanguard has two large broad-based portfolios of overseas stocks and two index funds, one that specializes in the Pacific and the other in Europe.

The Freedom to Switch Your Money In and Out by Phone

When you pick an international fund that is a member of one of these families, you normally are given the freedom to call their 800 number and switch money you have in their money market fund, for example, into one of their international funds. Perhaps more important, if you are a market timer, you also get the freedom to switch *out* once you think that foreign stocks are high and vulnerable to a big correction.

Of the twenty-one top-rated international stock funds in the April 1991 *MMF* report, only five did *not* offer you the freedom to switch into and out of the fund with an 800 number call. Switching can be a two-edged sword, however.

The freedom to switch in and out of a fund is an invitation to get involved in short-term fluctuations of the market and the short-term performance of that particular fund. And that might not be good either for the soundness of your sleep or for your financial health.

Some fund companies wisely limit the number of switches you can make in any year. When you send for the fund's prospectus, which you must in order to start investing in it, pay particular attention to any restrictions on the number of switches you can make. And if the fund does *not* impose a restriction, you could end up richer if you impose restrictions of your own and use the privilege sparingly.

What Other Funds Do They Offer?

If you pick your international fund in part because it allows you free passage to other funds, make sure the other funds include a money market fund and at least some of the specialized funds you think could strengthen your performance now or in the future: a gold or natural resource fund, for example, an aggressive growth fund, a small-cap fund, or a tax-free bond fund.

Of the major fund groups that offer top-performing international mutual funds, Dreyfus allows you to switch among about twenty funds, a fairly broad menu for investment. Fidelity allows switches among its more than fifty mutual funds, although switches into certain areas require an additional sales charge. You can switch out of Harbor International, an *MMF* five-star fund, to seven other funds but that could be enough for you. Shareholders in the Japan Fund have the privilege of switching into any of twenty-six funds that bear the Scudder name.

Should You Pick a Fund by Its Manager?

Very often, fund companies have had to go a great distance to get managers who are effective in managing portfolios of foreign stocks. Vanguard, for example, entrusts the management of their International Growth Portfolio to Richard Foulkes of the London firm of Schroder Capital Management; he's been in charge since 1981 and works out of London. T. Rowe Price joined forces with two of the world's most esteemed international investment organizations, Robert Fleming in London and Jardine Fleming in Hong Kong, to create Rowe Price–Fleming International, which runs all T. Rowe Price international funds. John Templeton lives and works outside the United States, as do most of his top managers. While Scudder's top managers are headquartered in the United States, three of its management stars, Nicholas Bratt, Willie Holtzer, and E. Mark Turner, all cut their professional teeth not here but in London. And even before it offered its Europe Growth Fund to the public, Capital Management of San Francisco turned over stewardship of this fund to John R. Legat; he still runs it out of London.

Some fund companies keep their managers for a long time. Some (like Fidelity) are known for frequent changes. Some use a team method and don't name their managers. This will not always be made clear by the prospectus. But both *Barron's* and *MMF* make clear the fund manager's name and the date he or she first took charge.

Picking a fund whose successful manager has been in place for some time is just another assurance you can give yourself when making your selection.

What Can You Learn from the Prospectus?

The Securities and Exchange Commission requires all mutual funds to send you a prospectus before you invest money with them. Especially among international and global funds, the prospectus can provide surprising information.

You may learn, for example, that the fund you are about to invest in is authorized by its charter to invest not only in stocks but also options, warrants, repurchase agreements, stock index and currency futures contracts, etc. This may give you pause because—even though most international funds use these investment instruments—they do entail risk (especially to the degree they employ leverage) and/or extra cost. The prospectus of a fund may seek to reassure you by saying that the managers of the fund are *not* permitted to buy currency futures or otherwise engage in currency hedging procedures. Over time this prohibition may indeed work to the shareholders' benefit, but during a period in which the dollar is rising, that provision could put a dent in the fund's performance. The choice is yours: to pick such a fund or not.

The SEC wants you to read the fund's prospectus (which must reveal any unusual risk in the fund's normal operation) so that you can avoid risks you don't want to take. The funds are probably glad that the SEC does this. Much like the wording on a bottle of medicine or the installation instructions for a new computer, a candid prospectus does more than just protect the *shareholder:* it can be the *fund's* best protection against suits by shareholders who have lost money.

Invest in Haste, Repent in Leisure

Picking an international fund is, in a way, like picking a marriage partner. If you consider all the factors and avoid an impulsive selection, you may live to exult in your profits rather than repent in your leisure.

In the next chapter we offer profiles of thirty-two top-rated or top-performing funds and include (to the extent possible in so small a space) some factors that could help you pick a fund more wisely.

CHAPTER 16

▼

Thirty-three
Top-Performing
International
Stock Funds

It is often said that common stocks are your most promising long-term investments. Recently many investors have seen more promise in foreign stocks than in their domestic counterparts.

New, fast-growing stocks keep turning up along the Pacific rim, from Korea to Singapore; within the newly unified European Community; in the formerly communist bloc of Eastern Europe, freshly open to capital investment; and in the emerging economies of Latin America and South Asia. While this is an enormous hunk of geography to scout in order to find outstanding values, that is where international funds have to go to do their job. Judging from the results, they've done a commendable job of it.

In the ten-year period that started in 1979, international mutual funds outperformed the S & P 500 index (and most domestic mutual funds) by almost 4% a year. In 1986 leading international equity funds beat the rise in the S & P by almost 25%. And they outperformed again in 1987, beating the S & P average by almost 7% more.

This better-than–Wall Street performance sent mutual fund investors flocking to international funds. Fund companies responded with a whole raft of new products: international equity funds, global equity funds, equity funds specializing in one corner of the world or another, international bond funds, even international money-market funds.

International equity funds now manage over $25 billion in assets for 3 to 5 million American shareholders. According to some observers that's only a timid beginning.

The Tough Job of Running an International Fund

The men and women who run international equity portfolios face daunting challenges. They have at their disposal fewer experienced analysts, since fewer cover foreign stocks. It's more difficult and more expensive to visit the far-flung companies whose stocks seem attractive. Brokerage commissions are strikingly higher overseas, often making portfolio turnover an unattractive option. And overseas portfolio managers have to zig and zag around currency fluctuations in order to protect their dollar-based shareholders when the dollar rises or to exploit more fully their gains when the dollar falls.

How Morningstar Rates Overseas Funds

In this chapter we discuss the thirty-one funds that received either a four- or five-star rating for total risk-adjusted performance in one of the recent *Morningstar Mutual Funds* rankings. We also discuss two promising funds too new to have been rated, for a total of thirty-three.

MMF's ratings are arrived at by first tracking each fund's total return (net asset rise plus dividends and capital gains) against the average return of all international stock markets, against all mutual funds, and against all funds with the same investment objective. Then, after measuring the frequency and magnitude of each fund's past losses, *MMF* is able to identify what it considers the funds that reward their shareholders the most for the risks they have taken with the shareholders' money.

If you are a risk-adverse investor, you will like the fact that *MMF* gives heavy weighting to a fund's ability to avoid losses. If you are a more adventurous investor, the rankings will be helpful to you because we include those funds that get four or five stars even while they take greater-than-average risk.

Eleven of the thirty-three funds we survey fall in a category we call "devotedly international" because less than 5% of their assets are normally held in U.S. securities. A second group, "global equity funds," seeks profitable investments wherever they can find them and therefore do, on occasion, hold a substantial number of U.S. securities in their portfolios. There are nine global funds in our list. Lastly, we discuss twelve funds that seek to grow assets in special corners of the world, generally Europe or Japan or the far reaches of the Pacific.

How to Use Our Directory of Top-Rated Funds

The following miniprofiles of *MMF*'s top-rated international equity funds were abstracted from four recent reports (February 1990, April 1991, September 1991, and January 1992.) According to Kenneth L. Fisher, writing in *Forbes, MMF* provides "the best mutual fund coverage ever done. . . . Awe-inspiring is the only way to describe the information it offers." Its ratings, of course, do change as new information is received. While acknowledging that changeability, we salute past performance by showing the highest ranking each fund has achieved in any of the several ratings surveyed.

What follows should be considered merely as a starting point for your search. We advise you to:

1. Avoid trying to find a superwinner. The funds are listed alphabetically within their categories, not according to the number of stars they were accorded in any particular report. What you see next to the fund's name is the highest rating it has gotten in *any* recent ranking. So do not pay too much attention to the number of stars. What matters is whether the fund seems worthy and whether its objectives and its stomach for risk seem to match yours.

2. Go beyond our samplings. Most reports include the name of the fund manager and the year he or she took over responsibility for the fund. You will also find the 800 number to call for more information. We suggest that after reading this chapter, you make an initial selection of funds that appeal to you. Then go to a library and get a copy of the most recent *Barron's* quarterly survey (January, April, July, October). Check the recent performance of the funds you like. Also make sure that the fund manager we name is still running the fund. The *Barron's* listing will tell you that. Then call the 800 numbers of the funds that still attract you and request the funds' prospectuses. Be sure to ask any other questions you may have about fees, performances, privileges, etc. The telephone people are used to answering an amazing variety of questions from investors of all levels of sophistication. In our experience they do a good job.

If you like the kind of detail that *MMF* provides, you can try to find the most recent issue at your library or you can send for their trial subscription (call 1-800-876-5005) and get both the most recent and the upcoming issue. Together with what's here, that would give five different rankings of a fund to guide your judgment.

The Eleven Best "Devotedly International" Funds

There are three reasons to pick one or more of the funds in this category:

1. By including in your stock portfolio a number of foreign stocks, you make yourself less vulnerable to a major fall in the U.S. stock market.

2. Diversifying internationally allows you to share in faster-rising stock prices when other economies have a growth spurt and their stock markets outperform Wall Street, a not unusual happening in recent years. There wasn't a single year during the 1982–90 bull market on Wall Street in which our stock market was the top performer of all world bourses. In six of those eight years Wall Street's performance actually ranked close to the bottom of the world markets.

3. These devotedly international funds have the potential to deliver a currency advantage. As the managers move their assets around the world in pursuit of the fastest-growing overseas stocks, their portfolios are valued in foreign currencies (rather than in dollars); and very often the strongest stock markets also are valued in relatively strong currencies. That could make a big difference in the value of your holdings when the dollar takes a big fall and the currencies in which your foreign stocks are valued take a corresponding rise. Of course, when the dollar rises, you lose that advantage and could see your total return eroded unless your fund manager hedges the dollar's rise or moves into markets whose currencies are more closely aligned to ours. You have a right to expect your manager to do this. Ask about it when you call for fund information, and read the prospectus.

EuroPacific Growth Fund (☆☆☆☆☆), **1-800-421-0180.** This fund's largest holdings have often been in the United Kingdom, Germany, Japan, France, and Australia, giving U.S.

shareholders both broad geographical spread and strong diversification. Its gains have been gratifying as well, with shares almost tripling over the first six years of the fund's existence. Run by Capital Research and Management, Euro-Pacific charges a sales load of 5.75%. Shareholders have telephone switching to dozens of excellent domestic and international funds. Your initial investment need only be $250, and additions of as little as $50 are allowed. Multiple managers run this fund.

G.T. International Growth Fund (☆☆☆☆☆), **1-800-824-1580.** This fund's recent portfolios have often been heavily weighted in such major markets as Germany, Japan, Hong Kong, and the United Kingdom. At a time that was favorable, it also included a surprising 6% holding in Mexico. Started in mid-1985, the fund saw its assets per share just about triple in five years. The fund (run by G.T. Capital Management in San Francisco) charges a 4.75% sales load. It allows telephone switching to other G.T. funds. You can start an account for $500 and make additions of $100 or more. Manager: F. C. Wignall (since 1986).

Harbor International (☆☆☆☆☆), **1-800-422-1050.** This relatively small, young fund (started late in 1987 by Harbor Capital Advisors in Toledo, Ohio) won the hearts of the analysts at Morningstar by its underweighting in Japan when that market fell precipitously; its overweighting, at times, in such oft-neglected markets as Norway and Mexico; its prudent use of cash; and its more than doubling the returns of shareholders in three years. The fund charges no sales load and permits telephone switching. Minimum investment is $2,000; additions of $500 are permitted. Manager: Hakan Castegren (since 1987).

International Equity Fund (☆☆☆☆), **1-800-334-8332.** This fund, started late in 1985, came racing out of the starting gate with a 49% gain in 1986. A recent defensive posture has slowed its gain against the pack, but it still rates your consideration for its earlier performance. International Equity is a no-load fund but is not part of a group, permits no telephone switching, and requires a $2,500 initial investment. Manager: Mark J. Smith (since 1989).

Ivy International Fund (☆☆☆☆), 1-800-456-5111. *MMF* calls this fund "a class act," praising its portfolio's low turnover ratio and its dedication to high-quality, predictable earnings. The fund's occasional overweighting in such tiny markets as Spain and Singapore indicates a willingness to place unusual bets. The fund charges no sales load, offers telephone switching, and requires a $1,000 minimum purchase, with additions of any amount. Manager: Hakan Castegren (since 1986).

Kemper International Fund (☆☆☆☆), 1-800-621-1048. While this fund is included in our "devotedly international" category because it normally has a very small investment in the United States, portfolio manager Gordon Wilson (since 1989) hedged a large portion of the fund back into the dollar in 1991, which turned out to be a very good bet as the dollar firmed against other major currencies. Kemper International charges a 5.75% load, requires a $1,000 initial investment, permits telephone switching to other Kemper funds, and boasts one of the best ten-year total returns in its field while trying (but not always succeeding) to maintain a low-risk posture.

T. Rowe Price International Stock Fund (☆☆☆☆☆), 1-800-638-5660. Martin Wade and his team have run this fund since its inception in 1979. The fund has seen its share value rise almost fivefold, its total assets top a billion dollars, and the number of its shareholders reach more than 100,000. The fund is fairly broadly invested. It made a large and early bet in Mexico as that market took off. At one point, in fact, its $24 million investment in Teléfonos de México was among the fund's largest holdings. This is a true no-load fund, and it permits telephone switching to more than a score of well-managed domestic and international funds. Minimum initial purchase is $2,500 with additions of $100 or more after that.

Scudder International Fund (☆☆☆☆), 1-800-225-2470. This is the oldest of international mutual funds and one of its star performers. Nicholas Bratt has guided Scudder International since 1976 (he's now president of the Scudder mutual fund family). Bratt has a reputation as a trailblazer, having fathered the Korean Fund and exhibited a pioneering spirit in such emerging markets as Hong Kong, Thailand, Brazil, and the smaller markets of the Pacific rim. The fund is true no-load as are all of the Scudder-managed funds, both domestic and international. Shareholders have telephone switching privileges in and out of all these funds. The minimum initial purchase is $1,000, with additions of $100 or more after that.

Templeton Foreign (☆☆☆☆☆), **1-800-237-0738.** *MMF* has consistently given this fund its highest rating, taking note of its continuing top-quartile performance against all international funds (average total return for five years was more than 18% per year) and its lower-than-average risk exposure. Except for short-term defensive moves, this fund will not hold securities issued by companies or political entities in the United States. So U.S. shareholders are assured both diversification and a hedge against any big drop in the dollar. The fund charges a hefty 8.50% sales charge, the maximum allowable, and permits telephone switching to other Templeton Funds. A $500 investment gets you started, with additions of only $25 or more allowed. Manager: Mark Holowesko (since 1987).

Trustees' Commingled Fund International (☆☆☆☆☆), **1-800-662-7447.** This fund is part of the Vanguard mutual fund family. Batterymarch Financial Management, which has advised this fund for nine years—using a computer, rather than jet travel, to search for values—racked up an enviable record with an almost fourfold increase in share value. Through most of this period, Jarrod Wilcox has been the day-to-day manager. Vanguard levies no sales charge, permits telephone switching to a large number of domestic and international funds. Minimum investment required is very high, $10,000 or more, with additions of a not inconsiderable $1,000.

Vanguard World International Growth Fund (☆☆☆☆), **1-800-662-7447.** Schroder Capital Management of London and Richard Foulkes have run this fund since 1981 and have seen the net asset value of its shares grow almost five times.

The fund deems the United States off limits, which gives its American-based shareholders both market diversification and protection against a falling dollar. About 65% of fund assets are in long-term core holdings, with the rest poised for opportunistic investment. The reason *MMF* dropped this fund out of the "Winner's Circle" in its late 1991 ratings is ironic, considering the fact that the fund is managed out of London. *MMF* noted a wrong bet on currency risk that year and a failed guess that interest rates in Europe would drop that year, which only shows that being so close to the action with its London base didn't enable Schroder to guess right on Europe. Like all Vanguard funds, Vanguard World is no-load and gives shareholders wide telephone-switching privileges. Initial investment is relatively high, $3,000; $100 or more after that.

The Ten Top Global Funds

Global funds are hybrids. Portfolio managers try to blend the best values they can find all over the world, and should that include some (or quite a few) in the United States, that's just fine with them.

If at this moment you don't have a large stake in Wall Street, choosing a top-performing global fund could be the only stock market investment decision you have to make for quite a while. As Wall Street outperforms, you can expect to see more of your global fund invested on Wall Street. And as other markets show more promise, more of your investment should theoretically go there. As the dollar strengthens, more of your portfolio will tend to be denominated in dollars. When the dollar falls, you can expect more of your funds to scamper overseas, where they will deliver a currency bonus to you. Below are the ten top global funds as recently rated by MMF.

Dreyfus Strategic World Investing (☆☆☆☆☆), 1-800-782-6620. This fund, which doubled shareholders' reinvested val-

ues in its first four years, is ideal for very conservative investors. Portfolio manager Fiona Biggs has been in charge since
1987. Using the freedoms allowed her by the fund's charter,
she will hedge, short sell, trade, allocate her assets more dy-
namically than most managers, and go heavily into cash if
that seems advisable. Yearly turnover of more than 500% is
not uncommon here. This may limit Biggs' portfolio performance in big up-years but also cushions it during periods of
market shock. The fund beat 98% of its competitors during
1990, a down market for most of the world. The fund's sales
load is 3%. Shareholders have telephone switching access to
other Dreyfus funds. It takes $2,500 to get in, $500 after that.

    First Investors Global (☆☆☆☆), **1-800-423-4026**. This is
a fund with a glittering past and, for a brief period, a future
clouded by the departure of the portfolio manager that made
it famous. First Investors has since put the famous Wellington
Management and Jerrold Mitchell in charge, and that should
be a comfort to shareholders. *MMF* tracked Mr. Mitchell's
performance over two recent ranking periods and found he
didn't let shareholders down. Also a comfort to investors who
want a truly global reach to their investments is the fact that
a few years ago, First Investors merged some of their domestic
funds into First Investors Global, theoretically making it a
stronger performer on Wall Street. (Recently U.S. securities
made up over 30% of the portfolio.) Shareholders pay a 6.9%
sales charge and have telephone switching to other FI funds.
Initial investment is only $200, and $50 after that.

    Merrill Lynch International A (☆☆☆☆), **1-800-637-3863**.
The fund's recent below-average performance is surprising
considering Merrill Lynch's vast stock market connections
worldwide. Still, such desirable access to local information
gives shareholders reason to hope for better returns in the
future, while they continue to benefit from the fund's risk-
averse stance. Sales load is 6.5%. No telephone switching
privileges. Initial investment must be $1,000 or more; $50
after that. Manager: Fred Ives (since 1984).

    New Perspective Fund (☆☆☆☆☆), **1-800-421-0180**. This

fund's quadrupling of reinvested shareholder stakes in a ten-year period was done largely without portfolio fireworks. (Thirty percent or less turnover is more the rule than not.) A good slug of the portfolio is often in the United States, and the fund generally avoids emerging markets. Excellent performance and low risk has made this the largest fund in our survey, with more than $1.5 billion under management. The fund charges a 5.75% sales load. There is telephone switching to other Capital Research & Management funds. It takes only $250 to get in; $50 after that. Multiple managers.

Oppenheim Global (☆☆☆☆), 1-800-525-7048. Ken Oberman, who has managed this fund since 1981, is not afraid to base the more than one hundred issues in his portfolio on strong (occasionally trendy) themes, which he first identifies then fleshes out with the best stocks he can find in the category. One such bet, health care (both domestic and overseas), was a big winner. Oberman has shunned the pack by often avoiding the Pacific, despite its (at times) attractive rate of growth. The fund's five-year record puts it in the top third of all international funds. Sales load is 5.75%. Shareholders can telephone switch. Minimum purchase is $1,000 to start and $25 after that.

Paine Webber Atlas Global Fund (☆☆☆☆), 1-800-647-1568. Nimrod Fachler, overseas manager of this fund since 1986, scours the world for bargain stocks. He emphasizes low P/Es (ratio of the stock price to its recent annual earnings) but gives greater rein when he finds a powerful theme, like renewing a nation's infrastructure. He is also not averse to going heavily into cash, which mutes fund performance in quickly rising periods and helps a lot when markets fall out of bed. The fund also has a United States market manager, Ellen Harris, who prefers classic blue-chip growth stocks. The fund charges a 4.5% sales load, extends telephone switching privileges, requires an initial investment of $1,000 or more, then $100.

Putnam Global Growth Fund (☆☆☆☆), 1-800-225-1581. This fund has often had a large stake in the U.S. market, mixing such institutional favorites as Philip Morris with, for example, a basket of beaten-down technology stocks. The fund charges a 5.75% sales load. Telephone switching is allowed. Initial purchase must be $500 or more, with $50 the minimum after that. Managers: Regan/Beck (since 1988).

Scudder Global Fund (☆☆☆☆☆), 1-800-225-2470. Recently, this fund's performance put it in the top 10% of all international funds, quite an accomplishment considering its conservative emphasis on the private market value of the stocks it picks. Portfolio manager William Holtzer (since 1986) early declared his disenchantment with what he deemed overowned telecommunication stocks, the level of inflation in Europe, and the overheated economies of some emerging countries. All of which is meant to say that he is a cautious investor. Like all Scudder funds, this is true no-load, with full telephone switching. Minimum initial investment is $1,000; $100 after that.

SoGen International Fund (☆☆☆☆☆), 1-800-628-0252. This fund is not designed to outperform in bull markets, but it is widely respected for its steadfastly conservative nature. Manager Jean-Marie Eveillard has traditionally avoided firms with excessive debt levels, overvalued markets, and of course, the prospects of recession. His typical allocation is 40% to 50% in stocks, 25% or so in bonds, and the rest in cash. Through the years, the fund's performance has been very good despite its strong aversion to risk. The fund charges a 3.75% load. It offers no telephone switching privileges. Minimum initial investment, $1,000; $100 after that.

Templeton Growth Fund (☆☆☆☆) 1-800-237-0738. In 1954 this pioneering fund so successfully found fast-rising stocks outside the United States it sent other fund groups scurrying offshore, too. Managed since its inception by the venerable Sir John Templeton, the fund traditionally holds a substantial stake in the United States market, heavying up there when Sir John finds attractive values on Wall Street, and moving out when he sees greater values elsewhere. In the past fifteen years, it has given shareholders an average total return of over 16% annually. Sales charge is 8.5%, minimum initial investment is only $500 with additions of $50 or more after that. Telephone switching to other Templeton funds.

Ten Funds That Specialize in a Corner of the Globe

A specialized portfolio (the hallmark of the funds we next cover) is by its very nature low in diversification. As such, these funds also are vulnerable to a general downturn in the region in which they are required to invest. Most of the funds next listed once performed spectacularly but, in their most recent ranking, showed the scars of investing either in Europe or Japan when those areas were having a bad year.

DFA Japan Small Company Portfolio (☆☆☆☆☆), 1-310-395-8005. This fund is a no-fooling risk taker, and its performance has varied from incredibly good to awful. Its early five-year performance earned MMF's highest rating, but its showing in the most recent three or four years dropped it to below average. Still, if you believe in the future of the Japanese economy (and many experts do) and if you see greater long-term growth in smaller companies, this is worth looking into. The fund is marketed primarily to institutional investors and requires a $50,000 initial investment. But there is no sales load. No provision is made for telephone switching or even an 800 number. This fund is clearly for heavy hitters in for the long pull. Manager: Rex Sinquefield (since 1986).

Fidelity Europe Fund (☆☆☆☆), 1-800-544-8888. The promise of this fund is the promise of a unified and booming Europe. And the problems of this fund's performance mirror the problems Europe has had absorbing the formerly communist eastern half of the continent. Manager changes are frequent. Fund performance has been hurt on occasion by a policy that prevents currency hedging. The fund charges a 3% sales charge and offers telephone switching to other Fidelity funds. Minimum initial investment is $2,500, $250 after that.

Financial Strategic Europe Fund (☆☆☆☆), 1-800-525-8085. Invesco Funds offers this portfolio aimed at Europe, and another (listed next) with holdings in the Pacific. Again the recent weak performance can be traced to high interest rates and weak economies in Europe. But if you believe in Europe, look forward, not back. This fund has done well in the past and could again. The fund charges no sales load. Telephone switching is possible. Minimum purchase is only $250 to start, $50 after that. Multiple managers run the fund. (since 1990).

Financial Pacific Basin Fund (☆☆☆☆), 1-800-525-8085. Shareholders saw their holdings triple in the first three years (1984 to 1987) giving their fund the highest rating possible. They then had to settle for much more anemic gains, and the rating dropped to below average. The fund is still positioned to gain and lose with the Pacific as a whole. The fund levies no sales charge, permits telephone switching, has a low $250 minimum initial investment, with $50 after that. Manager: Paul Parsons (since 1988).

G.T. Europe Growth Fund (☆☆☆☆), 1-800-824-1580. Like all Europe funds, this one had to step lively during the morning-after effect that followed the post–Berlin Wall euphoria. It also had to deal with the unfamiliar phenomenon of a surging dollar (first half of 1991). Because of the dollar damage to shareholder assets, the fund scampered back into as much as a 50% dollar hedge. In late 1991 it was still convinced that investments in Europe, while not wildly promising, would show slow, steady asset gains. The fund charges a 4.75% load. Telephone switching is permitted. Minimum investment is only $500, with $100 or more after that. Manager: John Legat (since 1984).

G.T. Japan Growth Fund (☆☆☆☆☆), 1-800-824-1580. At the beginning of 1991, G.T. Japan's new manager, Marshall Auerback, took a dim view of the Japanese economy and shifted more of his portfolio to the stocks of Japanese companies whose sales do not depend heavily on the local economy; he took a further defensive stance by favoring stocks with unusually low P/Es. He also hedged his Japanese currency exposure back into a firming dollar. After a five-fold growth in as many years, the value of shareholders' holdings took a fall in 1990 (that may explain the new manager) but then started to come back. At the end of 1991, G.T.'s top management decided that Japan was bottoming out and increased their exposure to Japan in many of their funds. If that guess turns out to be correct, this fund—as G.T.'s flagship in Japan—will benefit the most. The sales load is 4.75%. Telephone switching is possible. Minimum investment is $500; $100 after that.

G.T. Pacific Growth (☆☆☆☆☆), **1-800-824-1580**. Unlike G.T. Japan, this fund has free rein to roam the Pacific for undervalued stocks. When the Japan market started to look dangerous, F. C. Wignall, portfolio manager since 1987, underweighted Japan, concentrating mostly on the bluest of the Japanese blue chips, and placed the extra cash in Hong Kong, Singapore, and Malaysia. With his emphasis on emerging markets, the fund is not immune from volatility; that comes with the territory. Like other GT funds, the sales load is 4.75% and telephone switching is permitted.

Japan Fund (☆☆☆☆), **1-800-535-2726**. Japan Fund, a pioneer in the region, started its life as a closed-end fund more than ten years ago and did so well the shareholders forced it into open-end status to realize their gains. It is still pioneering, often holding aggressive positions in the stocks of smaller, faster-growing Japanese firms. With that weighting and with attendant currency risk, Japan Fund is not for light sleepers. It has the power to dazzle (bringing in returns that put it close to the top of funds that invest in Japan) but also to disappoint. The fund does not charge a sales load and permits telephone switching among all Scudder funds (the family that attended at its birth). A thousand dollars gets you in, with $100 additions after that. Multiple managers run the fund (since 1990).

Merrill Lynch Pacific Fund (☆☆☆☆☆), **1-800-637-3863**. From 1981 to 1987, shareholders in this fund saw their reinvested assets rise fourfold. Since then the growth has slowed, and in 1990 it actually retreated, but not by much—indeed, much less than the Japanese market, which accounted for 70% of its assets. The fund's portfolio manager since 1983, Stephen Silverman, is brusquely candid about the Japanese market. But his posture of "no illusions now" (reflected by his willingness to put a lot of money into "puts" on the Japanese market as a whole) "but grand expectations later" could set the fund up for better-than-average performance in the years ahead. The fund does not permit telephone switching. That and its hefty 6.5% sales load makes it less than ideal for any but long-term investors. Minimum initial investment is $250; $50 after that.

Nomura Pacific Basin Fund (☆☆☆☆☆), 1-800-833-0018. Like most funds that trawl in the Pacific, Nomura Pacific was able to boast a better initial five-year performance than it managed thereafter. Being of Japanese parentage, this fund offers its shareholders expert knowledge of the market. It levies no sales load. But it doesn't allow telephone switching and requires a whopping $10,000 initial investment, with additions that have to be $5,000 or more. Manager: Takeo Nakamura (since 1985).

Index Funds: Like Flying on Automatic Pilot

A recent newspaper headline said a lot about the performance of many mutual funds, particularly in the United States: "Funds *finally* Beat the Averages."

This has led some investors to wonder: "If beating the Dow-Jones Average is so tough for a fund, why should my fund manager even *try* to pick the right stocks? Why doesn't he just buy every stock in the Dow-Jones Index (or the Morgan Stanley International Index)? Then both of us could sleep better."

Some years ago, the people at Vanguard took precisely that point of view. They brought out a fund that closely matches the stocks in the S&P 500 Index. Since they don't have to pay a gang of analysts to select the stocks, the fund's expenses are lower, allowing shareholders to end up with more of their stock market gains. Vanguard index funds have done well, and recently management pushed that idea into the international arena. In 1990, under the direction of George Sauter, they started the Vanguard International Index Fund. This fund is still too new to get a *MMF* rating, but shareholders have reason to be satisfied. Lack of a rating should not concern you because these funds employ no sophisticated strategies. They merely try to reflect the markets they cover as accurately as possible. You can buy either this fund's European portfolio or its Pacific portfolio. Or, of course, you can mix both parts and decide whether you want to favor one region or the other.

   Vanguard European Index Fund (not rated), 1-800-662-7447. This fund generously samples the European section of stocks that make up the Morgan Stanley EAFE (Europe, Australia, Far East) Index and fairly represent the index by country, capitalization, industry, and fundamental investment characteristics (earnings, P/E, and the like). The fund expenses at the start were running as low as 0.3% (against an average of close to 2% for most international funds). This partly explains the gratifying 11.73% returns that shareholders enjoyed in just the first six months. There is no sales charge. Telephone switching to the full roster of Vanguard funds is permitted. Minimum initial investment must be $3,000, with additions of only $100 after that.

   Vanguard Pacific Index Fund (not rated), 1-800-662-7447. This is the Pacific counterpart of the fund described above. Expenses were almost as low as the European index fund, and returns to shareholders were even higher, 21.95% in the first six months. Because this fund so closely follows the fortunes of the volatile Japanese market, you might sleep better if you bought it in conjunction with the European index fund. This fund also charges no sales fee. Telephone switching is allowed. Your first investment must be $3,000 or more, with additions of $100.

▼

CHAPTER 17

The Best
International
Bond Funds

In 1990 the dollar fell with a thud. So did American interest rates. Many American investors fell into a panic, searching for any fixed-income vehicle outside the falling dollar that would give them a decent return on their savings. They discovered international bond funds and, in that year alone, poured over $10 billion into them. Even though the dollar bottomed in early 1991 and started to rise again, there was no stopping the stampede into global bond funds. In the first five months of that year, Americans invested $6.4 billion that way, a 72% increase over the same period in 1990—even though the former currency windfall had turned into a currency risk.

Why Americans Are Drawn to International Bond Funds

Perhaps your simplest way to earn high interest rates while escaping a falling dollar is your own "Swiss" bank account (not necessarily in Switzerland) denominated in any rising currency (not necessarily the Swiss franc). In 1990, however, foreign bank accounts were still a relatively esoteric investment for most Americans. They preferred to dial an 800 number and switch out of their U.S. government or municipal bond funds (denominated, of course, in dollars) into an international bond fund. These promised higher yields and were denominated in a basket of currencies that, at the time, were rising in value against the dollar.

Over time, good foreign bonds have yielded 50 to 75 more basis points (0.5 % to 0.75 % more interest) than comparable U.S. bonds. So they have represented superior real return on your money and a good long-term investment regardless of short-term fluctuations in the dollar. But if you pick the right year to go into international bonds (ideally when the dollar is starting to fall) you can do exceptionally well. In 1982, 1985, and 1986, for example, those funds produced an average total return of about 30 % per year. In 1983 and 1984, however, as the dollar was rising to a temporary crest, the total return of these funds almost disappeared after currency conversion was taken into account. But then they bounced back when the dollar fell again. And fell when the dollar rose again.

Obviously, with that kind of currency fluctuation, the skill of the fund's portfolio manager becomes very important. The manager must not only find bonds of the right issuer, the right maturity, and the right currency, but he or she must also be quick to either hedge those investments once their currencies come under pressure, or switch the threatened part of the portfolio into dollar-denominated or dollar-related instruments.

One manager who caught the tide of a tumultuous year for international bonds, 1990, and made his shareholders a lot richer was F. Mark Turner. A youngish Englishman who came to the United States about seven years ago, Turner rose to managing director of the Scudder International Bond Fund. Turner's portfolio ended 1990 with almost 30% of its bonds in European currencies, a bit more than that in North America, with the rest in the Pacific and in Scandinavia. And it led the pack for the year with a total return of 21.1%, reflecting in part the decline in the dollar that year.

A firming dollar in 1991 put a crimp in the performance of most international bond funds, including Scudder's. But by hedging his international positions and switching some funds into dollar and dollar-related investments, Turner still landed on his feet. In fact, in mid-1991, when *The New York Times* ranked all bond funds—both domestic and international—an international bond fund, surprisingly, stood at the top of their list. It was Scudder's.

The Currency Advantage Versus the Currency Risk

International bond funds (like their domestic counterparts) should be thought of as long-term investments. Foreign bonds not only normally pay their holders higher dividends, they also have the potential to benefit from growth of an economy and a rise in its currency.

When the dollar is falling, the total return on these bonds will be higher because they will benefit from the conversion of rising foreign currencies into (more) dollars. And when interest rates are falling overseas, your investment in foreign bonds will be worth more because you have locked in the old, higher rates; so the net asset value of your international bond fund will rise.

When the dollar is rising, the currency advantage will, of course, not be there. And the managers of your fund will have to utilize sophisticated hedging techniques to protect your investment (which is in foreign currencies) against the erosive effect of a further rise in the dollar. These hedging techniques, while necessary as the dollar rises, do not come without cost. It is not unusual for hedging to dent total return by 2%. But then again, when the dollar is rising quickly (as

it did for a short period early in 1991, by as much as 15%),
2 % seems like a very small price to pay.

The Top International Bond Funds

In their late 1991 report on international bond funds, *Morningstar Mutual Funds* avoided giving either of its top ratings
to any international bond fund. This was in contrast to earlier
that year when five international bond funds were accorded
either a four- or five-star rating, and in contrast, too, to a
very recent report which gives a long overdue five-stars to
Scudder International Bond Fund.

What led to the change in 1991? After the dollar started
to rise in early 1991, *MMF* saw risk in these funds—not just
interest-rate risk (which all bond funds are exposed to) but
especially currency risk—that was out of line with the profits
the funds were delivering.

It is true that naive investors who just chase higher interest rates available in international bonds without any heed to
fluctuations in currencies are exposing themselves to risks
they have no way of assessing; such investors had best stay
out of the category entirely. But for investors who take a
long view of bond investment—and long-term bonds are, of
course, long-term investments—international bonds and the
best funds that invest in them are well worth looking into.
What's more, for investors who follow the major trends in
currencies and so are in a position to profit from them (after
reading this book, you should count yourself among them),
the opportunity that international bonds offer is especially
attractive. It is the chance to earn a higher-than-average rate
of interest and to gain on foreign currency valuations whenever the dollar takes a dive. That chance has been very profitable for some in the past and, no doubt, will be once again.

With that in mind, we list below the international bond
funds that *MMF* mentioned favorably in their recent rankings.
Fidelity Global Bond Fund, 1-800-544-6666, delivered

an average return of nearly 11% in its first four years, charges no sales load, and requires a $2,500 initial purchase, with $250 additions after that. Free telephone switching to all Fidelity no-load funds.

Freedom Global Income Fund, 1-800-225-6258, had an average total return in its first four years of nearly 14%. The fund charges a delayed 3% sales load, permits telephone switching, and requires a minimum $1,000 initial investment, with additions of $100 or more after that.

MFS Worldwide Governments Trust, 1-800-225-2606, formerly called Massachusetts Financial International Bond Fund, has merely changed its name, not its focus on total return (as opposed to income). And it has taken some risks to achieve the impressive total return that shareholders enjoyed during the fund's first nine years in business—an annual average of 16.7%. Sales load is 4.75%; minimum initial investment is $1,000, with $50 increments after that; and telephone switching is allowed.

Paine Webber Global Income Fund, 1-800-647-1568, in its first three years, had an average total return of 12% on relatively short maturities (four years or less) that yielded about 10%. The rest of the return came primarily from currency conversion as the dollar fell. The fund's focus remains primarily on income. It charges a deferred sales load of 5%, fairly hefty for a bond fund. No telephone switching is possible. Minimum initial purchase is $1,000, with increments of $100 or more after that.

Putnam Global Governmental Income Trust, 1-800-225-1581, has an affinity for bonds from the English-speaking world, often holding a large chunk of its portfolio in the United States, Canada, Australia, and the United Kingdom. Its average total returns of over 12% per annum since inception in 1987 makes its 4.75% sales load more palatable. Shareholders can switch by phone to other Putnam funds. Minimum investment to start is $500, and only $50 after that.

Scudder International Bond Fund, 1-800-225-2470,

charges no sales fee at all. Purchases and redemptions are made at net asset value. Telephone switching to dozens of Scudder Funds is permitted. Initial minimum investment is $1,000, with additions of $100 or more after that.

Templeton Income Fund, 1-800-237-0738, has been good enough at anticipating currency and interest rate changes to deliver a more than 10% return over five years. It charges a 4.5% sales load, requires $500 initial investment (with $25 additions), and allows telephone switching to some of the most respected overseas funds.

Van Eck World Income Fund, 1-800-221-2220, which was previously accorded the highest *MMF* rating, delivered an average total return of about 13% in its first four years, mostly with short maturities and a U.S. position close to zero. The fund charges a 4.75% sales load (slightly on the high side), but for that price, shareholders have enjoyed a high return with lower than industry-level risk. Phone switching is permitted. Minimum investment, $1,000; $100 after that.

Of all the bond funds covered in this chapter, the only ones you can buy without a sales charge are: Fidelity Global Bond Fund and the Scudder International Bond Fund.

Should You Be Long-term or Short-term in International Bonds?

There are domestic short-term bond funds (fully invested in dollar instruments) and global short-term bond funds. Both usually deliver higher yields than money-market funds and maintain an asset value that is almost as stable. Their net asset values do fluctuate with the market value of the portfolio's holdings. But they do not fluctuate nearly as much as medium- or long-term bonds.

Short-term global bond funds offer greater stability against unwanted changes in interest rates. What interest rates they lock in are locked in for only a year or so. So compared to bonds with longer maturities, the value of the bonds doesn't rise as much when interest rates fall in a country, nor does it fall as much when interest rates rise there. They are, as the name suggests, an investment made to capture a superior yield for a relatively short period of time.

But being denominated largely in foreign currencies, they are as open to the whipsaw effect of changing foreign exchange rates as are long-term international bond funds. So not uncommonly, they also utilize the hedging techniques mentioned above to protect the dollar-adjusted net asset value that is paid to shareholders when they redeem shares.

In November 1991, for example, the two most popular short-term global bond funds—the Blanchard Short-Term Global Bond Fund (1-800-922-7771) and Scudder Short-Term Global Income Fund (1-800-225-2470)—were dealt a shock to the value of their portfolios when tiny Finland, whose currency had been linked to the Common Market's, suddenly decided it had to let that currency float. That sudden action knocked down the exchange rate of the markka by 12%. The effect on Blanchard and Scudder investors was a 0.5% loss off the price of their shares.

Even Experts Take Unwise Risks

What is surprising is that both funds were reported to have 10% of their portfolios invested in the obligations of such a tiny country. Normally, they would probably not have invested so much in Finland but for two conditions: first, the yield on Finland's three-year government notes was above average (about 12% at the time of the float that devalued the currency); and second, being linked to the European Monetary System gave the markka the illusion of greater stability than Finland was able to maintain.

There were danger flags flying shortly before the float. Interest rates on one-month notes had risen all the way to 27% and overnight rates went to 40% just before the government's action—surely a sign that something was rotten very close to Denmark. If some of the most prestigious money managers in this field were not able to protect their funds against an action such as Finland's, surely you could not be expected to do better on your own. And both Blanchard Short-Term Global and Scudder Short-Term Global—despite their lapse on the Finnish markka—continue to deliver consistent profits for their shareholders.

Since short-term international bond funds are clearly short-term investments, one should probably avoid investing in them without a good sense of how the dollar is likely to perform in the immediate future against the currencies that the fund's portfolio reflects. A big currency shift would make them less attractive than a simple domestic money-market fund.

This, of course, brings up the question of whether you should even try to time your investments to take advantage of or protect yourself against short-term fluctuations in the value of the dollar.

Should You Try to Time Your International Bond Investments?

Peter Lynch, who ran the remarkable Magellan Fund for more than a decade and delivered tenfold profits and more to his shareholders, has been quoted as saying, "We don't market time. We don't know how to. When I think the market is going to go up, it goes down and the other way round. So, we stay fully invested all the time."

To time internationally, you would have to know a lot about a lot of markets. You avoid this need when you invest for the long haul and leave market timing to the manager of your international mutual fund. His or her need to perform against competing mutual funds should put the pressure on to do whatever timing seems advisable.

Later in the book we'll try to show you how to time the dollar against other currencies. Once you master that, you can

TABLE 6

Return of International Funds

Year	Bond Fund Total Return	Stock Fund Total Return
1982 (weak dollar)	29.46%	9.85%
1983	1.55%	29.87%
1984	2.34%	−3.87%
1985 (weak dollar)	29.79%	40.81%
1986 (weak dollar)	30.17%	43.12%
1987 (weak dollar)	21.33%	12.14%
1988	6.33%	16.46%
1989	6.16%	24.13%
1990 (weak dollar)	13.88%	−11.90%

raise your investment in international mutual funds whenever you feel the dollar is far too high and due for a fall, and you can cut back a little on those funds when you feel the dollar is clearly too low and due for a rise.

Look at table 6 to see the average total return of the international funds covered by *MMF* during the years 1982 to 1990. As you can see, bond funds were a purer play on the weakness of the dollar. Stock funds rose and fell largely on the performance of the foreign markets themselves, although the dollar had its effect too.

CHAPTER 18

▼

Those Sexy
Single-Country,
Closed-end Funds
and ADRs

When you receive the prospectus of a United States—based international (stock or bond) mutual fund, you will discover that the prospectus takes some pains to point out that international investing has costs and risks that investing solely in the United States does not entail. That is why, earlier in the book, we made it clear that we do not recommend the average U.S. investor go into foreign investing on his or her own. We also said that there *are* ways that more adventurous U.S. investors *can* handle their own overseas investments without the extra costs and with fewer of the risks that are encountered when trying to buy securities on foreign courses.

This chapter will cover two of those ways:

1. Closed-end funds. If you know in which parts of the world you want to invest your money, you'll find *single-country* closed-end funds a convenient instrument for pinpoint investing. Closed-end *regional* funds do a similar job

but take in a little more territory and thereby add some diversification. By buying closed-end foreign funds, you do get an opportunity to exercise your judgment about when and where to invest. You also enjoy professional help—a trained portfolio manager who selects the most promising securities for you and also promises to stay on top of them.

2. American Depositary Receipts. If you find specific companies overseas attractive, it's quite possible for you to invest in their stocks without going overseas or without paying a lot of money in commissions. Hundreds of foreign stocks are now traded on the New York Stock Exchange, the American Stock Exchange, or Over-the-Counter (OTC) through American Depositary Receipts or ADRs. You can buy and sell them much the way you do any American stock.

Closed-end Funds

Closed-end funds (originally called trusts) have been around for almost two hundred years, starting in the early nineteenth century in Belgium. Usually, closed-end funds are started to satisfy a narrow investment purpose and with a specific pool of money to invest, a pool that only gets larger if the assets are successfully invested. Unlike open-end funds (usually called mutual funds), closed-end funds get their pool of money by selling shares on a stock exchange. Thereafter, unless the fund decides to raise more money through a subsequent public offering of stock, the only way you can buy or sell shares in the fund is on the open market through your broker, just like any other stock.

The three principal reasons for buying a closed-end fund are:

1. You want to achieve the same narrow investment purpose the fund's managers are pursuing. If, for example, you want to invest in gold-mining stocks or utility stocks or

stocks in an emerging economy like Korea's or Malaysia's, you can find closed-end funds aimed at each of those objectives.

2. A closed-end fund can provide you with an "open sesame" to promising stock exchanges that are (by local government regulation) largely closed to Americans. The Korean and Brazilian stock markets are just two of these. Fortunately, the Korea Fund and the Brazil Fund solve the problem very nicely, and they have been popular with American investors.

3. Closed-end funds can sometimes be bought at a substantial discount from what the stocks in the fund sell for on the local exchange—i.e., at less then their "real" worth. That's because the fund shares are traded here, in the United States, not in the country where the underlying stocks are traded. When interest in the fund drops here, so will its publicly traded shares. Sometimes that will bring the price down 15% to 20% below the net asset value of the fund's holdings on, say, the Seoul or Zurich or São Paulo exchange. Then the fund is said to be trading at a discount to its net asset value, and you have an apparent or real value open to you.

Cherchez le Discount or Not?

Because closed-end funds represent a portfolio of actual stocks, you can say that a share in the fund's portfolio is worth a specific amount at the end of each trading day. The portfolio of the Korea Fund, for example, might on a specific day be worth $10.57 a share in Seoul. But because Korea limits the amount of outside investment in their stock market and because the country has had a strong, emerging economy, investors in this country have generally been willing to pay quite a bit more for the portfolio of the Korea Fund than what the same stocks are selling for in Seoul. American investors might, for example, pay $13.25 a share for the Korea Fund on the same day that the stocks in the fund's portfolio were selling in Korea for $10.57 a share. The difference be-

tween the two prices represents a 25.35% premium above a
net asset value of $10.57. The premiums (or discounts) for
many closed-end funds are computed for you each week in
Barron's, Wall Street Journal, The New York Times,
and other publications. In this instance, the quotation in the
paper would read "Korea Funds NYSE 10.57 13
¼ +25.35%."

If you are a value investor, this Korea Fund premium
may be unappealing to you. (But be aware that its premium
has run as high as 120% and most of its shareholders are
quite happy with the profits they have made.)

Some other (often *most* other) closed-end funds trade at
a discount to their net asset value, as in "Chile Fund -
NYSE   33.79   26 ¼ – 20.83%" In this case the holdings of
the Chile Fund were selling for over $7 a share less than what
the same group of stocks were selling for in Santiago.

Since a discount represents real money, it's worth considering when you buy shares. If you invest in a discounted
country fund that you feel has a very good future—a future
the general investing public apparently does *not yet* see (else
the fund would not still be selling at a discount)—you can
hope that as soon as the investing public catches up with
your judgment, the discount will narrow or disappear or even
become a premium over the value the portfolio's stocks have
on their local exchange. As that happens, whatever gain you
make on the fund itself is increased by the degree to which
the discount has narrowed and/or been replaced by a premium. For example, let's say you had bought the Mexico
Fund when its net asset value was $12.00 a share in Mexico
City and the shares in the fund were selling in New York for
$9.60, or at a 20% discount. Then, let us also say that after
two years the net asset of the holdings in Mexico City rose
to $17.00 and the former discount completely disappeared;
you could then sell your shares for $17.00 each. So while the
stocks in your fund had gone up only about 40% in two
years, you could have netted a more than 75% gain by buying
at $9.60 and selling at $17.00 a share.

The foregoing example is typical of the way closed-end funds trade. When shares in the fund's holdings are going up in value, the market will likely be aware of this and the fund's discount in New York is more likely to narrow or disappear, thereby increasing the profits you have made. And when shares in the fund are falling on its local exchange the discount at which you bought will cushion your shares against a fall here—at least until the New York market takes note.

Generally, as the price of a fund that had been selling at a premium in New York begins to fall and approaches what the portfolio will fetch on its local exchange, its rate of fall slows. In effect, reality sets in. Not so when the public is wildly bidding up its shares and giving it a higher and higher premium. Reality has nothing to do with such a situation, and the local value at such times seems to have little effect on the fund's selling price. When shares in the Korean Fund were heading toward a 120% premium in New York, the Korean market was not bidding up its shares nearly as sharply. They knew what those companies were worth. We here only fantasized what the future held for them.

There are dozens of single-country, closed-end funds to choose from. Many of these represent emerging economies, and it is not uncommon for those to sell at a discount to their net asset value. When any of these economies takes off (as Mexico did in the late eighties), you can expect the local stock market to explode upward. And the closed-end fund that covers it—especially if you bought it at a discount—could become an investment that gives you a lot of pleasure.

We can't mention emerging economies without mentioning the special risks you face when investing in any currency that has a bad history of sudden devaluation or continuous erosion of value against the dollar. In chapter 14, you will find a listing of the safest and the most risky currencies. Take that into consideration before you buy the shares of a closed-end fund that are denominated in a currency you're not sure of. You buy the shares in dollars, to be sure, but that is not the base currency of your holding; rather, you are invested in the currency of the local foreign market.

There is another reason to be cautious about emerging-country funds. In any world wide downturn they can be expected to be hit hardest, especially if they have had a big run up. It is the opinion of some analysts (Chris Weber among them) that the unwinding of the huge world debt created in the eighties will tend to depress world markets until a healthier debt-to-asset ratio is achieved.

How the Typical Closed-end Fund Is Launched

How a closed-end fund starts and when you are best advised to buy it might be clearer if we concoct a fictional example. The facts presented here about the Peru Fund are bogus, but they are descriptive of many closed-end, single-country funds.

There is no Peru Fund, and given the level of political unrest in that country and its poor reputation in the international banking community, it would be nearly impossible to sell such a fund now or in the near future. But for the moment let's imagine that the Peru Fund had been launched early in 1989, when single-country, closed-end funds were sprouting like crabgrass in June and Americans couldn't get enough of them.

The Launching of the Peru Fund

It is late in 1988. A large financial institution in Boston with special ties to Peru (Back Bay Capital Management, let's call it) notes that the political situation in Peru is trending better and that stocks on the Lima exchange are selling at ridiculously low P/Es.

Back Bay decides the time is ripe for Americans to invest in Peru. They appoint as the fund's adviser a highly respected Lima-based money manager. They also pick two large brokerage firms in New York to be the lead underwriters of an issue to be called the Peru Fund, which will list as PRU on the New York Stock Exchange.

June 15, 1989, is the date set for the public offering of 10 million shares. With the offering price set at $10 a share, $100 million is to be raised. The fund's prospectus limits the investment of this money to the purchase of stocks, bonds, and short-term instruments on the Lima exchange, but also permits the investment of no more then 5% of its funds in Peruvian companies that are still privately held.

The underwriters advertise the new fund in large ads, and working through two dozen brokerage firms across the United States, they easily sell 10 million shares of the fund, raising $100 million. The adviser is given $91,500,000 (after the underwriting commission of 7% and other expenses are paid out), and he is told to start putting together the fund's portfolio of choice securities listed on the Lima exchange. The first purchases include such blue chips as the leading copper mining companies, as well as Aero Peru, Banco Nationale de Lima, Teléfonos de Peru, etc.

When the New York Stock Exchange sounds the day's opening bell at 9.30 A.M. on June 15, investors who bought the Peru Fund through the original offering (at $10.00 a share) put up 200,000 of their shares for resale to the general public. There is a backlog of still-interested investors who couldn't get the stock at the offering price; so the price of PRU rises to $11.50 on opening day and doesn't stop there. In the next three weeks, the price of PRU rises to $12.00 a share, then $13.25, and reaches a crest of $14.00 by midsummer.

In *Barron's* of July 30, 1989, the Peru Fund is listed at "$13.75   +48.6%," meaning that the price at which the shares sold the previous week represented a 48.6% premium over the net asset value of all securities in the fund's portfolio.

Then things suddenly get very quiet. There is no longer a clamor for shares in the fund. The underwriters no longer have inventory, so their brokers stop pushing the issue. Investors who check *Barron's*, *Wall Street Journal*, or *The New York Times* can clearly see that the Peru Fund has a way-above-average premium and is no longer a bargain (if it ever was). Over the next six months, the price of PRU ebbs to $12.00, then $11.50, then $10.75, and on down.

This does not mean that the fund's portfolio on the Lima exchange has not been doing well. In fact, because its portfolio management in those first six months had been skillful, the net asset value has risen 8%, for a projected annual return of 16%. The fund's portfolio is now worth $9.99, up from the $9.15 per share that the adviser started out with.

But a rising portfolio value of a closed-end fund does not always produce a rising selling price for its shares in New York. In fact, the December 16 listing of closed-end funds shows PRU selling at only "$9.50 −5.01%" (or a discount of slightly over 5%.) This means that after six months of unusual investor attention, the new fund, PRU, is getting back to the norm for most closed-end funds. Most sell at a premium when they are first launched and soon decline to sell at a discount.

Now Back to the Real World

On August 17, 1990, Smith Barney Research completed a study of the premium-discount range of the major closed-end funds for the previous fifty-two weeks. At one point, the Germany Fund sold at a premium as high as 100% (after the Berlin Wall came down, euphoric investors were willing to pay twice as much for its shares in New York as its securities were selling for in Frankfurt). At another point in the same fifty-two-week period, shares in this fund dropped to a selling price on the New York Stock Exchange that enabled investors to buy the portfolio at a *discount* of 15% from its net asset value. The people who bought the Germany Fund at a 100% premium surely did not get a bargain, but those who bought it at a 15% discount fared much better: the fund subsequently got back to selling at a premium, albeit a more modest one.

The same Smith Barney study shows the Italy Fund selling at anywhere from a 38% premium to a 21% discount. The Korea Fund is shown trading at premiums anywhere from 16% to a premium high of 129%. The Taiwan Fund ranged from a discount of 23% to a premium of 98%.

One should not take the premium or discount lightly or follow its pattern for only a few weeks. The drop in the Korea Fund premium from 120% to 87%, for example, did not represent a buying opportunity; it later dropped even more. A big discount offers the chance for double gains if the portfolio rises (one gain) and if the discount narrows (a second gain). A big premium, on the other hand, opens you up to a much bigger loss if the portfolio's value drops and so does the premium. A third gain is possible if the fund-country's currency rises against the dollar, as this tends to increase the premium or to reduce the discount.

The conventional wisdom about closed-end funds is that you buy them at a discount and sell them when they trade at a premium. But not everyone agrees with that strategy. Writing in his *International Fund Monitor,* Jon Woronoff had this to say:

> We think it is justifiable for foreign funds (as opposed to domestic funds) to have at least a modest premium. After all, if you want to buy foreign stocks you would have to cover hefty commissions plus the cost of currency conversion and sundry items. It would cost you at least 5%. So why shouldn't you to pay 5% or so to get into a fund that does all that for you and which can be bought on The N.Y. Stock Exchange in U.S. dollars? If the corresponding market is closed to foreign investors *except* through a country fund (as is Korea)—why shouldn't you pay even more. . . . Limiting yourself to funds selling at a discount keeps you out of many, including the most successful.

Single-Country Closed-end Funds

Single-country funds are now covered by two rating services. For some years the *Value Line Investment Survey (VLIS)*, which is widely available in public libraries, and its analysts Norman Tepper and Marc H. Gerstein have covered some of the largest and most interesting single-country closed-end funds, much as *VLIS* rates single stocks on the major U.S. stock exchanges. Morningstar, Inc. recently brought out a new service to cover closed-end funds. Like their other fund service, this one, called *Morningstar Closed-End Funds (MCEF)*, offers reports every two weeks, with international closed-end funds in most issues. You can get a three-month trial subscription for $35 (1-800-876-5005).

Among the funds covered by *VLIS* and *MCEF* are these:

Brazil Fund (NYSE: BZF). This fund, which *VLIS* rates as a very high-risk/high-reward investment (*MCEF* gives its lowest rating to it), has indeed has its ups and downs, with yearly changes of over 50% not uncommon. The attraction of the fund has, in recent years, been threefold. First, it gives average U.S. investors access to the Rio exchange, which is normally closed to them. Second, a new president of Brazil managed to squeeze out some of the country's traditionally high inflation, a very surprising development in Brazil. And third, the price-to-earnings ratio at which Brazilian stocks usually sell are among the lowest in the world. Some Brazilian stocks have sold for less than their yearly earnings on occasion (in the United States a P/E ratio of thirteen to eighteen times earnings is more common). Of course, what the low Brazilian P/Es reflect is the expected effect of inflation, there, which in the past has been horrendous. But that bias seems to continue even as inflation has begun to ebb. Through the Brazil Fund Americans were able to enjoy those lower P/Es even after inflation began to abate.

If inflation ever enters a normal range in Brazil, real corporate earnings can be expected to rise. This would nor-

mally bring about a rise in the P/Es of Brazilian stocks. Both
of these happy developments would increase the desirability
and the selling price of shares in the Brazil Fund. When that
happens, you can expect to see the discount at which BZF
shares are traded to narrow and become a premium (still
another bonus for BZF shareholders). Something else might
happen; Brazil's currency might strengthen in relation to the
dollar, which would also make the Brazil Fund shares more
desirable. But that day is not yet here. Read in chapter 14
why you should approach this fund (or the fund of any other
country with an endangered currency) cautiously.

  Germany Fund (NYSE: GER). When the Berlin Wall fell,
the German stock market boomed and American investors
fell all over themselves to get shares in this fund, catapulting
its premium to 100% over net asset value. That premium
later shrunk and became a 15% discount, making it a more
sensible investment, and then returned to a modest premium.
The fund's enormous success also helped launch its clones—
the New Germany Fund, the Future Germany Fund, the
Emerging Germany Fund—all of which managed by top-
notch advisers, have less of a blue-chip focus, and often sell
at a discount. (The Germany Fund was given a below-average
rating by *MCEF*, which notes its average return and above-
average risk.)

  Italy Fund (NYSE: ITA). In 1990 this then four-year-old
fund sold at a premium as high as 38% and at a discount of
as much as 20%. "Profit gains of Italian companies have been
among the best in the world in the past decade," observed
VLIS's Tepper not long ago. He also sees the lira's inclusion
in the European Monetary System as likely to lessen the traditional volatility of stocks on the Milan exchange. However,
Morningstar is not impressed by the recent performance of
the fund, noting below-average returns and above-average
risk-taking.

  Korea Fund (NYSE: KF). The stock market in Seoul has
been largely closed to foreigners except through this fund.
That fact and the ebullience of the Korean economy pushed

up the share price of KF by tenfold from its inception in 1984 to its three-for-one stock split in 1989. KF's share rise reflected at times an incredible premium that investors were willing to pay: as much as 120% over the portfolio's net asset value. Norman Tepper of *VLIS* has expressed confidence that long-term prospects for the Korean economy are bright, projecting average profits for investors in this fund of close to 20% per year through middecade. His advice is to buy when the premium narrows. *MCEF* is less enthusiastic about this fund, calling its returns only average and its risk-taking above-average.

Malaysia Fund (NYSE: MF). The net asset value of this fund's portfolio rose from less than $7.50 at its birth in mid-1987 to almost $15 at the same point in 1991. By then it had also lost its traditional premium and was selling at a discount of almost 10%, making it, according to *VLIS*, an attractive investment for aggressive investors. The fund offers Wall Street investors a good tool for diversification but no shield against a fall in the dollar: the Malaysian currency is pegged directly to the dollar.

Mexico Fund (NYSE: MXF). Original stockholders of this fund have gone through a roller-coaster ride since its inception in 1981. They bought in at about $12 a share but soon (in part because of a devaluation of the peso) saw their fund's share price plunge to less than $2. The price fully recovered by 1987 only to plunge again when world markets fell apart that October. With the election of President Carlos Salinas de Gortari (a no-nonsense Harvard-trained economist) faith in the Mexican economy strengthened and investors bid up the Mexico City exchange to huge gains for three years straight. The fund nonetheless often sells at a discount as do its semiclones, Emerging Mexico Fund and the Mexico Equity Income Fund. *MCEF* rates this fund above average, something (in its customary loathing of risk) it does for very few country funds.

Spain Fund (NYSE: SNF). The Spanish economy was one of the stars of Europe in the late eighties and early nineties

(and so was its stock market), pushing up the market price
of this fund at one point to a premium of about 150% over
the net asset value. That premium later simmered down, as
outsized premiums usually do. The fund has many attractions.
It deals in a stock market where the P/E multiples are usually
sensible, often about eleven times earnings; its portfolio tends
to concentrate on high-quality stocks that generate income
(making it less vulnerable to market drops); and it promises
to share Spain's better-than-average prospects in post-1992
Europe. *VLIS*'s Tepper recommended the fund for three-to
five-year commitments whenever the fund's selling price gets
close to or below its net asset value. *MCEF* rates the fund
below average because of recent low returns and its above-
average risk.

    Swiss Helvetia (NYSE: SWZ). This fund, reflecting the
doughty country it invests in, has had a slow but steady
growth and continues to enjoy good prospects. *VLIS*, noting
its almost insignificant premium above net asset value and its
occasional discount, finds it a good alternative to the Germany Fund (and that fund's customary healthy premium) for
investors who want to gain the most from post-1992 Europe.

    Taiwan Fund (NYSE: TWN). Despite the Taipei stock
market's fall from grace in 1990—when its low touched 70%
below that year's high—*VLIS*'s Tepper saw still-good prospects for the Taiwan economy until at least middecade. But
because of the fund's traditional premium over net asset value
and the more muted growth that he saw ahead, Tepper re-
frained from recommending purchase of shares in this fund.
And *MCEF*, in one of their earliest reports, simply hated it.
Only for the truly aggressive investor, they said.

Major Political Change Often Leads to Market Rise

Sometimes a change in political leadership provides a tonic
for a country's currency and its stock market. By buying a

single-country, closed-end fund at such times, you stand to profit from the change in more than one way.

Late in 1979, for example, Margaret Thatcher became prime minister of Britain and reigned without interruption for the next ten years. From 1981 to 1990, the U.K. stock market outperformed every other major stock market in the world. It beat the U.S. market, which was in an historic bull market. It beat the German stock market. It even trounced the gains made by the high-flying Tokyo stock exchange.

Mexico and the Mexican stock market had an even more dramatic reaction to the election of a new president. In the three years following the 1988 election of President Carlos Salinas de Gortari, the Mexican currency stabilized and its stock market took off with yearly gains of 50% and more.

You could have made a simple and pure play on the change in Mexican leadership by buying shares in the Mexico Fund in the summer of 1988. Within two years the net asset value of your investment would have doubled, and the selling price, once the premium was added, would have been even greater than that.

Holders of shares in the DFA United Kingdom Small Company Portfolio had a similar lift in the early days of Margaret Thatcher's regime. Their shares more than doubled in value in two years.

In 1990 the appointment of a tough-minded finance minister in Japan led Mark Turner and his team at Scudder International Bond Fund to make an early and hefty bet on Japanese bonds. He remembers this as perhaps the fund's best pick in a year when it led all international bond funds in total return.

Multicountry and Regional Funds

In the late eighties some fund families supplemented their general international stock funds with funds specializing in one region of the world or another. Fidelity, for example, added a Pacific basin fund, a Canada fund, a Europe fund, and several portfolios that invested in currencies such as the British pound. These were all open-end mutual funds, but a number of closed-end funds specializing in a region of the world (rather than a single country) were also started.

In their book *Investing in Closed-End Funds,* Albert Fredman and George Cole Scott offer brief profiles (adapted here) of the following regional and global closed-end funds:

Asia Pacific Fund (NYSE: APB). This regional fund seeks long-term capital appreciation by investing mainly in equities of companies doing business in emerging equity markets in the Asia-Pacific region. These include Hong Kong, Korea, Malaysia, the Philippines, Singapore, Taiwan, and Thailand. APB does not invest in Japan. Morningstar—taking note of this fund's nearly 19 percent average net asset growth over three years—recently awarded it 3 stars.

Clemente Global Growth Fund (NYSE: CLM). CLM seeks long-term capital appreciation through investment in equities of small and medium-sized companies. A global fund, CLM concentrates on securities in the world's major stock markets and in many of the smaller and emerging markets. The manager normally aims to invest at least 85 percent of CLM's assets outside the United States. Over thirty countries are generally represented, half in emerging markets, with (historically) a large exposure to Japanese securities. The fund is growth-stock oriented. Morningstar feels this fund's returns are below average and rates its risk-taking above average.

Europe Fund (NYSE: EF). This fund, started in April 1990, is managed out of London, and is the first overseas fund to adopt a fixed payout—with annual distributions set at 7% percent of the amount you have invested. This could be a great convenience to someone who has retired and is willing to withdraw part of his invested funds periodically to provide income on which to live.

G.T. Greater Europe Fund (NYSE: GTF). Developed by a fund family in San Francisco that offers ten open-end funds as well, GTF was given a closed-end format because it wants to be free to include in its portfolio some less liquid securities. GTF seeks to identify those countries and industries where the economic and political changes affecting Western and Eastern Europe are likely to produce above-average growth. The fund's first investment in Hungary, for example, was a private placement in a floor and textile manufacturer that the fund's portfolio manager described as "a very westernized company with 40 percent of its products sold to western companies." It is perhaps the future focus of the fund that has accounted for the substantial discount from net asset value at which its shares have often sold.

Scudder New Asia Fund (NYSE: SAF). This fund often invests at least 50% of its assets in smaller Japanese companies and holds equity positions in Hong Kong, India, Indonesia, Korea (a Scudder stronghold), Malaysia, the Philippines, Singapore, Thailand, and (oddly) the United Kingdom. The fund is popular with institutional investors, who often hold about 38% of its shares. Morningstar calls this fund's 3-year average return of over 18% above average and its risk-taking moderate.

Scudder New Europe Fund (NYSE: NEF). This fund's focus is on securities traded on smaller or emerging European bourses, and it seeks as well to make specialized investments in privately held European companies, those who have recently gone public and those that are now government owned and being privatized. This fund had a bad beginning with returns that were actually negative but that only reflected the short-term performance of markets in Europe.

Templeton Emerging Markets Fund (NYSE: EMF). This fund normally does not invest in the United States but is chartered to invest in the low- or middle-income economies around the globe (as defined by The World Bank). There are currently ninety-five such countries, and EMF is willing to invest in the forty-two of those where investment is more feasible. Despite its adventurous posture this fund often sells at a robust premium to its net asset value, in part because of the Templeton name. *MMF* gives this fund its highest rating and asks subscribers to be on the lookout for the chance to buy when the premium narrows or disappears—which would indeed be a bargain since Templeton *open-end* funds offering the same approach and expertise normally carry a 8.5% sales charge.

Small-Cap Foreign Funds

After being trashed through most of the eighties, small-cap stocks—often defined as stocks in corporations that do less than $200 million or so in yearly sales—became, in the early nineties, star performers on Wall Street. They also became favorite picks of overseas portfolio managers.

You can buy a portfolio of small-cap foreign stocks, either in closed-end form or as an open-ended (mutual) fund. The *International Fund Monitor* lists the following closed-end funds that focus on smaller companies: Alliance New Europe, Clemente Global Growth, Scudder New Asia, Scudder New Europe, and Templeton Value. The newsletter also lists these open-end funds: DFA Europe, DFA United Kingdom, Alliance Global Small-Cap, European Emerging Companies Fund, T. Rowe Price International Discovery Fund, and Templeton Smaller Companies Growth Fund. Some of these have not yet been rated by *MMF* and so were not covered in chapter 16.

ADRs: When You Want to Invest in Sony, Glaxo, Heineken, and Hundreds of Other Foreign Companies

In the past, if you wanted to buy shares in Heineken on the Amsterdam exchange, you would have to find a broker there and pay his outsized commission. The same went for buying Sony on the Tokyo stock market.

Not anymore, however.

You no longer have to go abroad to buy shares in some of the most important corporations around the world. American Depositary Receipts (ADRs) enable you to buy on American stock exchanges (through a proxy device) shares in hundreds of foreign stocks that are traded every day on foreign exchanges. You buy ADRs like any other stock through your regular broker. And you sell them the same way.

The underlying mechanism is simple: An American bank (known as the "depositary bank") issues negotiable certificates that circulate in the United States and are traded on our stock exchanges. The actual stock certificates of the company you want to buy are held at a "custodian bank" in the country where the stock is traded. The custodian bank takes care of any local taxes and fees. It collects dividends, proceeds from rights offerings, and shareholder reports and passes them on to the depositary bank in the United States, which then channels them to the ADR holders here. The depositary bank also can "bundle" shares so that an ADR represents five, ten, or more foreign shares when the share price abroad is unusually low by our standards.

According to Jon Woronoff, founder of *International Fund Monitor*, "There is a temptation to think of ADRs as behaving like any American stock. You should never forget that they are foreign stocks which are traded more intensively in the home country. That means that prices abroad basically set the prices you pay here for ADRs. Arbitrage helps keep those prices in line."

Your broker may have some investment suggestions that involve buying an ADR. You also can get analyses of ADRs through *Value Line Investment Survey*, which covers a fair sampling of them (and which, as noted earlier, is available in many libraries). For an analysis of leading South African gold mining stocks, also available through ADRs, consult the monthly *Gold Stocks Advisory*, published out of Lafayette, California.

One of the best sources of information on ADRs is also

a good place to find fearless recommendations about closed-end funds. It is a newsletter called *Global Investing* that comes out twice a month and is just about as feisty as anything we've seen among the handful of advisories on international investing. A year's subscription costs $225. But since you have probably never seen it, why not write to the publishers (Global Investing, 35 Sutton Place, Suite 14F, New York, NY 10022) and ask for a sample copy? Then you can judge for yourself.

PART V

▼

Making Money on Margin

▲

CHAPTER 19

▼

Using Leverage to Buy Currencies

Have you ever wondered why so many of the big players of the eighties ran out of money in the nineties? Donald Trump, Rupert Murdoch, Robert Maxwell, Charles Keating, Robert Campeau (he bought Bloomingdale's)—the list is long.

All of them were brought down by leverage. Their debts grew to overwhelm the amount of assets they owned. This may seem like a strange way to open a chapter about the profits that can come from using leverage. But if it scares you enough to skip this chapter, that's all for the good.

Here we leave the realm of investment and enter that of speculation. It is possible to buy a currency with less than 100% down. People who do this through banks can put down 50% or less. Depending on the bank, it is possible to put down as little as 11%.

Of course on futures markets one usually puts down 5% or even less. And you can buy currency futures through European banks because banks there act as stock and commodity brokers. But that kind of speculation is beyond the realm of this book. It better befits a book on gambling.

When you buy, say, DM100,000 and put down half, you are using two-to-one leverage. If you put down one-third, you're using three to one; 25% down means four to one. People are familiar with leverage in stocks, where it is usually called margin. It is not generally known that the same thing can be done with currency deposits, CDs, or government bonds.

Using *Moderate* Leverage

It is possible to use moderate leverage with a portion of your funds to augment the return on foreign currencies when they are rising against the dollar. If that idea appeals to you, let's start with some basics.

Certificates of Deposit (CDs) exist in many currencies. Buying one currency's CD while borrowing another currency to pay for it has been an excellent way over the years to make impressive profits from even minor (10% to 25%) changes in exchange rates. Our aim in this chapter is to show you how you can do that.

Suppose, for example, you bought a one-year SFr10,000 CD in March 1985 (the start of a big rally in the franc). The franc was at 33¢ then. You would have done very well with this investment. You would have paid about $3,300 buying it outright with no leverage. If you sold it—or had it come due—one year later when the franc was at 55¢, your pure currency profit, in dollars, would have been 67%, i.e., $2,200. Add to this the approximate 6% interest rate, and your one-year total return would have been 73%. That would have been the kind of return even stock market investors rarely get in one year.

Your Gain Would Be Much More, of Course, with Leverage

Suppose you had bought that same SFr10,000 CD and put down only 20% (SFr2,000 or a mere $660 at the exchange rates then). You borrowed the other SFr8,000 in equivalent U.S. dollars, a currency that you thought would decline in value over the next year, borrowing $2,640. Obviously, you don't buy Swiss francs (with borrowed dollars) without hoping that the franc will rise against the dollar. At the time you'd have paid an 8% annual interest rate to borrow the dollars.

Buying any investment instrument with only 20% down is risky, of course. But let's see what would have happened that year. You would own the SFr10,000 CD, worth at the new rate U.S. $5,500. You borrowed $2,640 in March 1985, and you paid 8% on it. You would have to pay back a total of $2,851.20 a year later. At the end of the year you owned a CD worth SFr10,600 (the SFr10,000 plus interest). Converted back into dollars at 55¢, this would now be worth $5,830. Subtracting the loan of $2,851, you would have been left with $2,979. (Remember you only put down $660.) This translates into a gain that totals 451%. A profit of 451% in just one year buying one currency with another currency.

Begin to see the possibilities?

In real life, however, you can't expect to hit it that right. But even using more moderate leverage and catching only a part of a currency rise, you can end up with more than respectable profits, as the following real-life examples demonstrate.

How Charles G. Made $40,000 in Three Months

On July 27, 1990, Charles G. purchased about $300,000 worth of German marks and Swiss francs at a Swiss bank. He placed about two-thirds of his funds in the most liquid and conservative form possible, and one-third in a more speculative fashion. Let's see how he divided his purchases.

The Conservative Portion

Charles bought DM110,000 on a forty-eight-hour "call." What this means is that instead of a CD, which lasts three months, money on a two-day call rolls over every forty-eight hours and gets whatever the interest rate is at the time it rolls over. It is about the most liquid way to hold money; you can "call" it in at any time with minimal penalty, and with no penalty if you wait for the two-day period to end. Technically, this is a fiduciary time deposit because your bank is lending your funds to another reliable bank for a two-day period.

On July 27 DM1 equaled 51.4¢, so DM110,000 equaled $67,540. That is the price Charles paid.

Charles sold his position on October 19, 1990. At that time the mark's price had risen to 66.27¢, so DM110,000 was worth $72,896. Interest payments during that twelve-week period pushed the total up to $73,101. He'd made 8.23% on his money in just under three months, or an annualized gain of 33%.

On that same July day he also bought SFr190,000 on a forty-eight-hour call. At the time one franc was worth 73.26¢, so he paid $139,196. On October 19, 1990, he sold these francs after the franc had risen to 78.6¢, so SFr190,000 now equaled $149,348; interest payments over that period pushed it up to $150,495, for a profit of $11,300—8.1% gains, or almost 33% annualized. Again a nice gain. With no use of leverage. And Charles stayed essentially liquid.

The Speculative Portion

With the rest of his money, Charles bought two time deposits. The first was for DM191,300, to mature three months later. (It carried an interest rate of 8.0625%.) At the time this sum was worth, in U.S. dollars, $117,458. But Charles didn't put up 100% of the amount, as he had done with his DM110,000 call deposit. He only put up one-third of this sum, or $39,153. He borrowed the other two-thirds ($78,305) from the same bank. He was hoping to pay it back in cheaper dollars. That is exactly what happened.

On October 19, 1990, the DM191,300 he started with were now worth $126,772.70 in U.S. dollars. That was the value of what Charles "owned." But he did not own it free and clear; he had borrowed $78,305 against it. He had to pay back that sum, leaving him with $48,468. He had put up only $39,153, so he made a profit of $9,314, or 23.8%.

Likewise, on the same day, he bought a Swiss franc time deposit worth SFr217,983.93, which cost $159,700. He put up only a third of it, or $53,233, and borrowed the other two-thirds, or $106,467. When he sold, the franc's price had risen, so his SFr217,984 was now worth $171,651, not the $159,700 he started out with. And after Charles paid back the $106,467 he owed, he was left with $65,174, for a 22.4% profit of $11,941.

Starting off in late July 1990 with $300,000, Charles G. had, in less than three months, made almost $40,000, or over 60% annualized profits. And this is all based on catching a fairly small part of the huge rise in the Swiss franc and the mark since 1985.

How Ronald W. Made 25% in Three Months

For another recent example, let us see what Ronald W. did with a more conservative approach. From his Austrian bank account, on July 9, 1990, he bought $75,000 worth of German marks and Japanese yen: $50,000 in marks and $25,000 in yen. On that date the yen was at ¥151 per dollar, so $25,000 bought him ¥3.775 million. And the mark was worth 60.6¢, so $50,000 got him DM82,500.

Unlike what Charles did about the same time, Ronald actually bought twice these amounts, borrowing the other half in U.S. dollars. Using two-to-one leverage, he actually bought DM165,000 with the $50,000, and ¥ 7.55 million with the $25,000. For every dollar he invested, he borrowed another dollar to provide the leverage. By putting up half of the money, instead of one-third (as Charles had) Ronald was actually more conservative than Charles.

How did he do through October 19, 1990, when he sold? On that day the yen conversion rate was ¥128.6 per dollar, so ¥7.55 million was worth $58,709. He also earned about 7% per year on his yen and paid 10.5% per year to borrow dollars. So he actually received about ¥7.686 million for holding them just over three months. At ¥128.6 per dollar, his yen holdings were worth $59,767. Subtracting his $25,700 loan, he is left with $34,067. He only put up $25,000, so his $9,067 profit represented a 36.3% gain over about three months. On an annual basis his gain was a stunning 245%.

Ronald's mark position had grown from DM165,000 to about DM168,300, due to the 7.75% interest he earned. And his loan of $50,000 had grown to a total debt of $51,375 (also because of interest). At 65.88¢ per mark, the DM168,300 Ronald sold equaled $110,876. Paying back his $51,375 loan left him with $59,501. His $8,126 profit represented a gain of nearly 16%; at an annual rate his gain was 80%.

The mark's gain was only half the gain (in percentage terms) of his yen purchase. This is because in the three months and ten days from July 9 to October 19, 1990, the mark had risen 8.75% (from 60.6¢ to 65.9¢), but the yen, with an 18% gain, had risen more than twice as fast (from 0.66¢ to 0.78¢).

Ronald did even better than Charles in more ways than one. He had diversified geographically much better than Charles had. While Charles bought two similar currencies, Swiss and German, Ronald bought Japanese and German money. Swiss francs and German marks usually fluctuate much the same against the dollar. It is rare for one to rise or fall much more than the other, although it does happen.

The yen's history, however, shows a different picture. It can easily rise against the dollar while the two European currencies are falling, and vice versa. So to buy both yen and marks or yen and francs gives you greater assurance of ending up with the profit you seek.

It may not have turned out that way, of course. Charles with his francs and marks may have gotten lucky and seen those two Germanic currencies rise more than the yen. But it was riskier to do that. Spreading your currency purchases geographically spreads your risk. In this case it was also more profitable. On his total holdings Ronald did quite well. He had put up $75,000 in early July 1990. When he sold on October 19, he had $93,568, or a near 25% increase (a 142% annual rate)—better than Charles had done, and with less risk.

The Danger of Leverage: The Margin Call

You can get a margin call if the value of your equity falls to a certain point. Each bank's policy is different, so it is wise to "check before you pay."

Let's say a bank has the right to issue a margin call if the value of your equity falls below 20% of the total value of what you've bought. This means that if you go in with a down payment of 50%, you have a very large cushion. The value of the currency you bought would have to decline by over 30% against the currency you have borrowed. The chances of this happening—if you have chosen a good currency at a good time—are slim.

If you get a margin call, you will usually be asked to bring the value of your equity up to where it was, or at least to some minimum. In an alternative to issuing a margin call, the bank will sometimes reduce the amount of your equity by issuing a CD of lesser value.

If you had bought a SFr100,000 CD and the loan was 75% in U.S. dollars, the bank could reduce the CD's value to SFr90,000 if the dollar should rise. Remember, you want to be borrowing a currency that will fall in value, and buying one that will rise. That's obviously the surest way to avoid margin calls.

The best banks make it possible for you to switch at any time both the currency you own and the currency you owe. This enables you to take defensive action whenever the market changes.

The three best rules for avoiding margin calls are these:

1. Limit the leveraged part of your currency portfolio to no more than 10% to 20% of your total currencies.

2. Keep the percentage of debt comfortably below the level that would cause the bank to issue a margin call.

3. Be prepared to switch currencies owned or owed to either lock in profits or cut losses.

Leverage is a double-edged sword. It is not for everyone. But at times that seem especially favorable, it can be a very profitable way to deploy a portion of what you invest in currencies.

▼

PART VI

Developing a Knack for Timing Currency Markets

▲

CHAPTER 20

▼

What Makes
Currencies Rise
and Fall

From now on, since your expertise on currencies has grown so much, you're bound to get curious whenever you read in the paper that the dollar has gone up or down or that the yen or the mark has hit an all-time high. It will be almost impossible for you not to wonder why that happened.

Very often, the newspaper report will quote some expert saying lower interest rates or balance of payments or unrest in Eastern Europe brought on the change. Don't swallow that whole. What makes currencies rise and fall, unfortunately, is a complicated matter. But you should have a rudimentary knowledge of the major factors that push around the price of the dollar and the other major currencies, and these are discussed below.

Economic growth and productivity. If a nation is on the rise from a very low level of material production—such as Germany and Japan after 1945—their currency will generally rise rapidly. On the other extreme, a nation that had been riding higher than any other and finds itself over a couple of generations losing that preeminence (such as Great Britain since 1914) will generally suffer a weaker currency.

During the past four generations, no major currency has lost more of its value and fallen farther from a high plane than the British pound; from $5.60 in 1945 to $1.05 in 1985. Even so, Britain's relative growth in economic productivity led the pound from $1.05 in 1985 to $1.95 in 1991, nearly doubling.

Monetary discipline. In the long run a country that prints more of its money than another country is going to cheapen the value of its money against the other. It may take years of monetary inflation to bring down the exchange rate—it took thirty years of U.S. monetary inflation before the dollar was finally devalued in 1971—but the effects of inflation can also sometimes take place quickly.

For example, when the ruling Socialist French government announced an inflationary program in 1981, the French franc quickly plunged, falling so far that Paris was persuaded to scrap its plans. So while respective money supplies are important in the long run, this factor alone cannot be used to time which currency to get into.

Trade deficits. A nation that imports more goods than it exports is always subject to a weaker currency for two reasons. First, this trade deficit usually means that the world doesn't want to buy the products of the country—because either they are shoddy or they are too expensive. (In response, governments often force their currencies to fall in value, in order to make their exports more competitive.)

The second reason a big trade deficit causes a falling currency is that when the people of the deficit country buy imports, they are essentially selling their currencies and buying foreign currencies. They are ultimately sending their currency into the hands of the foreign producers of those products, who in turn convert it back into their own currencies, the money that they use. This massive selling of one currency and purchase of another exacts a big pull up or down on the deficit currencies. It is no wonder that the dollar has lost so much of its value.

Purchasing Power Parity (PPP). A very helpful tool to measure whether a currency is too cheap or too expensive is the PPP. The theory is that, over time, one country's exchange rate relative to another will adjust so that the same item costs approximately the same amount of money (allowing for restrictions, taxes, etc.) in both countries.

For instance, if today the same products can generally be bought much cheaper in the United States than in Japan or Western Europe, the incentive to buy these same products cheaper should lead the rest of the world to convert their currencies to buy dollars, or so the PPP theory goes.

But it would be foolish to make a major investment decision based on PPPs alone. A currency that becomes cheap according to a PPP level can, and usually does, become much more cheap before it works its way back to parity. You're better off waiting until a definite trend is under way before investing in it. As a rule, once a currency trend is under way, it will go dramatically above or below the theoretical PPP level.

Interest rates. Investors instinctively seek the highest income with safety, so obviously if more interest can be earned while holding one currency instead of another—all else being equal—this will cause money to flow into the highest currency. But the interest rate must be a "real" rate of return (after inflation). Argentina's interest rate may be 250%, but that's a negative return if inflation is 300%.

High interest rates by themselves are not reason enough to desert one currency for another. Far more money is made or lost on the rise and fall of exchange rates than on interest income. In fact, in one recent case, buying Singapore dollar CDs yielding only 3%, and borrowing pounds at 17% to pay for them, resulted in big profits! The fall in the pound against the Singapore dollar more than overwhelmed whatever interest rate differential there was.

Productivity. Just as a share of stock represents ownership of the assets of a company, holding a foreign currency represents ownership of the productive power of the nation that prints the currency. There are aspects of a country's economy that can work to either strengthen or undermine its currency. For example, it's a good thing if a nation's industry has high productivity and a work force that doesn't press its demands higher than the economy can bear. Since 1973, for example, U.S. productivity has not kept up with Europe and Japan. The gap has grown in recent years. That gap is reflected in the currency gains of the Japanese yen, German mark, and Swiss franc.

Political stability. The fate of economies and currencies ultimately rests in the hands of politicians. For the investor, bad politics mean bad economics and a failing currency. Currency traders are constantly surveying the political landscape of every major country to see if the legislative decisions are promoting noninflationary growth and productive industries, or whether they promote excess consumption, noncompetitive services, or make-work projects.

The election of Ronald Reagan to the presidency in 1980 demonstrates the power politics has over a currency's value. His election marked a shift in preference toward the dollar as the currency of the most stable nation on earth. In the eighties the United States gained respect from such former naysayers as France, China, the Soviet Union, and Latin America. All are now trying to emulate America's economic success. All things being equal, this trend would mean a higher dollar.

But all things are seldom equal. This factor, too, can be pushed too far. The first Reagan term (1981–1985) saw the dollar soar. The second term saw it plunge right back down again. No one can say that the United States became significantly less stable beginning in 1985. Obviously there was something more important at work here. Perhaps the world's perception changed in 1985. It began to realize that the Reagan policy would mean bigger deficits and international borrowing. It may have seen that America was not ready to pay as it went but wanted to finance the good life on credit.

In any case, the dollar has generally fallen ever since 1985. And the political paralysis shown in the U.S. budget debates most years since then is even more disheartening to foreigners. The world can see that no U.S. politician wants to really cut the deficit. The United States is still viewed as a country wanting to live beyond its means. That has meant a weaker dollar since 1968, with a particularly significant drop in 1985.

What Goes Up Must Come Down

It may sound simplistic, but a currency will rise when it has fallen low enough, and will fall when it has risen high enough. That is just another way of saying that no major currency— or any other investment—rises or falls forever. Minor currencies, like the Argentinian peso/austral, seem only to go down. But those are the exceptions.

The United States and the top four or five other countries of the world are not about to disappear as economic powers. To see any of their currencies double in value over another of this group in three or four years is not usual. It should prompt you to examine if such a move is justified by any dramatic trends in the two nation's relative productivities, money supplies, trade deficits, PPP levels, or any of the other factors we've discussed.

If not enough of a deterioration has occurred, or if the bad trends are in the process of correcting themselves (e.g., the rate of increase in the growth of one country's money supply has slowed sharply relative to the other, or the trade deficit is generally narrowing), then chances are that the weaker currency is not in as bad a shape as the markets are saying. Chances are great—certainly better than even—that the currency is severely undervalued and will work its way back up to a normal level.

This has happened a couple of times in the past decade just between the U.S. dollar and the Swiss franc. By early 1985 the dollar had risen 88% against the franc (SFr1.54 to SFr2.90) in just over five years. This was almost a doubling. Now, Switzerland was not about to go under as an economy; it remained as stable and sound as it ever was. The chances were that the franc had fallen too far and would rise again.

The Swiss franc did indeed recover, to such an extent that by the time three more years had passed, the franc had risen 123% against the dollar. This phenomenon was even more unusual in that it was so great a move in such a short time. Sure enough, after early 1988 the dollar strengthened, but only for about a year; then it began to plunge again.

Herd instinct. Finally, there is the "herd instinct" factor. We can see in hindsight that, like clockwork, near every peak of a currency trend, almost all advisers and investors say that however much the currency has increased in the past, the rise can only continue. Thus in early 1985, though the dollar had nearly doubled against strong European countries, the journals were full of articles saying why the dollar's rise would continue, as it was the world's only great currency. It is best to enter a market and buy when everyone is bearish, and sell when all are bullish, provided, of course, that the factors discussed above are also on your side.

Sometimes the majority can be right; generally, however, they are only right in the middle of a trend, not at the top or bottom. As a rise or fall gathers speed, more and more investors will come to believe that the move can only go further. As they pile on, the move can indeed continue and even be accelerated to an unrealistic level. By then the bull market is generally over, and the majority are left with sudden losses. The period from when the majority piles on to where they are proven wrong can last months and even years.

Think of any great bull market of the recent past. In the late eighties it seemed as if the Tokyo stock market could only rise, as well as real estate in New York City or California. Then, in the early nineties, those markets collapsed by 25% to 50%.

When prices are soaring, everyone is interested. Everyone buys, and too often hindsight shows that "everyone" bought too high. When prices are cheap, or have fallen much, few want to buy. But this often turns out to be the smartest time to have bought.

One of this book's authors naively wanted to write a book on foreign currency assets in 1985. He quickly found that no publisher was interested. After all, the dollar had been rising for six years, and other currencies were very low. This was the time for investors to buy, but few of them were interested either.

It may be a wicked thing to suggest, but if this book sells like hotcakes, the dollar may be in for a period of strength. It may start rising just at the time when most people have given up on it. If so, however, the rise will unfortunately probably only be temporary. The United States has too many fundamental problems to expect anything else.

CHAPTER 21

How the Experts
Spot Market
Tops and Bottoms

There's no foolproof way to get in or out of a market at the absolute best time. The best you can hope for—and this can turn out to be anything from pretty good to fabulous—is to catch the lion's share of any bull or bear move.

Your general aim is to be out of the dollar when the dollar is falling, and in the dollar during those times the dollar is rising. In this chapter we'll look at various approaches to the question of when best to switch from the dollar to another currency and when back again.

Basically, you have three choices for timing the currency markets:

1. You can stay abreast of the markets by reading periodicals that report the currency markets and that have columnists and analysts who observe what is happening and predict what is likely to happen next. Only remember that the market does not respond the way most observers say it will. Indeed, the theory of contrarian investing suggests that you go against

the crowd—and analysts, in general, are part of the crowd too. As *The Economist* wrote in January 1992, "Currency forecasters seem to be in unusual agreement that the dollar will pick up in 1992—which on their past record, may be the best reason for expecting it to tumble."[1] A list of publications we've found useful can be found at the end of the chapter.

2. You can leave the timing to a portfolio manager. We'll cover that later.

3. There are some analysts that have a very good track record. They are worth listening to even though their timing may not be as precise as you hope for. If they even come close, you will be way ahead of the game.

A Couple of Currency-Timing Experts with Good Track Records

One way to get sharp at timing currency movements is to follow an analyst who specializes in currencies and has a very good track record. Two we think highly of are *International Bank Credit Analyst* and *The Aden Analysis*.

You will find the *Bank Credit Analyst* and its global counterpart, the *International Bank Credit Analyst (IBCA)*, on the desks of central bankers around the world. For over forty years, the *IBCA* has been clearly and shrewdly forecasting major moves in interest rates, stocks, and bonds. Since currencies began to float in the early seventies, *IBCA* has included them as well. A look at their chart "D-mark Currency Model" (chart 13 on page 282) will show you that their methods have done very well since 1970 in forecasting major moves in the relationship between the dollar and the mark.

They switched from the dollar in 1970 to the mark and Swiss franc. There was a quick switch out in 1976 and then back in again a few months later at a (rare) small loss. Another

---

[1] Indeed, the dollar fell to record lows by 1992's summer before recovering during the last quarter.

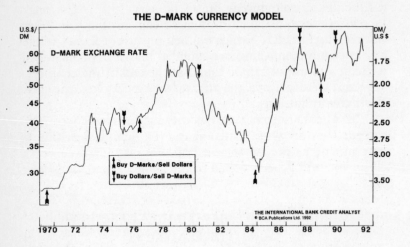

Timing the mark against the dollar: Up arrows show when BCA flashed a buy signal on the mark (and sell on the dollar). Down arrows indicate the reverse. Except for one miscall early in 1990, BCA's calls have been great.

switch out of the mark was made in early 1981. So with just four switches in eleven years, *IBCA* caught virtually all of the more than 100% increase of the mark over that time.

That, as we have said earlier, is just about as good as you can get.

The *IBCA* model was in the dollar when it was going up in the early eighties. They were able to buy the mark again, when they finally switched back in early 1985, at a price half of what they'd sold at in 1981. Thus, their model had them in the D-mark all of the way up to 1988; back in the dollar from then to early 1989, when the dollar was rising; then into the mark in early 1989, when the mark was rising. This lasted until early 1990, at which time the model turned bearish on the mark, at a price of about 60¢. (They've been bullish on the dollar ever since.)

Three switches in three years. This is very little for a commodities trader, but quite a few for a sound longer-term currency investor. That kind of higher than normal switching activity shows how, from 1988 to at least 1992, the currency markets were choppier than normal and lacked the clear multiyear trend we had in the seventies and eighties.

Maybe by the time you read this a new trend will have emerged. We will be watching the *IBCA* model closely for any sign of a major change.

The Aden Analysis, published by two sisters (improbably based in San José, Costa Rica), has also done well in its forecasting during the same period. The Adens, too, caught the big 1985–87 rise in the European currencies, and they've done well since. In 1988 their currency recommendations equaled the U.S. T-bill rate; in 1989 they doubled that rate; in 1990 they tripled the T-bill return.

How *IBCA* Times Its Switches

In its November 1989 issue the *International Bank Credit Analyst* described how it constructed its various currency models. We quote only from the first paragraph and paraphrase the rest because the language is fairly technical.

"The investment opportunity in forex [foreign exchange] markets lies in knowing which way the crowd is likely to move the currency and also in recognizing when the rush of hot money has pushed foreign exchange prices to an extreme. Exchange rates can stay at extreme levels for unexpectedly long periods. But extremes in market prices always present favorable risk/reward tradeoffs, especially if [you're willing to wait.]"

The current volatility of money, credit, and liquidity is given 50% of the weight in the *IBCA* currency model. Growth in any of these that is too rapid usually affects the value of the currency, depending on the point of the business cycle at which it comes. You can find more about this approach in chapter 28.

Another 25% of the weight is given to a currency's fundamental value, which derives from a country's indebtedness and the rate of change of prices relative to other countries. The next chapter, finding currency bargains, goes into more detail on this.

The last 25% of the model centers on the technical element, or the rate of change of the currency. But this only becomes important if the fundamentals have changed. If they have, but the prior trend is still in place, then timing a switch to catch a new trend can be helped by studying such technical factors as the rate of change in a currency's prices.

How the Adens Make Their Calls

The Adens pretty much put all their emphasis on this technical analysis. They do not generally include fundamental factors in their currency forecasts. They use all the traditional tools of technical analysis plus their own developed methods. These involve moving averages, percent rates of change in these moving averages, momentum, and relative strength indication, that is, many of the same things *IBCA* takes into account in its technical component. The difference between the two is that *IBCA* uses both fundamentals and technical analysis, and that the Adens make actual forecasts at precise prices for the many investments—stocks, bonds, precious metals—that they survey. Over the years the Adens have come to disregard fundamentals entirely in their calls. While they keep up on news, the Adens say they have regretted every move made by overruling the message of their charts and following fundamentals.

The Limits of Technical Analysis

A word about the limits of technical analysis is called for here. One of the most renowned analysts using these techniques, Ian McAvity, is a frequent guest on "Wall Street Week" and has been in the business for at least a generation.

He warns against anyone expecting to find a foolproof timing system for any investment area. As he puts it, "Every time I think I find the key, they change the lock." And at times, the Adens have been buffeted by false technical signals.

So the best overall way to judge when to buy is to study fundamentals, buy good value (cheap, if possible), and be prepared to wait. That's what works for billionaire Warren Buffett.

Warren Buffett's Rules for Investment Success

Warren Buffett has been called "the greatest investor of all time" by Peter Lynch, himself the investment genius who made Fidelity's Magellan Fund the largest in the country. Buffett is, according to *Forbes* magazine, the second-wealthiest American. He made all his money over a thirty-five-year career as an investor. His investment vehicle is a company called Berkshire Hathaway. It was worth $20 million in 1965, and more than $9 billion today.

Buffett lives and works in Omaha, Nebraska. He specializes in U.S. stocks. Until recently, he never owned any foreign currency or bought a single share in a company outside the United States. Nevertheless, what he has to say about how he chooses what to buy has a wealth of value to anyone deciding in which currency to denominate their savings.

An interview with him in the London *Financial Times* (June 22, 1991) was striking in that so many of the things he believes about companies are applicable to currencies.

Buffett has achieved success by "picking a few heavily under-valued securities, putting a lot of money into them, and holding on to them." He buys and holds until the market values them as he believes they should be valued. "Over time—and it may be a long time—the price . . . will move toward [its] intrinsic value." The combination of sound fundamental analysis—picking the right stock in the first place—and patience almost guarantees exceptional returns in the long term, Buffett believes.

The same is true when buying currencies. You must first throw yourself into a profound study of all the factors that lead you to believe the price is undervalued. Only when convinced do you buy it. Then you go on about your life and have patience through the inevitable period where the price isn't zooming up—and may indeed even be falling amidst general pessimism.

This last is very hard to do. Institutional pressures and human nature's preference for quick profit are often enemies of successful long-term investment. Just imagine the fate of a pension fund manager who admitted (as Buffett did in 1985) in his annual letter to shareholders that he had "no good ideas this year."

Most investors tend to have too many ideas. They usually trade more than they should. This makes profits for banks and brokers, but not usually for the investors. As the *Financial Times* noted, "Buffett's objective is to make *at most* a handful of investment decisions each year" (emphasis added), instead of switching and trading.

He will only switch and make a move when a great "buying opportunity 'shouts' at him from the marketplace." There are some years when no opportunity does, so he does nothing but sit tight in what he already has. To write "there are some years" is easy and quickly done. But to live "some years" day after day without making any changes, this can be excruciatingly hard. So it comes as no surprise that "self-discipline" is fundamental to his success. More than half of his personal net worth can be attributed to fewer than a dozen investment decisions." For instance, in mid-1991 almost 85% of his entire equity holding was in just four companies: Coca-Cola, Capital Cities, the *Washington Post* newspaper, and the insurance company GEICO. All are blue chips. In 1992 Buffett bought a foreign stock for the first time when he took a large position in Guinness, the blue chip British-based brewery.

Similarly, if you had put most of your long-term savings into the top-four least-risky blue chip currencies—the Swiss franc, yen, Austrian schilling, and deutsche mark—and just left them to accumulate interest, you would have done very well. Of course, currencies don't have the leveraged growth that the best companies have. You never hear of a currency going from $1 to $10 in a year. But what we are talking about here is the principle of picking a few such choices and sticking to them. These insights can be applied to any investment area.

These are times when there will be no good new ideas in any area. For example, Buffett said that he had no good ideas in 1985. Had he been aware of how high the dollar was at that time and what good values the best foreign currencies represented, he could have just switched cash from U.S. dollars to yen, francs, marks, or schillings. Doing so, he could have easily made 50% on his money in 1985.

One of Buffett's hallmarks of success is that he invests only in those things he knows a lot about. At the time, he stayed only in U.S. dollar-based assets. It was no crime that he did so; he stayed with what he knew until he was ready to learn about something else.

There will always be some market opportunity somewhere. If you have abstained from a market that's going gangbusters because you don't know a lot about it, do not lose sleep. Buffett could have switched into other currencies in 1985, the single best year for them ever. But he didn't because he doesn't know much about them. Nevertheless, he made out well anyway. The things he did know about did very well.

Another lesson is that diversity and diversification may not always be best. The *Financial Times* interview comments on what distinguishes Buffett's position from most: "Diversification, while a sound principle for an average investor, may be more of a hindrance than a help to those who know what they are doing."

We've found this true with currencies. Diversification in ten to fifteen currencies is safe, and a good way for people who don't feel totally comfortable with them. But picking out the handful of best—maybe four at most—is more profitable. If you don't know what you are doing, then please don't be afraid to diversify. But when you are convinced of a currency trend, never be afraid to zero in on one or two of them, the ones that look the strongest.

Letting a Currency Portfolio Manager Do Your Timing for You

Another way to improve your timing of the currency markets is not to try at all yourself but rather to leave the timing to a portfolio manager who specializes in currencies. There are currency portfolio managers who will try to accomplish for you what you might ideally hope to do if you had optimum information and all the time in the world to apply it.

But how do you choose a currency manager? This is like asking how to choose any money manager because the goal is the same: to buy low, sell high, and get profits.

Unlike doctors or lawyers, there are no schools that accredit money managers. The United States has SEC-registered investment advisers, but the requirements for registration are extremely loose. If your grandmother could pay the $250 fee and had never been in trouble before, we're willing to bet she could register as an investment adviser. (In fact, a few years ago a pet owner tried to register her dog, and succeeded!) Moreover, many excellent money managers live and work outside the United States, and very often their home countries don't even require any registration.

So you have to be careful. Here are some pointers to consider with any potential managers:

1. How long have they been in business? Many managers fall into the pattern of being hot for a few years but losing big after that—at which point they find other work. The key is longevity. Making money in good times is wonderful, but did they avoid losing too much in bad times? Ten years or so is a long enough time to establish a track record over good times and bad. No one will have only great times. The test is

how they handle bad times. And the fact that they are still there after ten, fifteen, or twenty years says a lot about that.

2. Does their literature make sense? Ideally, managers should not promise the world—they won't be able to deliver it. Their logic and general approach should make sense to you. Don't be cowed by an expert talking down to you in jargon.

3. Never send them your money directly. For your safety, always open your own account at a safe bank and let them manage it from there. Make sure you give them only a *limited* power of attorney where they can trade and manage but cannot withdraw any of your money.

4. Will they help you in other areas? Even though you should open and control your own bank account, good managers can help you open and operate your account at a foreign bank. They can make the opening process easier for you and act as a go-between to communicate any special requests you have of the bank, as well as help with any problems or questions that arise (for example, explaining your quarterly statement). They can also help in getting your money back to you or getting a credit card attached to your account, among other things.

5. Will they let you start small? You should be able to start with a relatively small amount if you are unsure of a manager. Some will let you start with as little as $1,500 or so. Of course the options available won't be as many as you'd have for $150,000. One alternative is to see if the manager offers a pooled fund. Here, you still keep your own bank account, but you buy shares of a fund large enough to spread into many investments.

6. How are they compensated? A manager can get a flat percentage of the amount managed, a percentage of the profits, or both. But there is one thing a manager should not get: any incentive to trade investments. Switching from one currency to another costs you money. Managers should not benefit from this. They should not be brokers. In fact, they should have an incentive to switch as little as possible, and only when they believe it to be necessary. In general, the fee structure should mean that if you don't profit, your manager won't either.

7. Finally, how easily can you fire them? You should be able to tell your bank to withdraw your limited power of attorney with little or no notice. If you are in a pooled fund, you'll likely be able to exit only at the end of the next month, or calendar quarter. But this should be the limit; there is no excuse for having only one exit point per year, as we've sometimes seen.

The Weber Approach

One of the authors of this book, Chris Weber, is a money manager. In what follows, he describes his own personal approach in the first person:

I've been buying and selling currencies since the early seventies. While I've used technical analysis to time exact moves, I've employed a more fundamental approach in deciding whether the dollar was too high or too cheap.

I've made fairly few switches since 1971. Probably the best way to demonstrate my approach is to take you back to those points when I made the switches.

In 1971 I became convinced that the U.S. dollar was going to fall in value against the Swiss franc and deutsche mark. I'd been aware of the "German-speaking" currencies all my life because my parents were born in Germany and Austria and I had often visited Europe.

But a more fundamental reason made me begin buying Swiss francs. It had to do with the wrongheaded makeup of the world monetary system as it existed then.

In essence, the international monetary system from 1944 to 1973 gave the U.S. government a power no other government had ever had—and is not likely to ever have again: the power to print paper money and have it be accepted as gold all over the world. Just as $35 equaled one gold ounce at a fixed rate that soon became unrealistic, so too were the values fixed between the dollar and other currencies. From the thirties to April 1971, the Swiss franc, month after month, fluctuated only between 23.01¢, and 23.36¢. All foreign currencies were defined in terms of dollars at a fixed rate, and the dollar itself was defined in terms of gold.

The U.S. abused this power and printed dollars wildly during the sixties. Foreign governments were forced to inflate as well to keep the artificially high dollar exchange rate. But by the early seventies they'd had enough. They stopped supporting the dollar, and its value fell to reflect its years of inflation. It then began to take many more dollars to buy gold and the major currencies. By the decade's end gold had risen from $35 to $800, nearly 2,300%. The Swiss franc was the strongest currency of that era, rising from 23¢ to 70¢ from 1972 to late 1978: not even including interest, it tripled in value.

Back into the Dollar: 1978

I got out of the Swiss franc and back into dollars in November 1978. The reasons were not that the dollar's managers suddenly mended their profligate ways and resolved to inflate no more. It was that the various other currencies began inflating more.

In 1976 monetary inflation in the United States was expanding at an annual rate of 8%, which was then considered very high. In 1978 the money growth rate remained about 8%.

By comparison, in 1976 German money growth had been 6.5%. By late 1978 it was 13.5%. Over the same period Japan's went from 3.6% to 16.5%; Britain's from 11% to 21%; France's from 6% to 14.5%. But Switzerland's deterioration was most dramatic. In 1977 money growth was a tiny 0.4%, virtually zero inflation. By late 1978 money inflation had exploded, reaching annual levels of 33%. This was a real danger signal.

Also, I simply felt in my gut that after six terrible years for the dollar, its value had gone too low. No price goes in only one direction forever. We had made fabulous profits by owning the franc—it was time to take them and cash in.

I recommended that the Swiss francs be changed for U.S. dollar CDs, T-bills, commodities, silver, and gold. Two years later, in late 1980, I advised switching the commodities for long-term U.S. Treasury bonds.

It was not easy for me to be out of foreign currencies for all these years. After all, I'd long believed that the dollar had fundamental problems. But I had to set aside my biases and keep listening to what the market was telling me—that this was a dollar rally that would last years. During that time it was quite profitable to draw double-digit interest yields in safe dollar instruments, while watching the franc decline.

Finally, in late 1983, after watching the Swiss franc decline for nearly five years, losing a third of its value against the dollar, I bought it again. Part of what caused me to buy was pure contrarianism. Traveling in both Europe and North America, I heard talk of the strong dollar on everyone's lips. This gave me pause. When *Time* and *Newsweek* run cover stories on how the dollar's rise is inexorable, it's time to switch to other currencies. I was reminded of the cover stories and front-page newspaper headlines in late 1974 and early 1980 trumpeting gold's rise to the man in the street. Both times were followed by long periods of gold weakness.

I also saw how the Swiss had spent years putting their monetary house in order. No more the 33% money growth rates of 1978. By 1983 the Swiss had gotten a typically firm grip on the printing presses.

I also used the techniques described in the next chapter. Prices for the same items were becoming a real bargain in Europe, and this told me the European currencies were getting too cheap.

Sure enough, even though I switched early, patience paid off when the Swiss franc, along with all other major currencies, soared against the dollar from 1985 to 1987. They in fact doubled during this short time, which by 1988 made me take and bank sizable profits.

Since 1988 there has been no clear trend. The dollar gradually lost ground, but twice roared back by 20% to 25% over periods of six months. I was fortunate and caught the lion's share of both. But both dollar rallies turned out to be temporary, followed immediately by now-traditional rituals of dollar bashing.

It is possible that a new dollar rally will last longer than six months. The one that began in 1979 lasted six years, remember. After all, the dollar has fallen very far since 1985, and a correction would not be surprising. But since the long-term prognosis for the dollar remains bleak, any time spent in the dollar should be viewed as temporary and as awaiting opportunities to buy good currencies at lower prices.

All this is for short and medium holding. If you don't want to be bothered with any switches, you can simply buy Swiss francs, yen, and ecus and hold them for the long term. At least 10% of your holdings should be in these traditionally strong currencies. In the long term, they will likely be higher. What happens in the medium term may be something different, and you should be aware of how to profit from dollar rallies. That is, if you ever choose to switch back to the dollar. That is covered in chapter 24.

[Chris Weber manages a variety of currency portfolios ranging from conservative to speculative for both individual accounts or in pooled funds. For more information, contact his communications office at 1129 E. Cliff Rd., Burnsville, MN 55337 telephone: 612-895-8511, fax: 612-895-5526.]

Addresses of the Two Currency Timers

The monthly *International Bank Credit Analyst* costs $595 per year. Contact BCA Publications, Ltd., 3463 Peel Street, Montreal, Quebec., Canada H3A 1W7.

The monthly *Aden Analysis* is available for $250 at P.O. Box 84905, Phoenix, AZ 85071.

Other Publications

Barron's. Appearing each Saturday on newsstands, *Barron's* costs $2.50 a copy and contains about 150 pages of market news and analysis. Features of special interest to readers of this book include several weekly columns: "The International Trader," with summaries from seventeen markets; "Commodities Corner," which covers the dollar from time to time; "Tracking Closed-End Funds"; "The International Trader," a lively report (generally quoting money managers overseas) about what's happening in markets around the world. Also of interest are *Barron's* major reports: twice a year Barron's publishes its "International Roundtable," usually a cover feature, in which it interviews a group of the most respected money managers from around the world who normally specialize in the international arena and who inevitably give their predictions for the dollar and other leading currencies. You can subscribe to *Barron's* for $109 a year by calling 1-800-638-9320.

The Economist. Available for $3.50 a copy each week from good magazine stores and some specialized bookstores, this journal of international politics, business, and finance is edited in London, with British felicity of language and humor. It casts a wary eye on the Economic Community and the chances for that vaunted unified market and currency. The last two pages of this weekly gem are worth the price of admission. They contain economic and financial indicators that are a real help for guessing market tops and bottoms, and include these statistical updates: output, demand, and jobs; prices and wages; a commodity price index that focuses on the dollar and other currencies; world bourses (what happened in major stock markets that week); money and interest rates, which track money supplies in different countries and tell what you can earn on bonds and money on deposit in various currencies; trade, exchange rates, and reserves, with half a dozen revealing tables. You can subscribe to *The Economist* for $110 a year by calling 1-800-456-6086 or sending your check to P.O. Box 58524, Boulder, CO 80322-8524.

Financial Times (London). If you want to feel on top of what is happening every day in financial markets around the world—and particularly in Europe—there is no better place to go than to the pages of *Financial Times*, published in

London and distributed to newsstands in certain large metropolitan areas of the United States. Currency exchange rates, financial futures and options, money market rates, and world stock markets are all covered daily in great depth. But of even greater help in developing your knack for market timing are the shrewd reports on inflation, trade agreements, strikes, etc., from all the major financial centers—reports that are more current and more incisive than you can ever expect to get from an American publication. Single copies sell for $1.25. A year's subscription costs $420, and in twenty-seven major metropolitan areas it is delivered to you by hand. Outside of those areas, it is mailed to arrive the following day. Call 1-800-547-8833 for more information or to subscribe.

Forbes and *Fortune.* Both are published twice a month and are widely available. They attempt to cover world stock markets (*Forbes* publishes a Forbes International 500 of leading companies around the world), and neither gives ongoing coverage of the influences that change currency rates.

The New York Times. This daily covers the movement of the dollar against major world currencies. It now devotes a major overview to currency and stock markets around the world every Sunday as well.

International Herald-Tribune. With seventeen business and financial correspondents around the world, this paper gives a special Euro-American view of world currencies and markets that is skewed toward Americans who are living outside the United States and who are therefore already unshackled from the dollar. Available on newsstands in major American cities and by subscription. Call 1-800-882-2284. One year costs $349 in New York City and $369 elsewhere in the United States.

Investor's Business Daily. This publication covers world markets, currencies, and the dollar five times a week and is widely available at 75¢ a copy.

Wall Street Journal. Available five days a week for 75¢ a copy and by subscription for $139 a year (call 1-800-628-9320), this paper devotes two pages each day to international news and another page to world markets, including foreign exchange rates, futures, futures options and options, foreign stock market quotes and indexes, and key currency cross-rates.

Other Newsletters

Harry Browne's Special Reports. Harry Browne has been writing on and evaluating Swiss banking and advising on currencies for over twenty years. Occasionally, he rates all Swiss banks for safety. If you are interested in seeing the most recent Swiss banking liquidity report as well as the current issue, send $10 to P.O. Box 5586, Austin, TX 78763. Regular subscriptions (ten issues) are $225.

Adrian Day's Investment Analyst. Adrian Day wrote the book on international investing in the early eighties, long before the subject was fashionable. He now writes this monthly newsletter, a good part of which keeps one up to date on global investing. For a year's subscription send $87 to 824 E. Baltimore Street, Baltimore, MD 21202.

Gary A. Scott's World Reports. Full of interesting information on international investing; a year's subscription costs $99. Write to 3106 Tamiami Trail N.R., Naples, FL 33940. Telephone is 813-261-1222; fax is 813-261-2001.

Dr. Kurt Richebächer was an advisor to the German central bank for years. He has his own newsletter now:

Currencies and Credit Markets. It is truly excellent, and though written in Germany is available in the U.S. at Newsletter Systems, 5000 Green Lane, P.O. Box 11206. St. Paul, MN 55111-0206. $400 per year.

Christopher Weber's World View updates and expands on the insights found in this book. For a year's subscription, send $75 to 1129 E. Cliff Rd., Burnsville, MN 55337. Telephone is 612-895-8511; fax is 612-895-5526.

CHAPTER 22

▼

Finding Bargains: What That Says About a Country's Currency

If you're done a lot of traveling outside the United States, you've probably observed that an item that sells for one price at home can have a very different price abroad. Americans who traveled abroad years ago often have stories of bargains they've bought in other countries, things that would have cost them much more at home. (And almost as many have more recent horror stories about prices in another country being triple what they are in the United States—for the same item.)

The Winter of 1984–85: Our Last Chance at Great Bargains?

Any American could have lived like a king in Europe during the winter of 1984–85 and never felt the pinch of price. Imagine, for example, that you and some friends had decided to do what was very fashionable at that time: take a food tour through southern France, planning to eat lunch and dinner each day at Michelin three-star restaurants only. Had you gone ahead with that plan, your experience would have been both wonderful and overwhelming. In all likelihood you would have had to abandon the challenge of eating a daily round of these rich, six-course, two-hour meals; two a day probably would have been simply too much. But hardly too much in terms of price: with wine, the cost of your meals might have averaged no more than $17 a person. Yes, $17 a person for an elaborate meal, with a fine French wine, at what might well be one of the best restaurants in the world. Now, the same meal would run over $100.

Then, let's say—after all that eating—you and your friends decided to go on to Switzerland to slim down by skiing. Switzerland is known now as an expensive place for Americans to visit. But this was the winter of 1984–85. Things were different then. In Arosa, for example, a little-known but wonderful site near St. Moritz, daily expenses for everything—skiing, food, lodging, the works—would have cost you about $35 per person per day. Today, a day at a Swiss ski resort could run into the hundreds of dollars. Thirty-five-dollars was also roughly the price you would then have paid in London for the finest cashmere sweaters, and skirts were not that much more.

What Prices Tell You About a Currency

While those days are clearly gone now, they may come again. And the message of this chapter is this: when you find a bargain abroad, you can, of course, savor it for itself and gloat about it to your friends when you come home—but you can do something that would be more profitable. You can ponder what those bargains say about the currencies of the countries you visited.

Whenever you see a sharp discrepancy in prices between two major countries, it is a warning sign that the two currencies are seriously misvalued. One is too cheap, the other too high.

The dollar rose from 1980 to early 1985. By the end of that time its purchasing power was tremendous. That, more than anything else, accounted for the binge you could have enjoyed in Europe at very little cost during the winter of 1984–85. And the measly price you and your friends paid to vacation in Provence and St. Moritz that winter should have told you that the dollar was simply too high—that it was due for a fall.

Even when the contrast in prices between countries is not as dramatic as it was then, it's worth comparing prices as you travel. That's easy to do.

It's especially easy to do if you like hamburgers. Wherever you go, you can now price a McDonald's Big Mac—or for that matter, a movie ticket, a cab ride, etc. If you don't want to travel to foreign countries, then compare the cover prices between currencies for items such as books and magazines. Here is a specific example from the September 29, 1990, edition of *The Economist:*

> *The Mighty Fallen: King Edward VIII*
> By Philip Ziegler. Collins; 654 pages; £20;
> to be published in November by Knopf; $24.95

You can see that this book costs £20 in Britain and $24.95 in the United States. This is for exactly the same product, mind you. When £20 equals $25, what is being implicitly implied is that £1 equals $1.25. That's what the rate of exchange should be. But at that time in the currency markets, the pound was at $1.90; it was too high. The book was a bargain if bought in the United States. There it sold for $25; in Britain at that time it sold for the dollar equivalent of $38, or over 50% more.

If you were to observe a number of examples like this, you could come to a conclusion about the dollar and the pound. This *one* example suggests that the pound at that time was too expensive (it was time to sell it) and the dollar too cheap (it was time to buy it). And that was the case at that time; within months the two currencies moved into better alignment, the pound down and the dollar up.

The way the book was priced, it would have cost exactly the same in the United States as it did in the United Kingdom *only* if the dollar exchange rate was $1.25/pound. In other words, this was the theoretically correct currency price—the price at which the exact same things would cost the same in both places, or be priced at parity.

The Power of Purchasing Power Parity

Economists look at all of a country's goods and services, not just a single book, compare them to the same goods and services of another country, and try to calculate what the currency exchange rate of these countries would have to be in order for the same product to sell at the same price in both countries. Experience has shown that every time you can buy things in one country for much less than you can find those same things in another, the currency price will adjust to bring them into balance. Economists call this the Purchasing Power Parity (PPP) theory.

You'll remember that in the case of the book, if the pound exchange rate were $1.25 per pound, then that book would cost the same in both dollars and pounds. So just going by this, the pound's PPP would be $1.25.

Now this is just one item, and it would be foolish to base investment decisions on that alone. Therefore, economists and analysts try to take in, as much as possible, the whole range of prices for goods and services in one country and compare them to another.

There are always difficulties deciding what to include and how exactly to allow for price differences—how, for example, to factor in taxes or regulations in a particular country that would artificially drive up the price of a good. So even experts will disagree on the exact formula to use or follow in determining a currency's fundamental value. Don't let that faze you. Just look at a number of PPP projections and deduce for yourself some consensus about whether the dollar's value is too high, too low, or just about right against any particular currency.

Another solution is to rely on the evidence of your own eyes and wallet as you travel; you'll know when prices are out of whack. Experienced observers who know currencies will tell you this: you will never find huge bargains in a major country that do not eventually disappear as the currency subsequently strengthens.

There were amazing bargains in Switzerland in the early seventies, in Italy in the late seventies, and in Britain in 1985. All of those bargains disappeared when those currencies strengthened against the dollar (i.e., when the dollar fell against those currencies).

In the early nineties, if anything, it was the United States itself that was the cheapest country in the world. You may have seen Japanese and Europeans flocking to America and buying things at bargain prices, but by an odd fluke so too were Argentines and Nicaraguans! For them this just means that both of their countries have set their official currency rates artificially high; most likely their currencies will fall in the future.

But whenever the same quality goods can be bought in the United States for less than in much of the world, this just means that on a Purchasing Power Parity basis alone, the dollar is too cheap. That's an isolated fact and worth considering. But it doesn't mean that a holder of foreign currencies should dump them and only buy dollars. As the charts show, a currency that becomes cheap according to PPP theory will usually become much cheaper. Markets generally overshoot.

Eventually, parity will be restored, because it is just not

in the nature of things to be able to buy forever the same quality in one country for half of what it costs in another. Still these disparities can go on for some time.

They go on until the different prices in the countries involved reach the point of absolute absurdity. While absurdity is not a statistic that can be measured, you know it when you see it. Being able to dine at three-star French restaurants at prices not much higher than what you might have paid at McDonald's in the United States—now *that's* absurd! That was a time when you really could have "cashed in" on PPP theory because what was flashing was a screaming signal to get out of the dollar.

Cashing In on PPP: A Case History

Let's put ourselves in the catbird seat and turn the calendar back to the last time the dollar's PPP value was dramatically out of whack with currency prices—and then those prices adjusted to reflect reality.

By the end of 1984, the dollar was sky-high and had been rising for years. Its purchasing power overseas was tremendous. Americans who traveled through Europe in style for a pittance realized this in their guts. But what were the figures on the dollar's Purchasing Power Parity saying? How could an investor have profited from them?

Example: The German Mark

At the end of 1984, the German mark was worth about 32¢, or DM3.1 per dollar. Virtually every measure of the dollar/mark PPP value was flashing that the dollar was too expensive, that the mark's fundamental value was higher.

As usual, not everyone agreed on just how much the mark needed to rise to reach its fundamental value. But a look at two PPP forecasters with long track records revealed a sound consensus.

Charts 14 and 15 on page 304 show what you would have seen at the end of 1984. In each case, the solid line portrays the actual mark price at that time. The broken line represents the mark's PPP value estimated by the particular forecaster.

Chart 14 is from *International Bank Credit Analyst*. It estimated the mark's PPP rate was about 47¢, or DM2.13 per dollar. Chart 15 is from Harry Browne, who estimated it at 50.28¢, or DM1.99 per dollar.

The consensus was that the mark, at 32¢, was much too low.

What Actually Happened

Within two years the mark had risen to over 55¢, or 72% from those 1984 year-end levels. In three years the mark would be up over 100%.

This big swing characterizes PPPs. Once a trend is underway, a currency's price doesn't just go back to parity and stay there. Almost always the currency dramatically overshoots that parity. A currency that was for years too cheap can, when it begins to adjust back, rise so fast that in short order it becomes too expensive.

The flip side of this is that once a currency becomes too cheap or too high priced, there is no guarantee that the currency is about to correct—far from it. A glance at any of the charts will tell you that sometimes years go by with a currency either too high or low, according to where its Purchase Power Parity will tell you it "should" be.

Look at chart 16 on page 305. Imagine that by mid-1983 you'd been a dollar holder since late 1978. So far, so good. The dollar had risen during those four and a half years against the Swiss franc. By August 1983 it was overvalued by at least 20% against the franc.

The franc seemed cheap, so you bought it. Well, it was cheap, but it spent the next eighteen months getting even cheaper. By the time the Swissie finally reached its cheapest (33¢), it was a full 45% below its PPP. That is to say, at an

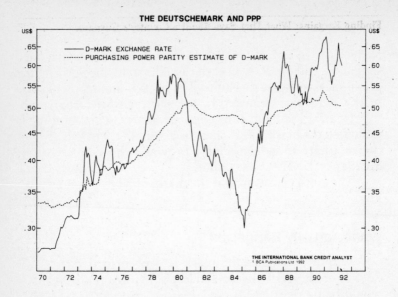

How two experts used PPP to predict a rise in the mark: The dotted lines show what each expert felt the dollar was worth (how overpriced vs. the mark) based on Purchasing Power Parity at the time. Sure enough, the mark rose (the dollar fell)—by 72% in two years, and by over 100% in three years—justifying the validity of the PPP measurement.

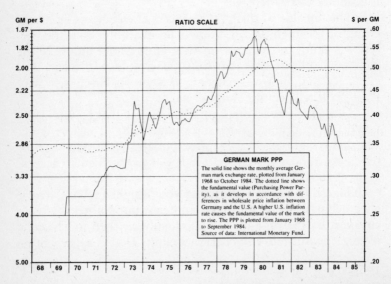

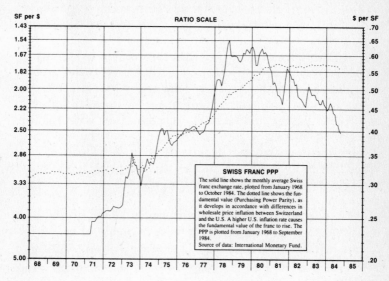

SWISS FRANC PPP
The solid line shows the monthly average Swiss franc exchange rate, plotted from January 1968 to October 1984. The dotted line shows the fundamental value (Purchasing Power Parity), as it develops in accordance with differences in wholesale price inflation between Switzerland and the U.S. A higher U.S. inflation rate causes the fundamental value of the franc to rise. The PPP is plotted from January 1968 to September 1984.
Source of data: International Monetary Fund.

Two great chances to make a killing on the Swiss franc: In this chart, Harry Browne plotted the dollar exchange rate of the franc (solid line) against his estimation of the franc's purchasing power at the time (dotted line). What this shows is that in two time periods—the first from 1968 to 1971 when exchange rates were artificially fixed and the second from 1982 onward— the franc was worth a lot more than its official exchange rate. The chart ends in 1984 but after that the dollar took another sickening fall against the franc. So using the franc's PPP (Purchasing Power Parity) as a guide, you could have bought the franc dirt cheap and made a killing.

exchange rate of 60¢—not 33¢—the price of goods would have been the same in Switzerland as in the United States. If you had started to buy at a franc price of 48¢ because it seemed low to you, you might have kicked yourself when the franc sank to 33¢. Of course, when it soared four years later to 80¢ the markets proved that 48¢ (the price you paid) was indeed low. But a franc price of 33¢ would have been better yet.

All this goes to show that you can be right in identifying a currency as being too cheap and still be too early. Indeed, you almost inevitably will be. That's why you needn't ever waste time kicking yourself for being eighteen months too early in getting out of dollars. For one thing, you will probably be earning interest while you are waiting for the market to catch up with your basically wise decision. Being early could, indeed, be thought of as a safer move than being too late and seeing the currency you should be in soar off out of your reach.

No one can switch all his currency holdings, selling high and buying low, at exactly the best moment. Even Joseph Kennedy, who apparently sold his stocks in May 1929, missed the exact peak of August. I doubt he ever griped. Indeed, he sold near enough to the peak to help ensure his family's fortunes for generations to come.

Summing Up Purchasing Power Parity

Purchasing Power Parity is one very helpful way to measure whether a currency is too cheap or too expensive. Briefly, the PPP theory states that over time one country's exchange rate relative to another's will move to a point at which the same item costs approximately the same (allowing for restrictions, taxes, etc.) in both countries.

For instance, when the same products can generally be bought much cheaper in the United States than in Japan or Western Europe, something has to give. The incentive to buy these same products cheaper (i.e., in this country) should lead the rest of the world to convert their currencies to dollars, or so the PPP theory goes. And this generally happens, over time.

It is, however, foolish to make any investment decision

based on PPPs alone. A currency that becomes cheap according to its PPP level can, and usually does, become much cheaper before it works its way back to parity. As a rule, once a currency trend is underway, it will dramatically go above or below the theoretical PPP level. It will overshoot, as dynamic markets generally do.

Use PPP as one measure. You should be able to see it at work wherever things are sold. Then when, after considering your other observations, you are sure about what the next trend will be, make your investment and have patience while the market catches up and verifies what you have done.

CHAPTER 23

▼

Are Recessions
Good for
a Currency?

Just as a share of stock represents ownership of the assets of a company, holding a foreign currency represents ownership of the productive power of a nation. Just as a stock price will increase if the company grows and prospers, so will a currency increase if the country's entire economy flourishes. There are aspects of a country's economy that can work either to underpin or undermine the currency.

This is just common sense. Over the long run you can easily see that a healthy economy translates into a strong currency. Again, compare the gains in productivity in Japan and the German-speaking countries to statistics from the United States, and it is no surprise that the dollar has lost so much ground against those currencies in the last generation. But also realize that however slowly America's economy has grown compared to Japan, it has actually grown more since 1970 than the economies of Britain, Australia, or Canada, countries where currencies have fallen against the dollar during that same generation. And even these relatively slow economies grew well when compared to Mexico, Brazil, or Chile.

As you would predict, the currencies of Britain, Australia, and Canada rose against the currencies of Mexico, Brazil, and Chile. And the economies of even these last three did well against Nicaragua's and Uganda's so their currencies did too. Over time the currency market does a marvelous job of rewarding those who hold the money of a healthy economy, compared to those who hold the money of the less healthy ones.

The Markets Always Catch Up

But keep in mind the first two words of that last sentence: *over time*. Even though America's productive growth has not matched Germany's since 1971, there have been years during that period when the dollar has nonetheless risen strongly against the mark. An investor who switched his savings to the currency of whatever country was reporting the best growth figures would usually have to pay a high price for it.

There are many reasons for this. For one, markets (including currency markets) anticipate what is going to happen. The savviest investors and traders look ahead and buy what they think will very likely go up in price. So a stock that is in a position to have a string of successful years would attract money early on from these professionals. Then as the company's performance strengthens, fulfilling the promise the pros saw, the stock would also attract a lot of general investor interest. People love to go with a "winner."

The only problem is that by the time a company's successes are widely known, the share price has risen to reflect this. Moreover, the price now also reflects the euphoria of grand future expectations.

It's the same thing with the share of a country—its currency.

In 1982 few people realized the powerhouse economy Japan was. But by the late eighties the spectacular performance of Japan had seared its way into the public consciousness. Early in the decade, as Japan was still laying the groundwork for its huge gains to come, the yen could still be had cheap. But by 1988, when the public awoke to the power of Japan, the yen was already very high and, in fact, has not in the years since bested its peak value in 1987.*

As long as Japan's economy continues generally to outperform America's, the yen will over time increase against the dollar. But again, like a stock that has gone too high too fast, there are times euphoria carries a price too high. Then the economy has to justify the euphoria before the price of the currency can again move ahead.

Are Recessions Good for Currencies?

If you believe in the widely held notion that it is good to buy a currency when the economy of the country is booming, then before you actually go out and buy, you should be aware of a phenomenon that makes that widely held notion less than persuasive.

The other side of this received wisdom is that you don't want to buy the currency of a country in a deeper recession than its major competitors. The argument is that, for example, a U.S. recession deeper than what is happening in Japan and Europe at the same time will cause the dollar to drop. The reasoning is that not only will the country's economy weaken, but interest rates fall during recessions, and "everyone knows" (or do they really?) that falling interest rates cause falling currency prices.

Well, it is true that interest rates fall during recessions. But you've seen that lower interest rates do not necessarily mean a lower exchange rate. It is also true that recessions may not cause a currency to fall in value. Let's see if we can make that clear.

Since the 1973 floating began, currency exchange rates

---

*Except for a few days in 1992, when it briefly bested it by only one yen or so.

have not responded to general changes in a major nation's economic climate. Indeed, during recessions a currency can rise!

In late 1974, for example, Britain hit the bottom of the worst economic crisis since the thirties. However, in that recession, which began around 1970, the pound did not really weaken. It had been $2.40 in 1970; by late 1974 it had dropped only to $2.30. And in the interim the highest it got was $2.60. The next two years, 1975 and 1976, saw a big bounce back from the recession. But during these two years of relative boom times, the pound plunged from $2.40 in early 1975 to below $1.60 by the end of 1976. Starting in 1977, the economy began to deteriorate again, paving the way for Mrs. Thatcher's 1979 victory. The economy did not improve immediately; not until 1982, when the corner was turned, did the economy pick up steam. But what happened during these bad economic times? The pound soared back up from $1.60 in late 1976 to $2.40 by 1981.

What was the pound's performance during the period since 1982? Extremely volatile: first plunging from $2.40 in 1981 to $1.05 in 1985 (a 56% drop), then soaring nearly 100% to $2.02 in the next seven years, during a period of both economic strength and slump. So there is no necessary connection between recessions and low currencies, just as there is none between lower interest rates and low currencies.

If there is any doubt about this, consider the 20% rise in the dollar against the D-mark in early 1991. This was a time when interest rates were falling in the United States and rising in Germany, as well as a time when the United States was in a full recession and Germany, while weakening, was not.

How the Dollar Fared in Four Recessions

The link between recessions and currency value is even more dramatically illustrated in the dollar.

Since the dollar began to float in 1973, there have been

four U.S. recessions. The first began in October 1973 and lasted until early 1975. Using the dollar's value versus the Swiss franc as a measure, we see that in late 1973 the dollar sharply rose, while through 1974 it gradually fell, and it ended the recession at about the same level it began. There was even less movement between the dollar and the pound, but the dollar likewise ended the recession at the same price as before.

Putting this period into perspective, we should be aware that a recession was not the only thing going on at that time in the currency markets. The overriding factor was the currencies being set free from their decades of fixed exchange rates. The dollar had been overvalued for many years, even decades, before 1971. Afterward it sank with a vengeance, to make up for all that time. From 1972 to 1979 the dollar fell almost steadily, from SFr4 per dollar to SFr1.6. In fact, there was only one major period in all these years when the dollar rose. This was in 1973, beginning just before the recession's start and continuing for several months into it.

Not only did the dollar rise during a recession; it rose during the *only* recession period in a decade during which overall it plunged precipitously. We clearly have to question the idea that currencies fall in recessions.

The next recession was the sharp but short one that took place during the first half of 1980. But during this precise time the dollar had its sharpest upward spike since—you guessed it—the 1973 recession. In fact, in the six months after the recession ended in mid-1980, the dollar fell back almost to the level it had been before the 1980 recession began.

After six months of economic recovery—and dollar weakness—another recession began. This was the long 1981–82 slump. What did the dollar do during this longest and deepest of postwar recessions? It rose; not dramatically, but it still ended the recession clearly higher than it had begun. Once again, a U.S. recession had not meant a falling dollar.

During the fourth recession, which began in mid-1990

and continues as of this writing in late 1992, the same pattern has held.

While it reached record lows against the fabulous five in 1992, in each case the new low was not very much lower than the low points of 1987. Also, in the midst of the recession there were two times when the dollar soared by over 20%. These were only temporary. But what is clear once again is that the recession had not caused the dollar to plunge.

Indeed, if there is a pattern through all this, it is that U.S. recessions seem to make the dollar stronger. But you wouldn't be wise to count blindly on this as a general rule; exceptions abound. During the first half of 1991, both the United States and Britain were in recession. While the dollar rose, the pound fell by 15% against the dollar. And Switzerland was in a recession in 1982 just as America was, but the dollar rose and the franc fell from SFr1.80 to SFr2.25 per dollar—fully 25%.

But two decades of fluctuating currencies and volatile economic cycles have taught the almost perverse lesson that the major country that is beset by the deepest recession will see its currency rise. You can put the theory to a test.

As of late 1992, the U.S. economy was still looking quite sorry. It had been performing much worse than other major nations since 1989. According to the theory the dollar should rise. It did rise during 1991. The rise was weak, and that may have been all the rise we'll get.

Again, by the time you read this, you will know. If it *has* risen, it will mean that the nondollar currencies will be much cheaper than they were just a couple of years ago. You will be able to buy them and begin a long-term foreign currency portfolio and invest in the other nondollar ways described in this book at much cheaper levels than you could have for two years before. Consider it a gift from the gods.

Whatever happens in 1993 or 1994, however, you sure can't believe the popular notion that U.S. recessions must mean a lower dollar. By now the popular notion may even have changed to its opposite: recessions must cause a currency to rise. That, in fact, is what people believed in the seventies.

Faddish theories abound, and the best an investor can do is have some historical perspective to help judge them as they come up. That warning given, experience seems to show that if a country suffers a recession deeper than other countries', that in itself will not cause its currency to fall very much; it might even make it rise.

The Cleansing Power of Recessions

Perhaps the key reason for this has to do with an understanding of what recessions are. They are usually seen as bad things. In fact, they are the result of mistakes that were made during the prior boom. If those mistakes are recognized and addressed, the seeming bad thing can become a good thing.

Though painful, recessions are cleansing processes that wring out the excesses of the previous boom. When over, they leave an economy more based in reality than the boom economy was at its height. Debt is reduced, productivity improves, resources that were misused are redirected. In general, recessions eliminate flab and trim the economy up. The deeper one country's recession is relative to another, then the "leaner and meaner" will be the economic machine, in general, that emerges from the slump.

So if you see a major economy that is deeper in recession than its fellows, look a little closer. Ask yourself if the uneconomic excesses are being wrung out to any great extent. Then look at the currency. Is it cheap: that is, did it spend the boom falling against other major currencies?

If both these things are true, then chances are good that this currency will rise over the next couple of years. Notwithstanding all the gloom about both the recession and a low currency, this is often the best time to buy. Chances are you won't get the absolute low, but chances also are that the currency will soon be higher.

▼

CHAPTER 24

How to Handle
Dollar Rallies

No investment goes up for-
ever. Even the strongest currencies can sometimes rise too far
too fast and simply have to fall back. And even though the
dollar has been fundamentally weak for years, there have
been times when its fall got ahead of itself.

Since it began falling in the early seventies, the dollar
has had only three general periods where it rose. The first
lasted the longest by far—about six years, from late 1978
to early 1985. Over this time the dollar doubled against
most major currencies. It seems hard to believe now, but
throughout 1984 "the King Dollar" was all Europeans
could talk about.

In 1989 and 1991 the dollar rose by about 20% and
25%, respectively, each time over a period of less than six
months.*

---

*In late 1992, as this book goes to press, another dollar rally has carried the
greenback up by 20% in just six weeks! It is not yet clear whether this will be the
start of a generalized period of dollar strength or just another flash in the pan.

When It Makes Sense for Americans to "Buy Dollars"

What does it mean for Americans to "buy dollars"? After all, we already have dollars. Further, when you buy them, where do you put them?

In practice it usually means just switching your foreign currency accounts back into dollars. But there's limited profit in that. If you buy the mark and the mark then rises 10% against the dollar, you've made 10% plus whatever the mark interest rate was. That's easy to see.

But see what happens when you "buy" the dollar—that is, hold dollars in your account for an expected period of dollar strength. If the dollar goes up 10% against the mark, all you make is the interest on the dollar. Of course, you do get to buy marks a little cheaper if you decide to switch back into marks. But while the dollar is rising, there are fewer ways to profit.

You could of course buy the Dollar Index* contract or sell foreign currency contracts on the futures exchange. If futures are within your comfort zone, that's fine. The contract's value fluctuates, usually hovering around $100,000. If you go two-to-one leverage, you'll have to put up 50%, or $50,000. Futures contracts by their nature expire no later than six or nine months in the future. When the contracts expire, you'll have to buy new ones, and that increases brokerage fees. Finally, the futures market allows you to put down only a fraction of the total contract value: 2% to 5% is common; 50% is rare. It is a great temptation to put down as little as possible. Most people cannot resist it. With such a small margin, it is no surprise that 90% of all investors lose at futures. This is because only a small decline in price can wipe out your equity. Most people are afraid of the futures

---

*The Dollar Index contract calculates the exchange rate of the dollar against a weighted basket of the ten most important trading partners' currencies.

markets for this reason. A few percentage points against you when you put down only the minimum, and your position is wiped out.

If you don't feel as comfortable in the options or futures market, holding CDs, T-bills, and T-bonds at safe banks can bring a very satisfactory return during dollar rallies.

There is a way to augment that return if you are willing to take on more risk than CDs or T-bills represent, but not as much as buying futures. During the eighties it became possible at some banks to buy these instruments on margin. You could, for example, buy a $10,000 CD, put down $5,000, and borrow the other $5,000 in a currency you believe will be the weakest and fall the most against the dollar.

Some banks we list in chapter 13 will let you put up as little as 20%. And the first of the case histories we'll examine uses this ratio.

Case History: 1988–89

On November 21, 1988, an investor bought a $121,000 six-month CD yielding 8% annually (or 4% over the six months that would end May 21, 1989). At that rate, the CD, held to maturity, was worth $125,840 on May 21.

Because he felt the U.S. dollar was going up, he paid only 20% down ($24,200) and borrowed the remaining 80% ($96,800) in Swiss francs at 4% interest from the same bank that issued the CD. At the time, the bank's retail rate for francs was 67.6¢. So he borrowed SFr142,167.20.

Sure enough, the dollar rose. In fact it soared. It soared against all major currencies, but particularly against the Swiss franc. On Monday, May 22 (the actual date of redemption), the bank's Swiss franc/U.S dollar conversion rate was SFr1.779 per dollar, or 56.2¢ per franc. On that date the investor owed SFr147,601.06 to repay the loan, including interest, and the CD's opening and closing costs. This was only 3.1% above the amount borrowed six months earlier.

TABLE 7

Profits on CD Investment

CD Value at Maturity		$125,840.00
Loan Repayment and CD Costs	SFr147,601.06 =	
	$82,968.56	
Conversion Fee	+207.42	
Amount Owed		−83,175.98
		42,664.02
Down Payment		−24,200.00
Net Profit		$18,464.02

Net profit represents 76.3% profit on a 20.3% currency move (downward) in six months.

Since the franc's price on May 22 was 56.2¢, the sum to be paid equaled $82,968.56. Add to this a final $207.42 conversion fee, and the grand total to be repaid was $83,175.98, a far cry from the $96,800 worth of francs borrowed six months earlier. If you subtract the money the investor owed ($83,175.98) from the full redemption value of the CD ($125,840), you're left with $42,644.02. This was what the $24,200 he had put down six months before was worth now.

The difference between these two figures is $18,464.02, which represents the amount of net profit this trade made. The six-month CD yielded a whopping 76.3% return, or a 152.6% annual rate of return. Not bad for a CD.

Case History: 1991

This case history adds a few wrinkles. On January 7, 1991, another investor bought a three-month CD in the amount of

$350,000. It yielded 6.62%, so if held until April 7, the CD would be worth $355,796.87.

Once again, the investor believed the Swiss franc would fall against the dollar, so he borrowed Swiss francs to buy the CD. The client put up $100,000 (or 28.5%) of the $350,000. He borrowed the remaining $250,000 in Swiss francs. At the time, the franc's exchange rate was SFr1.28 per dollar. (The all-time low of the dollar occurred days later at SFr1.25.) He borrowed SFr321,050.63 at an annual interest rate of 9.875%.

The franc did begin to decline quickly in the weeks after early January. Specifically, by March 22, 1991, the franc had declined to SFr1.388 per dollar. At this point the client decided to take his profits and put them (as well as another $100,000) into a new CD with a new loan in a different currency.

The first step was to "cash out" of the CD. It was sold prematurely, with two weeks to go in its term. This move may strike you as odd if you've bought CDs only at American banks, where CDs cannot be easily or cheaply sold or broken before the maturity date. But the best European banks do allow this, and for very small penalties.

Then the investor paid off the loan, which had grown to SFr328,385.41. At the new rate of SFr1.388 francs per dollar, this sum was actually less than the $250,000 borrowed: $236,588.91. Subtracting U.S. dollars *owed* from the value of the CD *owned*, we get:

TABLE 8

CD Cash-Out Value

Value of CD	$354,011.71
Loan Repayment	− 236,588.91
Net Cash-out Amount	$117,422.80

Remember that the investor put up $100,000 exactly eleven weeks earlier. This meant a gross profit over that period of 17.42%; on an annualized basis his gain was 82.36%.

If you think the dollar will rise, you have wide latitude in deciding which currency to borrow and how much.

What if you borrow yen, thinking that it will be the weakest currency, and then you see the deutsche mark falling twice as fast against the dollar as the yen? What can you do? There is a simple solution. Have your bank switch the loan from the one currency to the other. (There is, of course, a charge for converting from one money to another, and there is also a minor account closing fee. Interest services on the loan in the old currency are calculated quarterly. When you switch, you are charged for the unpaid part of the loan for the quarter.)

What if you are unsure which currency will be weakest? Then at the best banks you can diversify your loan, denominating it into two, three, four, or more currencies. You could denominate your loan in ecus, itself a basket of European currencies, if you think the dollar will rise against Europe's currency in general.

And what if you believe the dollar has risen enough? You can sell your CD, T-bill, or T-bond. Then you can decide whether to stay in nonleveraged dollars or switch into foreign currencies.

There is a chance your eyes glazed over while reading this chapter. If so, don't feel guilty. Leverage is only for those who want to gamble on extra gain and are willing to accept greater risk with even a small amount. If you ever plan to switch temporarily back into dollars, you can always stick to safe dollar instruments. There is no dishonor in protecting the profits you've made in foreign currencies by selling them and holding the proceeds in T-bills.

PART VII

▼

Clouds That Hang over the Dollar

▲

CHAPTER 25

▼

When Are We Going to Get Our Act Together?

There are so many fundamental problems across the American landscape today that it is hard to imagine that the U.S. dollar could ever rise again. Of course, this is an exaggeration—perhaps. No investment and no currency goes down forever. The dollar may well be rising as you read this. After all, it did rise strongly for a few years in the eighties. If it does again, chapter 24 has shown you how to profit from it.

But when one travels, observes, and compares other countries to the United States today, it's impossible to avoid being more than a little pessimistic about America's place in the world's future. We are not talking about the problems we can see hurting us right now—lack of competitiveness, a weak economy, political paralysis, even a lousy infrastructure.

No, to get really pessimistic about our country and our dollar, one need look at the only hope for our future: our children.

Our children are our future. And we haven't been treating them as well as Switzerland, Japan, or most of the other countries whose currencies have most risen against ours. Back in chapter 5 we called them the Fabulous Five. We could also call them the Fortunate Five, although good luck didn't have much to do with it.

America's neglect of its children begins when they are still in the womb. Each year a quarter million U.S. babies are born so seriously underweight that they go right into intensive care treatments costing an average of $3,000 a day. That's for nearly seven hundred babies born each day. Many of them will end up blind, deaf, or mentally retarded—most of them needlessly. The U.S. infant mortality rate is 9.7 per 1,000 births—the supposedly richest nation on earth ranks eighteenth in this. Japan, Switzerland, and Germany are in the top five, with a mortality rate a fraction of ours. It is a rare baby in those countries not inoculated against TB, polio, and measles; in California, our richest state, only half of the two-year-olds are fully immunized.

Even well-paid parents are not always able to afford all the medical care they'd like for their children. Fewer and fewer company health plans cover even routine medical care for children. In the other five countries full care is provided as a matter of course.

Where Are Their Mothers Today?

It is a fairly rare U.S. household now where a parent stays at home with the preschool children. In Switzerland or Japan a young mother who goes to work when her husband also works is very seldom encountered. In Japan, parents with children receive monthly subsidies from the government, and most employers pay them as well. Those societies deem it very important for a mother to be near her young children as much as possible.

Millions of young American mothers would love to stay home as well. But they can't afford to. While the Fortunate Five have been getting richer since currencies began floating

in 1973, we have gotten poorer. The real median income—
that's after inflation—of households with parents under age
thirty fell by 25 percent from 1973 to 1989. And that's with
two incomes, which almost all parents have depended upon
since 1973.

So even with mothers working, families have been getting
poorer. In fact, young families have been getting poorer faster
than most other Americans. And young children themselves
have become the poorest group in America. One-fourth of all
children under age six now live in households where total
annual income is below the poverty level—$12,675 for a
family of four.

In Germany, unlike Switzerland and Japan, it *is* fairly
common to see young mothers working. But German parents
may deduct the total cost of child care from their taxes. In
America a working mother cannot do this, but she *can* deduct
the cost of a new Persian rug for her office.

In Germany all day-care givers are regulated and regularly inspected in the very German way. In America parents
place their children in unlicensed home care or unregulated
nurseries and then just hope.

Don't Our Children Deserve More from Us?

In Switzerland a young woman fresh out of school now starts
at a $32,000 annual salary for teaching the youngest children.
In Michigan a preschool teacher with five years experience
earns $12,000 (though Michigan prison guards with similar
experience make nearly $30,000).

In Switzerland teaching is a respected job. In America it
seems that almost all jobs that mean coming into contact with
children are denigrated. No class of doctor earns less than do
pediatricians. Standards are extremely high for U.S. pilots (as
they should be), but almost anyone can get a job as a school
bus driver.

One could go on and on; the list of sins against children

in this country is a long one. One fact is particularly telling: school children in America simply don't know nearly as much about most *any* subject as do children in Western Europe and Japan. (Oops, that's wrong. School children in those other countries don't know about living with weapons in schools like ours do.) But given the small amount of effort and care that has surrounded them from birth compared to other countries' children, the state of our school children should surprise no one.

The lot of America's children has visibly worsened since you were a child, but that may only be a start. This neglect of what is our future in its most fundamental sense—compared to the rigid attention paid to the education, training, and general well-being of children in most other leading countries—is an ominous portent for America during the next generation.

We're Leaving Them Debt, Danger, and Decay

The things we are giving our children most enthusiastically are our debts. They'll be paying for the bailing out of our banking system until they start to turn gray, if not longer. We don't know how to pay our debts off, but we aren't providing the means for our children to pay them off more quickly.

Americans love debt much more than the Swiss, Japanese, or Germans and too often seem to embrace it with at least as much passion as they embrace their children.

But before leaving the generally sorry state of American children behind, let's put a small spotlight on one awful condition that, while it affects every American, affects children the worst. This is the level of sheer danger to be found in the streets, parks, and even schools of so much of America. If you travel to Tokyo, Zurich, Vienna, or Munich, you simply never feel unsafe, no matter what part of these big cities you're in.

Compare that to our greatest cities, where filth, broken

roads and bridges, inefficient public transportation, and mentally disturbed, homeless people will be hard to ignore. It is very hard to find *any* of these features in Tokyo or Zurich, but it is very easy in New York or Los Angeles. The first two are the major cities in the countries whose currencies have been the world's strongest for a generation. The second two are the major cities in a nation whose currency has dropped and dropped and dropped.

There must be a connection between the decay of our cities and the decay of our currency. The state of a nation's cities is the most public symbol of the physical well-being of a people. The state of a nation's currency is the most public symbol of its financial well-being. By that measure the great cities of Europe and even Asia now have it over American cities, just as the currencies of Europe and Asia have it over the dollar.

Take one American city that is widely admired here and abroad, San Francisco. It has been called both the most European and the most Asian of all American cities. It was called "the city that knows how" after it rebuilt itself so quickly and marvelously from the earthquake and fire that destroyed it in 1906.

That can no longer be said of San Francisco. Two years after the much smaller damage done by the 1989 earthquake, almost no damaged public structure was repaired. Yes, the vital Bay Bridge, which connects San Francisco to Oakland, was quickly repaired after part of it collapsed. But the four other damaged freeways had not been. On one major city freeway the only work has been millions of dollars wasted on what was discovered to be the wrong type of repairs. Another freeway's very future existence was in question for months before it was finally just torn down. A new one is promised, but meanwhile traffic in the area visibly worsens by the month.

Anyone who has lived in Tokyo or Zurich would find it impossible to imagine that damaged roads of importance would remain closed while months of dithering, dickering, waste, and simple incompetence all took their toll. In fact, recently the electric service of Zurich broke down for about twenty minutes, and residents were infuriated that such a thing was allowed to happen. It was unheard of and totally unacceptable.

The infrastructure is in dismal shape throughout America. It is, however, in terrific shape in Japan, Singapore, and (with the exception of Britain) Western Europe. You can't attribute this to the fact that much of Japan's and Germany's infrastructure was totally destroyed in World War II and thus had to be rebuilt recently from scratch. France was largely untouched by the bombing; Switzerland totally so, and yet both countries have kept their infrastructures modern. In contrast, while no American city has ever been bombed, many of its roads and bridges sure look as if they had been, and recently.

Have We Lost the *Will* to Solve Our Biggest Problems?

All the different fundamental problems we've touched on share at least two characteristics. First, in no area has there been any real remedy. If you think the problems will go away, think again. They all just keep getting worse. Second, these are all problems that most often affect us in localized and personal ways. But they are hardly small. Bad education and a crumbling infrastructure inevitably have larger economic consequences, but we seem unable to address even the local, immediate challenges that are so easy to see—from illiterate high school graduates to potholed roads. We are over-whelmed by the size of our problems, and in so many ways we seem to have given up.

There is, as well, an array of deep-seated economic problems, the consequences of which are harder to see. But they too will continue to exert a drag on the dollar's value for years to come.

CHAPTER 26

▼

The Price We Pay
by Refusing to Save

*D*ollar falls on fears of lower *interest rates.*" If you follow reports like this one in your newspaper, you might come to believe that high interest rates in a country make the value of its currency rise.

Just don't believe it.

All other things being equal, you would be much better off believing the following:

1. The more people save, the lower interest rates will be.
2. Conversely, the less people save, the higher interest rates will be.
3. Over time, as the pool of savings drops in a country, interest rates will be higher than they otherwise would be.

Those Who Love to Save Versus
Those Who Hate To

You can count on all of the statements listed above. And you can also count on this: as a low or falling rate of savings causes interest rates to rise, it will, over time, also have a bad effect on the value of that nation's currency.

You can prove this to yourself by asking, "If low savings levels cause interest rates to rise and [as superficial newspaper reports have led you to believe] higher interest rates cause a currency to rise, then wouldn't countries with the lowest savings rates—like Argentina and Israel—have the strongest currencies?"

They don't of course. They have troubled currencies.

Now let's look at the savings rates since 1950 of three major countries with strong currencies and see how they compare to the United States.

Japan's savings rate has been remarkably stable ever since 1950. Savings have fluctuated between 15 percent and 20 percent of income. This is an extraordinarily high percentage, and thus the fact that Japanese interest rates have generally been among the world's lowest since then should come as no surprise. Also no surprise is that during the past generation, no currency on earth besides the Swiss franc has been as strong as the yen.

Indeed, the two next strongest currencies are the two other "German-speaking" ones: the Austrian schilling and the deutsche mark. In the German-speaking world, savings have always been deemed important and admirable. Going into debt, on the other hand, has always been regarded as something to be ashamed of. (Remember, the word in German for debt is *schulden*, which also means guilt.) Clearly, cultures that encourage savings and downplay debt the way Japan and the German-speaking countries do are precisely those countries that enjoy not only generally low interest rates but generally strong currencies.

Now compare these experiences with that of the United States. From the fifties to the early seventies, the U.S. savings rate slowly increased. By 1973 Americans were saving around 10 percent of their income. But after that year a new trend began, one that is still with us. The saving rate fell to under 2 percent in 1987 and has not really recovered since.

Can it be a mere coincidence that the long decline in the U.S. saving rate from 1973 to 1987 exactly mirrors the long decline in the dollar, which also fell from 1973 to 1987 and has not really reversed since?

The Simplest Way to Pick a Strong Currency

If you are looking for a currency to invest in, one that will keep its value, the simplest way to decide is to remember this: over the long term a country with high savings and productivity and low interest rates will have a stronger currency than a country that won't save and has low productivity and high interest rates.

Around 1900 the great Austrian economist von Boehm-Bawerk offered his "law of decreasing interest." He believed that the lower a nation's long-term interest rates were, the higher the level of that nation's general intelligence, culture, and even moral values. He pointed out that the great civilizations of the past were characterized, in their periods of ascendancy, by generally low or declining interest rates. Their latter, decadent stages were characterized by high or rising rates.

Support for this can be found by reading Sidney Homer's excellent *A History of Interest Rates, 2000 B.C. to the Present*, in which he recounts the history of interest rates in three great ancient civilizations. Babylonian civilization began to hit its stride around 2000 B.C., and as it grew, interest rates generally declined. Hammurabi's Code (1800 B.C.) laid down sensible rules by which savings and productivity were encouraged. Rates over the next thousand years gradually declined from 25 percent to 10 percent or less. Then, in the generations just before Babylonia was conquered and destroyed by Persia in 539 B.C., rates rose sharply, to over 40 percent.

As civilization faltered in Babylonia, it was flourishing in Greece. Athens established democracy in 508 B.C., and for the next three hundred years saw its culture advance and its

interest rate decline (from 18 percent to 6 percent). But by
the time Greece declined and was absorbed by Rome (50 B.C.
to 50 A.D.), rates had risen sharply again.

In Rome the story was repeated. During the great years
of the Republic (200–50 B.C.) average rates generally declined from 18 percent to 4 percent. As the empire grew,
became corrupt, and declined interest rates made their inevitable advance (A.D. 50–400).

Every great civilization since Rome's has had a similar
experience. The Italian city-states, France, and Great Britain
all saw rates fall as their power grew, and rise as their power
declined.

Is the same likely to happen in this country?

The United States, 1792–1992: Rise and Fall(?)

American long-term government bond rates began their life
in the 1790s, with the Constitution. They were 8 percent at
that time, but fell over the course of the nineteenth century
to about 3 percent by 1900. By the early 1940s they averaged
only 1.95 percent. That was to be the low point in rates (and
perhaps the high point of American power). Since then, U.S.
rates have had a sustained climb never before witnessed in
our history. The phenomenon is disturbing.

It remains to be seen whether this trend can be broken
and convincingly reversed. Meanwhile, our recent, sorry savings rate and the high interest rates that have gone with it
will remain a cloud that hangs over the value of our dollars.

CHAPTER 27

▼

When We Can
No Longer
Borrow in Dollars—
Look Out, Dollar!

The dollar fell from 1985 to 1990 even while the American economy enjoyed good times almost unprecedented in peacetime. If the dollar fell when America's economy was strong, what will it do when the economy weakens? And most economists believe that our economy will be much weaker in the next five years than it was in the previous five.

Several things fueled the roaring eighties, America's longest-lived and most powerful peacetime economic expansion ever. But some of the forces that made us prosperous in the eighties probably will not be in place during the nineties. And the scariest of these is the likelihood that we simply will not be able to borrow money from other countries the way we have been to date.

Borrowing Your Own Money

The United States has been able to borrow vast amounts of money from Europe and Japan in dollars. That may not sound like a unique advantage, but actually it is an extraordinary one.

Say I borrowed money from you. But say also that I somehow was then able to print much more of the money, so it lost much of its value. When I repaid the loan to you, it would be money that was not worth as much as when you lent it to me. You wouldn't like that very much. Yet, that's exactly how our government has, for years, been treating foreigners who lend us money.

And here are the reasons we were able to pull it off. The dollar is still the world's currency. All central banks count their reserves in terms of the dollar. All the world's currencies are defined in terms of the dollar. Major commodities like oil and gold are defined in dollar terms. And the market for buying and selling dollars is gigantic compared to trading in any other currency. This remains the case even though the dollar's value has plunged over the past generation against other currencies, oil, and gold.

All this means is that the United States has been able (so far) to borrow dollars from foreigners, watch those dollars lose their value, and then pay back the debts in devalued dollars.

Let's say the U.S. government borrowed $500 billion from foreigners from 1985 to 1990. That's another way of saying that foreigners bought $500 billion in U.S. T-bills and Treasury bonds. What did those foreigners get in return? They, of course, received interest. But over those five years they watched the value of their principal fall by over half against their own currencies. So they ended up not making anything on those presumably safe investments; in fact, they lost and lost heavily.

No Other Nation Could Have Gotten Away with That

Take Argentina or Zambia, other nations living beyond their means. They cannot hope to get foreigners to accept

IOUs of australs or kwachas. No one in his or her right mind would agree to lend good money in exchange for promises to be repaid in currencies that are virtually worthless or will be soon. (The Argentine austral has lost 99.999 + % of its value against even the dollar since 1979; the Zambian kwacha has only lost 98.1% since then.) The dollar, to be sure, is not in such bad water. But the principle is the same.

Even major countries have a hard time borrowing in their own currency when the world perceives that they don't have their affairs in order. France in 1982 or the United Kingdom in 1976 are two examples. Not only did they face a run on their currencies when they tried to float foreign loans, they ended up borrowing (that is, denominating) most of their loans in U.S. dollars, Swiss francs, or marks.

Could the Same Thing Happen to Us?

The United States has never, at least in this century, been forced to denominate its foreign debt in foreign currency. Indeed, in the eighties it was able to borrow massively in dollars that were then devalued.

How long can we expect the world to extend us such largesse? If you were a foreigner who bought U.S. debt instruments like Treasury bonds and saw them devalued by over half in a few years, how would you feel? Would you be happy about where your capital has gone? Would you be willing to do the same thing again?

Obviously not. And even if there were no economy closer to home needing your capital today, you still would think long and hard about extending your loans to as risky a borrower as we must seem to be. It would be better to forgo the interest entirely rather than sacrifice huge hunks of your principal.

But our condition is now even more precarious than that. Neither Europe nor Japan has a current need to send their capital to the United States for investment. There is an urgent need for that capital close to home, a need that was not there in the eighties. Europe is unifying itself, and it's rebuilding an Eastern Europe that's been in ruin for decades. Japan saw half the value of its stock market—¥ 2 trillion—wiped away in 1990. Real estate prices there are falling as well. To shore up the system, Japan is raising interest rates to modern records to attract its capital back home.

So an historic shift has occurred that could do real damage to the value of the dollar. Instead of being net buyers of U.S. debt as it was since 1945, suddenly Japan has been a net seller of U.S. securities. That means it is getting out of the dollar. As Europe rebuilds its eastern sector, much the same could occur. It is already beginning.

The $70 to $80 billion worth of long-term U.S. debt that foreigners bought on average annually from 1984 to 1990 made life easy for us in many ways. Even though we saved only a pittance and, in fact, had record deficits, the U.S. economy was still able to grow on borrowed money. At any other time we would have been forced to change our ways; this time the world pampered us. It may not in the future.

No other nation exhibiting our unthrifty ways would have been able to borrow its own money as we did. They would have been forced to pay back their debts in a currency that everyone respects, in a currency that they could not then turn around and devalue. We were able to get away with our profligacy because of the residue of the dollar's past strength, as well as the fact that no other single currency was ready to take on a world role.

But the world is growing weary of watching the dollar fall, and the Japanese and Germans are becoming more comfortable with the growing global roles the yen and the mark are playing. Also, the ecu is growing daily in importance. And should it become the accepted currency in all of Europe, the dollar will suffer dramatically.

To sum up: when foreigners stop selling U.S. Treasury debt and start buying it again, they may force us to denominate our debt in yen, marks, or even ecus. This would be a national humiliation, to be sure. But worse yet, there's simply no telling what effect that would have on the value of the dollar.

In other words, when we can no longer borrow in dollars—look out, dollar!

PART VIII

▼

Conclusion

▲

▼

CHAPTER 28

A Bad Thing for Most Investors Could Be a Great Thing for You

This chapter is about money and credit—about having too much of them and not having enough; about what each does to the prices you have to pay and to the value of your currency. And it's also about how you, simply by putting your money in the right form and in the right place, can become richer just when most people are feeling poorer and poorer.

But, First, Let's Talk About Pizzas and Cars

If you're hungry and see a pizza, that first slice is going to taste great. Using financial terms, it will have a lot of *value* to you. The second slice will still taste good, but it will somehow not be as precious or valuable as the first piece. Once you get down to the sixth slice, you aren't as hungry as you were before slice number one. The value of the fifth and sixth slices have gone down a lot.

If you want a car and get one, you'll value it highly. If

you then get two, three, seven, or ten of the same cars soon after, there's no way you'll value each new addition as much as you valued the first.

The more of something there is, the less value each unit of it will have. The smaller the supply of something is, the more value each of those "somethings" will have. And this goes for money as well as cars and pizzas.

What a Flood of New Money Does to a Stable Economy

Pretend that you live on an island. The island enjoys a bustling economy: people make things, sell them, and buy things from other people. It's all pretty much like us. As money, they use the dollar, again like us. But unlike us in the United States, prices have been stable for a long time. One dollar buys, let's say, a nice new copy of the works of Shakespeare or a pretty good breakfast. In other words, in this country, a dollar still buys a lot.

Let's say that the total amount of all the dollars on this island nation add up to $1 million. Then one day a helicopter appears over the island and drops another million one-dollar bills. They scatter—everyone gets some. Let's say everyone now has twice as many dollars as before.

What is the end result of all that money? Is everybody now twice as rich? They may all feel so at first, but the amount of goods and services for sale hasn't changed, only the supply of money has doubled. But remember, the more of something there is in an economy, the lower the value each unit of it will have. And that, again, includes the value of money.

The supply of what it takes to serve you breakfast in a coffee shop hasn't risen, just the number of dollars. So with twice as many dollars chasing the same number of breakfasts, it suddenly costs two dollars for breakfast, not one.

When you have a rush of new money available to spend for the same amount of goods to buy, then each dollar will be worth less. It will buy fewer goods. Of course, if people got very productive and produced many more goods to buy, then the amount of goods that each dollar would buy would return to where it was. (But unfortunately for us in the United States in recent decades, it seems easier to create twice as much money than to produce twice as many goods. And therein lies part of our problem.)

Now, let's say that there was another island. Its currency is called the rock. Here, the supply of money didn't go up. The rock's value has not been diluted.

Intrinsically, a loaf of bread is pretty much worth the same in each island. It makes the same number of sandwiches. But the rock still buys a loaf of bread. The other island's dollar—where the helicopter had doubled the money supply—is worth maybe half of what it was. So a loaf of bread there now costs twice as much as in prehelicopter days. And that is not all that has changed on that island. The value of its dollar just *has* to go down against neighboring currencies.

After all, if you owned rocks (the currency of the island that did not increase its money supply), would you, when traveling to the first island, be willing to pay two rocks for a loaf of bread that you could get at home for only one? Of course not. Inevitably, the exchange rate between the rock and the other island's dollar has to change too.

We really don't need to talk about any mythological island, though. Real life is just as graphic. Let's look, for example, at what happened during the eighties in Brazil, Argentina, and Bolivia.

In 1980, the total supply of cruzados, the currency of Brazil, came to Cr$1.288 billion. The government began to print money like mad, and by 1987 there existed over Cr$1 trillion cruzados. In other words, for every cruzado that existed in 1980, seven years later there existed 100. Actually, in 1980, Brazil's currency was called the cruzero, but so many were printed that the government lopped off three zeros and called the "new" currency the cruzado. This is a common trick and fools no one, but still it is done. We're adjusting to

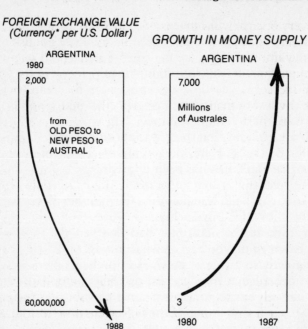

FOREIGN EXCHANGE VALUE
(Currency* per U.S. Dollar)

GROWTH IN MONEY SUPPLY

ARGENTINA
1980

2,000

from
OLD PESO to
NEW PESO to
AUSTRAL

60,000,000

1988

ARGENTINA

7,000

Millions
of Australes

3

1980   1987

*Recast to currency used in 1980.

How to trash a currency: Latin-American countries are great at printing vast amounts of new bills to spend their way out of problems. This does nothing but destroy one currency after another; Argentina, for example, has run through five different currencies in a very short time, making it almost impossible for investors and businesses to plan securely for the future.

what the total number of cruzados would have been in 1980, taking into account the accounting charge.

So the currency of Brazil grew 100-fold in seven years. What happened to the value of each one of those cruzados (against the U.S. dollar, let's say) during that time? In 1980 there was the equivalent of Cr$70 cruzados per dollar. By 1988 there were Cr$140,000 per dollar. The cruzado simply fell apart.

Argentina did much the same thing: In 1980 there existed a total of 3 million australs, by 1987 there existed 7 *billion*.

For every one that was in existence in 1980, there were 2,333 just seven years later. What did the exchange value of the currency do? No prizes for the correct answer—it went from an equivalent of 2,000 to 60,000,000 per dollar—a 3,000-fold increase!

Bolivia? For the Bolivian peso it's the same story: in 1980 there were $B15 billion in Bolivia. There were the equivalent of $B400 trillion (400,000,000,000,000) in 1987. (Actually, in 1985 Bolivia did the name-change accounting trick, lopping off six zeros from the peso, and renaming it the boliviano.) The currency value fell from $B24 per dollar to $B2 million per dollar in eight years. The charts show this very dramatically for all three countries. In each case, a huge increase in the supply of currency caused a massive collapse in the value of each one of those currency units versus the dollar.

It's easy to see here the connection between money supply and currency value. But for the major world currencies, there is rarely such a dramatic 1,000% increase in the money supply over a short time. If the U.S. were now to follow the Brazilian percentage increase of the eighties, the "narrow" U.S. money supply total, about $400 billion in 1991, would soar to $933.3 trillion by 1998. Things like that don't often happen. If median annual income today is $30,000, it would be $69,990,000 (almost $70 million!) seven years later. But no one would be any richer; a gallon of milk that costs $2 today would go for $4,666!

With our politicians in charge, you can't be sure it won't happen. But again, major governments don't usually inflate this crudely. They all inflate, however, even the best of them. You'll recall that even the Swiss franc has lost much of its value against gold over a few generations. But there is a great difference, as we'll see, between the comparatively small increase in the total Swiss franc supply and the increase in the U.S. dollar supply or most other currencies over any comparable period.

Now, in advanced economies, when politicians want to inflate, they don't normally just print it and release it, by helicopter or any other way. Instead, the central bank creates credit out of thin air and provides it to the banks. The banks pyramid this initial credit expansion by lending it to borrowers. Printed cash or currency in circulation is actually only a part of the total money supply picture. Bank credit—and that includes, of course, bank credit cards—is the way the lion's share of money is held. Your net worth in money assets is not the cash in your wallet. It is in the form of savings accounts, CDs, etc.—in the form of credits, so to speak, on your personal balance sheets at banks.

The point of the foregoing discussion is simply to show that the growth in what is called "domestic bank credit" is the way a nation expands the amount of its currency units. This action waters down the currency unit's value whenever the money supply increases faster than the production of goods. And if one country inflates its bank credit much more than another country, that first country's currency will fall apart against the second.

Let's take two more real-world examples, albeit extreme ones. From 1960 to 1990, Switzerland's supply of domestic bank credit grew by 1,049%. During the same time, Mexico's grew by 927,210%. That's about one thousand percent vs. nearly 1 million percent. What would you conclude happened to the respective values of their currencies from 1960 to 1990? Both inflated, and prices in both countries were higher in 1990 than they were in 1960. But what a difference. Mexico had hyperinflation, while Swiss price levels are not that much higher. How can this be, you ask, when the Swiss had a 1,000 % increase in bank credit? That 1,000 % increase in money supply in Switzerland did not destroy the Swiss franc because there was a big growth at the same time in the productive capacity of the Swiss economy. So the money supply increase wasn't all credit created and backed by nothing.

Don't get us wrong; Switzerland would be better off if they hadn't inflated at all in the past thirty years. Prices of goods for the Swiss would be a fraction of what they are today, because roughly the same amount of money would be able to buy vastly more goods and services.

But in this imperfect world, where even the best politicians are tempted to inflate, a tenfold increase over thirty years seems the best we can hope for.

Let's compare the figures (rounded to the nearest hundred) for a few other countries during the same period:

> United States: 1,200%
> Austria: 3,000%
> United Kingdom: 5,200%
> Italy: 6,500%
> Singapore: 10,000%

You might be shocked to see that credit expansion in the U.S. is very low over that thirty-year period. It is not much worse than Switzerland. So why have we and our dollar experienced so much pain?

The figures we have been looking at are for a long period—1960 to 1990. But recently (since around 1985) something very extraordinary—and potentially disturbing—has been happening to the growth of money and credit in the United States. Its growth slowed down tremendously.

During the sixties, seventies, and early eighties, the general path of money and credit growth were always up. You can see a distinct up-channel, for example, if you take a look at the M2 money supply.

A Trend Is Broken—What Does It Portend?

This generational trend of ever upward inflation was clearly broken by 1987. Had we measured the U.S. growth of credit expansion from 1960 to, say, 1985, we would have seen a much worse-looking figure. But since 1985, money and credit growth have drastically slowed. By the end of 1991, the annual growth of M3, a broader money supply measure, was under 1% and it has been slowing steadily for about ten years. General credit growth started slowing in the United States around 1985. It was growing at an inflationary 14% then. At the beginning of 1992, annual growth of money in the United States was down to about 4.5%.

If the U.S. drastically contracts its growth of money and credit on a more permanent basis, and the other major economies keep theirs growing and inflating at vastly higher rates, then sooner or later, the U.S. dollar will begin to rise against the major currencies.

Credit Expansion Around the World— And Then the Big Cutback

For the first few years after 1985, the other major economies not only failed to restrict money and credit inflation, they vastly expanded its growth. Switzerland's money supply, for example, was growing around 5% a year in the middle eighties. But by the beginning of 1990, it was briefly growing at a whopping 25% annual rate.

Japan's credit growth roughly doubled from 6.5% to 13% per year from 1983 to 1990. Germany, Britain, Australia, Canada—all the major economies—experienced big money and credit growth in the late eighties. (See chart 18 on pages 350 and 351)

And indeed, for a few years beginning in 1988, the dollar stopped its previous free-fall against those currencies. In the late eighties and early nineties, it even staged two impressive if temporary rallies. At the end of 1991, the dollar was actually higher against the Fabulous Five currencies than it had been at the end of 1987.*

---

*Well, four of them anyway. The mark was slightly higher. Germany is a special case and can't be truly compared to the other countries, because in the early nineties, West Germany incorporated East Germany and expanded its money supply to accommodate the worthless old ostmarks. But at the same time they pushed up interest rates and did anything else they could to protect the value of the mark. Also, market sentiment has been very bullish on the future of the new Germany.

But since 1990 all the major economies (except Germany, a special case) have drastically contracted the growth of money and credit in their economies.

Switzerland's money supply growth collapsed from 25% a year to virtually zero in less than two years, 1989 to 1991. This is unprecedented. Japan's credit contraction has been equally dramatic. Since 1990 we've seen not only the sharpest slowdown in its modern history, but credit growth has never been lower. By the end of 1991 it was 2% and falling. Compare this to the fact that until 1991 Japan's credit growth never fell below 8% and was usually in the double digits. Australia, Canada, and the United Kingdom—all of them are also contracting credit growth. In Britain's case the fall has come after years of ever looser credit in the eighties. Finally, even Germany is showing that its huge "unification" run-up in domestic credit will almost certainly be temporary. In 1991 the growth rate started falling fast. All this credit contraction may have two powerful effects. One concerns the U.S. dollar, the other the entire world economy. As far as the dollar goes, this means that its relative stability from 1988 to 1991 may be over. It can no longer count on being buoyed up because it was the only country where credit and money inflation was falling. Now all the major nations are seeing credit contracting with a dramatic force not seen since the thirties.

And this brings us to the second possible effect of this worldwide drop in new credit growth. The nineties may be in for the toughest world economy since the thirties, when depression contracted credit, inflation and business growth, and cash was king.

As millions of consumers learned in the eighties, credit is like a drug. The first bursts of it can make you feel wonderful, or at least richer than you really are. It was very tempting to go out and buy things you didn't really need. It didn't matter if you went into debt. Everyone was deeper in debt, it seemed, and besides, there was always more credit to be had. Millions of Americans took their lead from the Reagan ad-

UNITED STATES

CANADA

UNITED KINGDOM

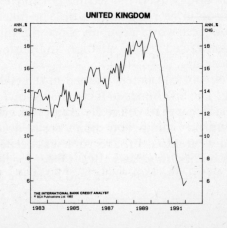

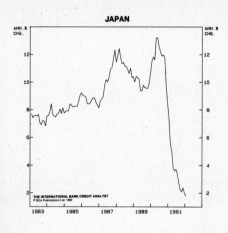

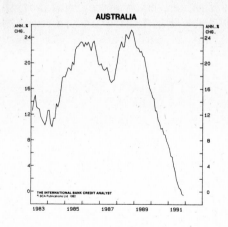

How the Fed tried to save the dollar: The chart at top of p. 350 shows how early tightening by the Fed managed to stem the dollar's awful fall after 1985 but perhaps set the stage for the ensuing recession. Notice how others have more recently tightened as well; this not only augurs for a world-wide downturn but may spell the end of the dollar's recent relative strength.

ministration, which ballooned the national debt to nearly $4 trillion—a level three times where it had been when Jimmy Carter left office.

Easy credit fuels a lot of financial and business activity that appears at the time to be healthy but is later revealed to have been uneconomic. Think of all the billions in loans bankers made that seemed smart in the eighties but had to be written off as near total losses in the nineties. Think of all the billions corporations borrowed to expand or buy out other companies in deals that just a few years later soured.

This is nothing new. It's happened before, so long as there have been credit institutions. But we had experienced nothing comparable to this kind of credit expansion since the twenties.

Credit cannot just become looser and looser. Sooner or later, debt excesses begin to be revealed. And it takes more and more of it to keep us in place. New domestic U.S. debt grew from 3% a year in 1981 to 14% a year in 1985, 1986, and 1987. Again, as with drugs, the "cold turkey" period begins.

Bankers, stung by mounting levels of bad loans, become afraid to lend even for good economic projects and call in loans already extended. Even if businesses are not hurt by this choking off of new or existing credit, they too discover weaknesses in the area into which they thought it wise to expand during the boom times (commercial real estate, hotels, airlines, etc.). And the consumer—even if he hasn't been laid off by a business that's cutting back, or isn't worried that he might be—is not typically expanding his debt or spending.

The world is very interconnected. It was unrealistic to expect a credit contraction to happen just in the United States. Besides, other major economies have their own reasons to worry about the credit growth of the eighties. Japan's stock and real estate markets took off like rockets in that decade. These rises were fueled by excessive debt. But with debt growth almost nil, a lot of air will be let out of the prices. And businesses will be hit as this happens, because the Japanese will feel poorer as they watch their real estate values plunge.

Germany has paid for unification by increasing taxes and borrowing more at higher interest rates. Rising interest rates may help the external value of the mark, but coupled with rising taxes, they can be hell on an economy. Retail sales and industrial production were booming in 1990; by early 1992 they were not just flat, they were declining.

The rest of Europe is tied to Germany, so interest rates have gone up across the Continent. Again, all good for the foreign depositors who reap the benefits of high yields, but not great for businesses in those countries who have to pay debts at higher rates while consumer spending stalls.

Stock Markets (Like Trees) Don't Just "Grow to the Skies"

Stock markets in Japan and Germany hit their record highs close to when the decade turned—the last days of the eighties and early 1990. Look at the stock charts that accompany each major currency in chapter 5. In most cases the big worldwide bull market that begin in the early eighties stalled as we entered the nineties.

This is not surprising. Loose credit policies usually make business and stocks boom—at first. But when credit tightens, so does business. It is hard to see corporate earnings holding up anywhere in the world where there is drastically tightened credit. And if the economies of Germany, Japan, and the United States all stall, it will be hard to expect great growth in the emerging stock markets of the smaller nations that did so well in the eighties.

It is usually too easy to call one decade all this way and the next decade all the other way. But sometimes it fits. The eighties were an era much like the twenties—lots of debt, good times for business, and booming stock markets all around the world. The nineties are showing all the signs of being more like the thirties: contracting debt, rougher times for business, and falling global stock prices.

There are probably too many institutional safeguards for the nineties to be as bad as the thirties were. But even if they aren't as bad, they will likely be worse than the eighties were, at least in terms of stocks. In country after country, stock prices had languished or grown moderately, only to boom in the eighties in an unprecedented manner. It is hard to think they can top themselves in the early nineties, especially with credit growth being choked off.

Stocks Crash While Currencies Rise

We have seen this pattern begin already. Both the Japanese and Taiwanese stock markets have fallen sharply so far in the nineties. But in both cases, the currencies of these two remained strong and, indeed, reached new record highs against the dollar. When stocks plunge in a deflation, cash is clearly king.

As an International Investor, You Have a Host of Choices

If the recent contraction in money growth does indeed slow down stock markets around the world, that needn't be discouraging to you. For one thing, such a cold-water bath may end up being the best thing in the world for the world economies. It may lead to more securely rising stock markets in the future.

There is no reason whatever—while credit throughout the world is contracting and stock markets are shaking in unison—that you should feel that opportunity is gone. Let the rigid-brained stock market investor feel that way. Real opportunity may just have started for you.

When credit contracts strongly and for a long period of

time, cash usually becomes king. And since you now know more about cash in all its forms, whatever cash you have at the time can be put to better and better use.

Now that you have read this book, you know how to tell a strong (and rising) currency from a weak one that is beginning to fall in value. You know which banks throughout the world will help you put your money safely into one of those strong currencies and move it around, if need be, as conditions change. You know how to get higher rates of interest than at home, either in a foreign CD or in the government bonds of a fiscally strong nation. You even know how to leverage your investable cash by buying the cash of a strong (and rising) currency with a small part of your money and borrowing the rest in a weak currency you feel certain will fall (leaving you the delicious pleasure of paying back less than you borrowed).

You know, too, that when stock markets fall steeply, a lot of escaping funds pile into bonds—which opens for you a chance that most investors fleeing the stock market are oblivious to. You know how to invest in high-grade bonds from countries with the strongest currencies.

Then, if the contraction in credit throughout the world does—by administering its cold bath of reason—put all markets on a more stable basis, thereby setting up the next period of expanding markets, you will know how to deploy your money to the best effect, which currencies to favor, and therefore which markets and which mutual funds will best help you do that.

A worldwide contraction in money and markets could be a blessing in disguise. It might make you a lot richer than you got during the go-go stock markets of the eighties—just when most investors are feeling the world has come to an end.

Chris Weber's Services

Chris Weber has a newsletter that updates all important information in this book, especially with regard to the best banks, currencies and interest rates, as well as the further adventures of Max Yield. Depending on the interest of the readers of this book, he may have a Max Yield fund that will duplicate the actions for investors who would not otherwise be able to buy sufficient amounts of the highest yielding currencies to get the best yields. This fund would be in addition to the managed funds and advisory service that Mr. Weber already offers.

Chris Weber's World View is a quarterly newsletter, at $75 per year.
All inquiries to:
1129 E. Cliff Road
Burnsville, MN 55337
Telephone: 612-895-8511
Fax: 612-895-5526